OLD MAN LOGAN

THE HUNTER AND THE HUNTED

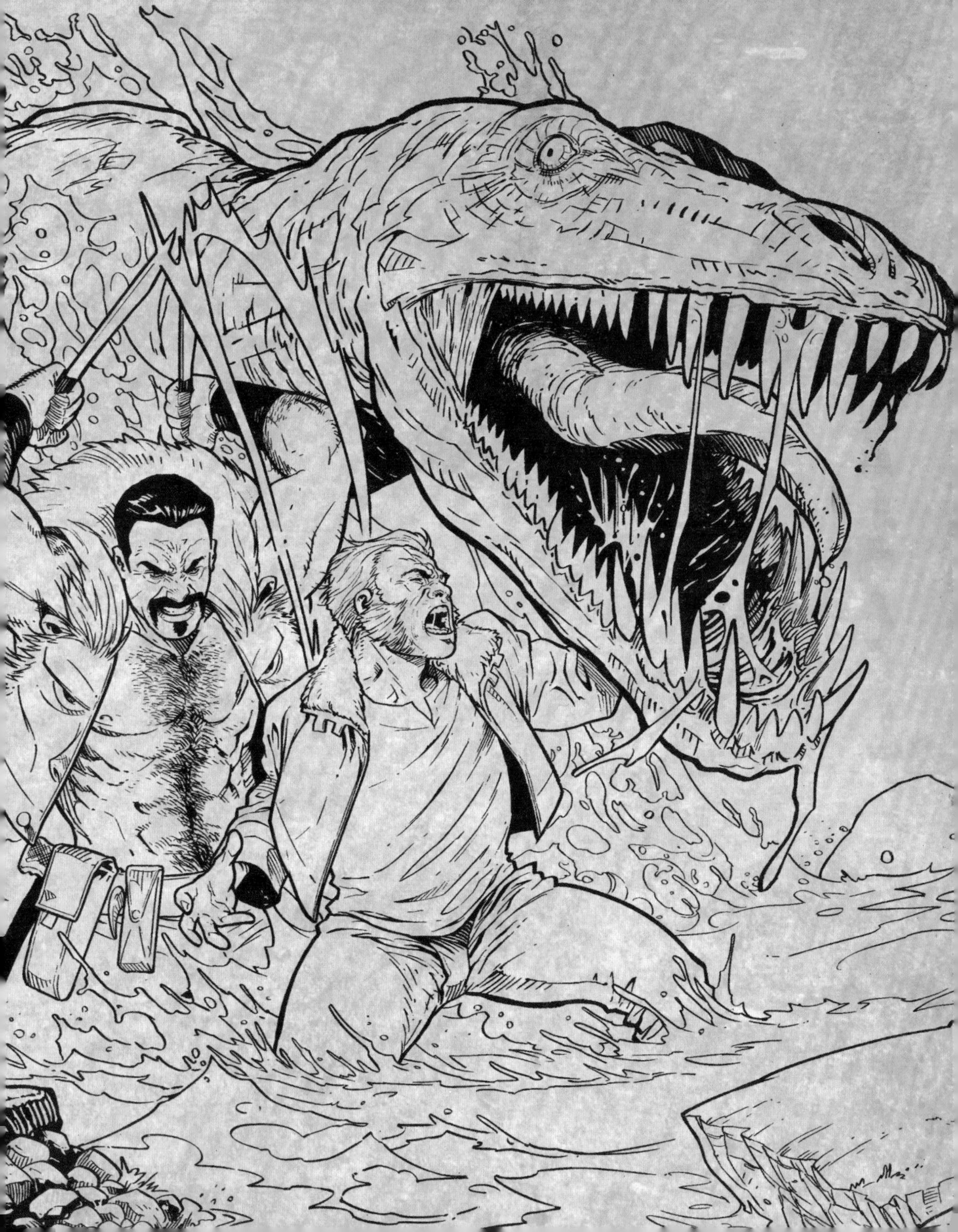

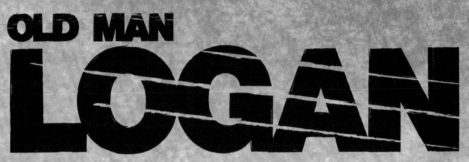

OLD MAN LOGAN

THE HUNTER AND THE HUNTED

WRITER **ED BRISSON**

LOGAN THE HUNTED (#41-42)

ARTIST **FRANCESCO MANNA**

COLOR ARTIST **CARLOS LOPEZ**

BULLSEYE RETURNS (#43-45)

ARTIST **JUAN FERREYRA**

LETTERER **VC's CORY PETIT**

COVER ART **MIKE DEODATO JR. & CARLOS LOPEZ**

ASSISTANT EDITOR **CHRIS ROBINSON**

EDITORS **CHRISTINA HARRINGTON & JORDAN D. WHITE**

COLLECTION EDITOR **MARK D. BEAZLEY**
ASSISTANT EDITOR **CAITLIN O'CONNELL**
ASSOCIATE MANAGING EDITOR **KATERI WOODY**
SENIOR EDITOR, SPECIAL PROJECTS **JENNIFER GRÜNWALD**
VP PRODUCTION & SPECIAL PROJECTS **JEFF YOUNGQUIST**
SVP PRINT, SALES & MARKETING **DAVID GABRIEL**
BOOK DESIGNER **ADAM DEL RE**

EDITOR IN CHIEF **C.B. CEBULSKI**
CHIEF CREATIVE OFFICER **JOE QUESADA**
PRESIDENT **DAN BUCKLEY**
EXECUTIVE PRODUCER **ALAN FINE**

WOLVERINE: OLD MAN LOGAN VOL. 9 — THE HUNTER AND THE HUNTED. Contains material originally published in magazine form as OLD MAN LOGAN #41-45. First printing 2018. ISBN 978-1-302-91096-9. Published by MARVEL WORLDWIDE, INC., a subsidiary of MARVEL ENTERTAINMENT, LLC. OFFICE OF PUBLICATION: 135 West 50th Street, New York, NY 10020. **Printed in Canada.** DAN BUCKLEY, President, Marvel Entertainment; JOHN NEE, Publisher; JOE QUESADA, Chief Creative Officer; TOM BREVOORT, SVP of Publishing; DAVID BOGART, SVP of Business Affairs & Operations, Publishing & Partnership; DAVID GABRIEL, SVP of Sales & Marketing, Publishing; JEFF YOUNGQUIST, VP of Production & Special Projects; DAN CARR, Executive Director of Publishing Technology; ALEX MORALES, Director of Publishing Operations; DAN EDINGTON, Managing Editor; SUSAN CRESPI, Production Manager; STAN LEE, Chairman Emeritus. For information regarding advertising in Marvel Comics or on Marvel.com, please contact Vit DeBellis, Custom Solutions & Integrated Advertising Manager, at vdebellis@marvel.com. For Marvel subscription inquiries, please call 888-511-5480. **Manufactured between 10/12/2018 and 11/13/2018 by SOLISCO PRINTERS, SCOTT, QC, CANADA.**

10 9 8 7 6 5 4 3 2 1

Surviving a future known as the Wastelands,
where everything good in the world, including his
family, was destroyed, Old Man Logan awoke in the
present determined to prevent this catastrophic
reality from ever coming to pass. Now, Logan tries
to find his place in a world not quite his own.

Logan's healing factor is mysteriously weakening.
Injuries that normally would have healed rapidly, aren't.
Without the help of a dangerous pharmaceutical called
Regenix to boost his healing, Logan is more vulnerable
than ever. During a recent altercation in Japan,
Logan's right hand and Adamantium claws
were severed from his wrist...

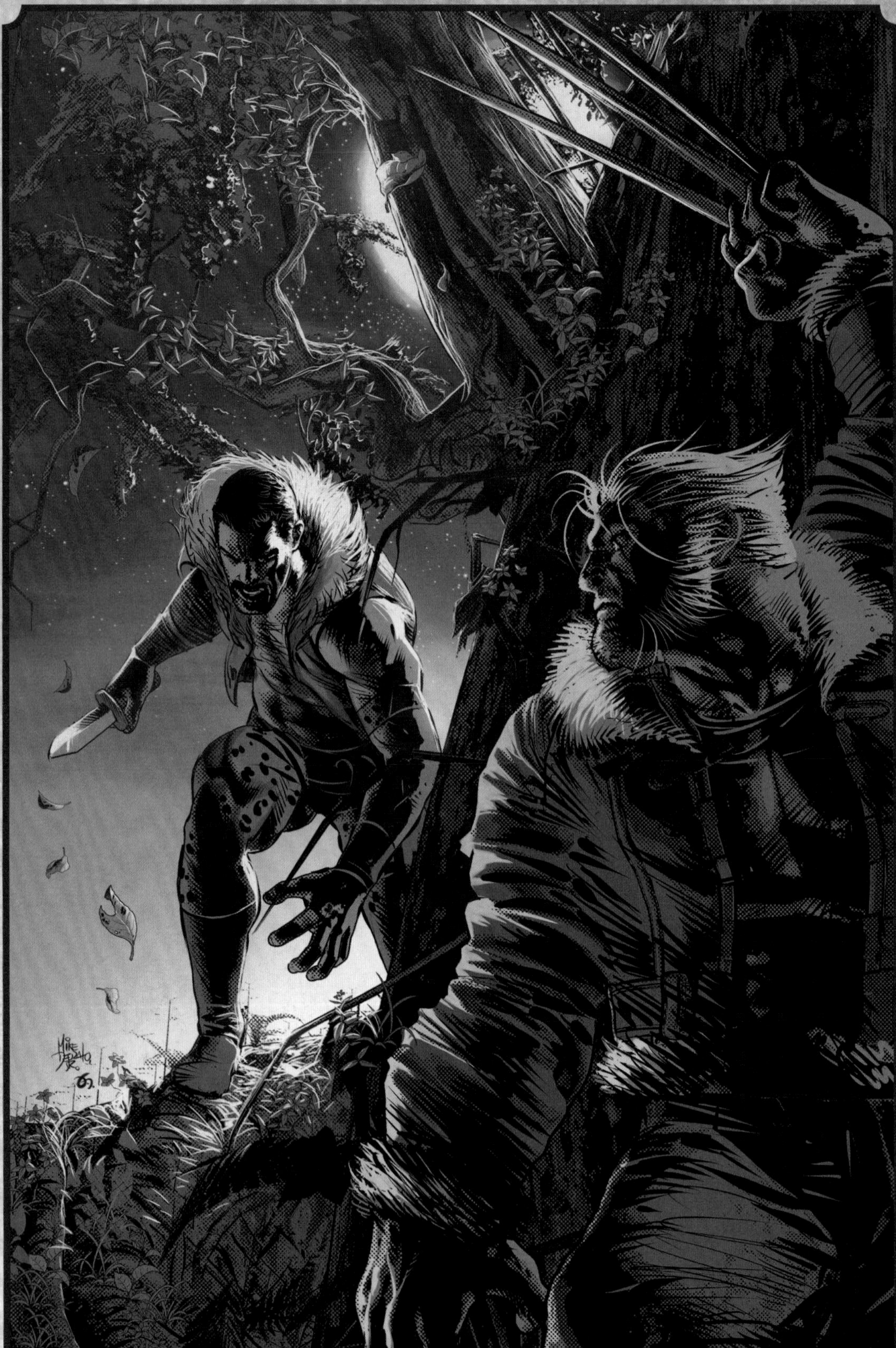

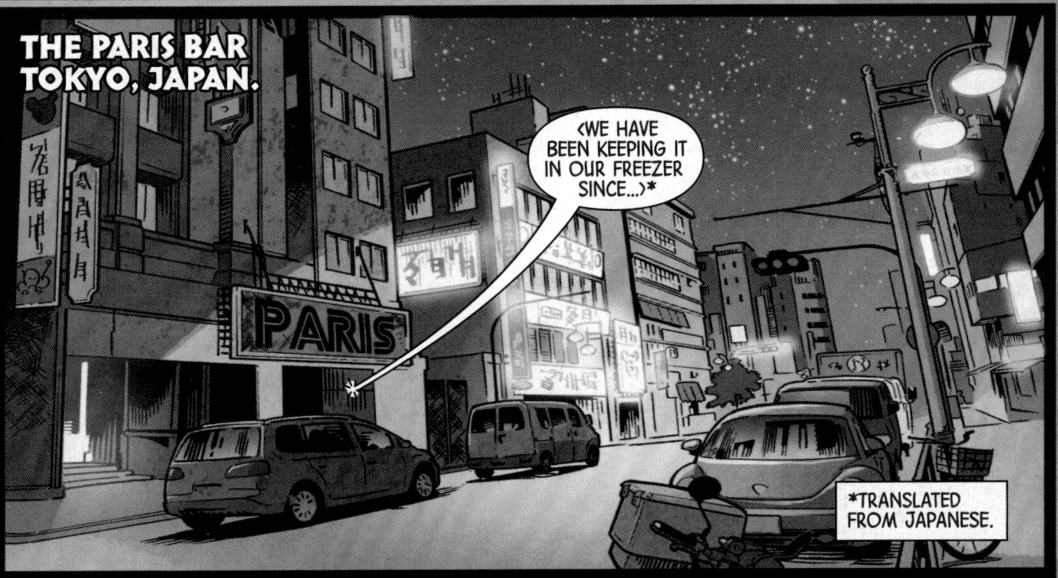
THE PARIS BAR
TOKYO, JAPAN.
PARIS
<WE HAVE BEEN KEEPING IT IN OUR FREEZER SINCE...>*
*TRANSLATED FROM JAPANESE.

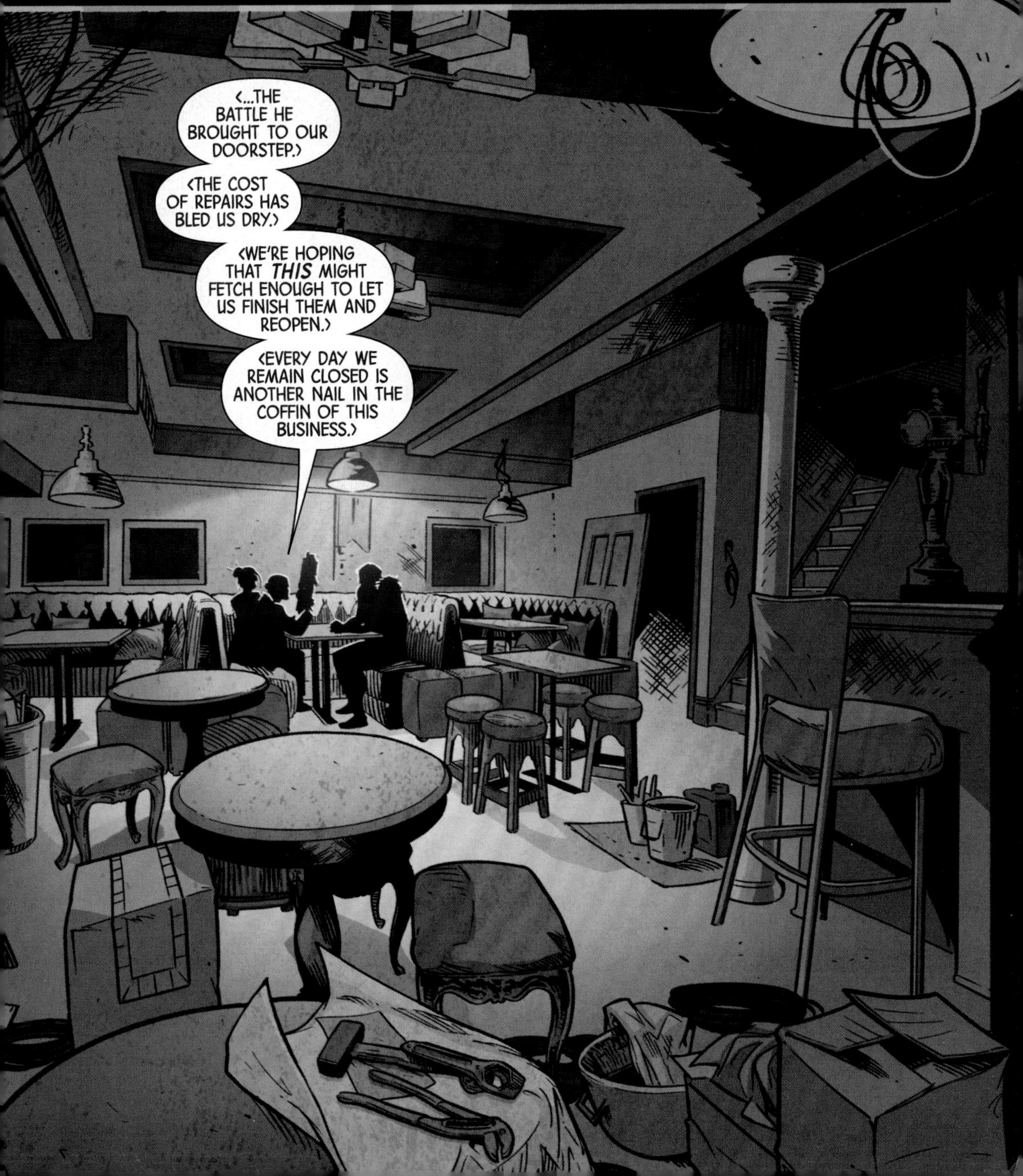
<...THE BATTLE HE BROUGHT TO OUR DOORSTEP.>
<THE COST OF REPAIRS HAS BLED US DRY.>
<WE'RE HOPING THAT *THIS* MIGHT FETCH ENOUGH TO LET US FINISH THEM AND REOPEN.>
<EVERY DAY WE REMAIN CLOSED IS ANOTHER NAIL IN THE COFFIN OF THIS BUSINESS.>

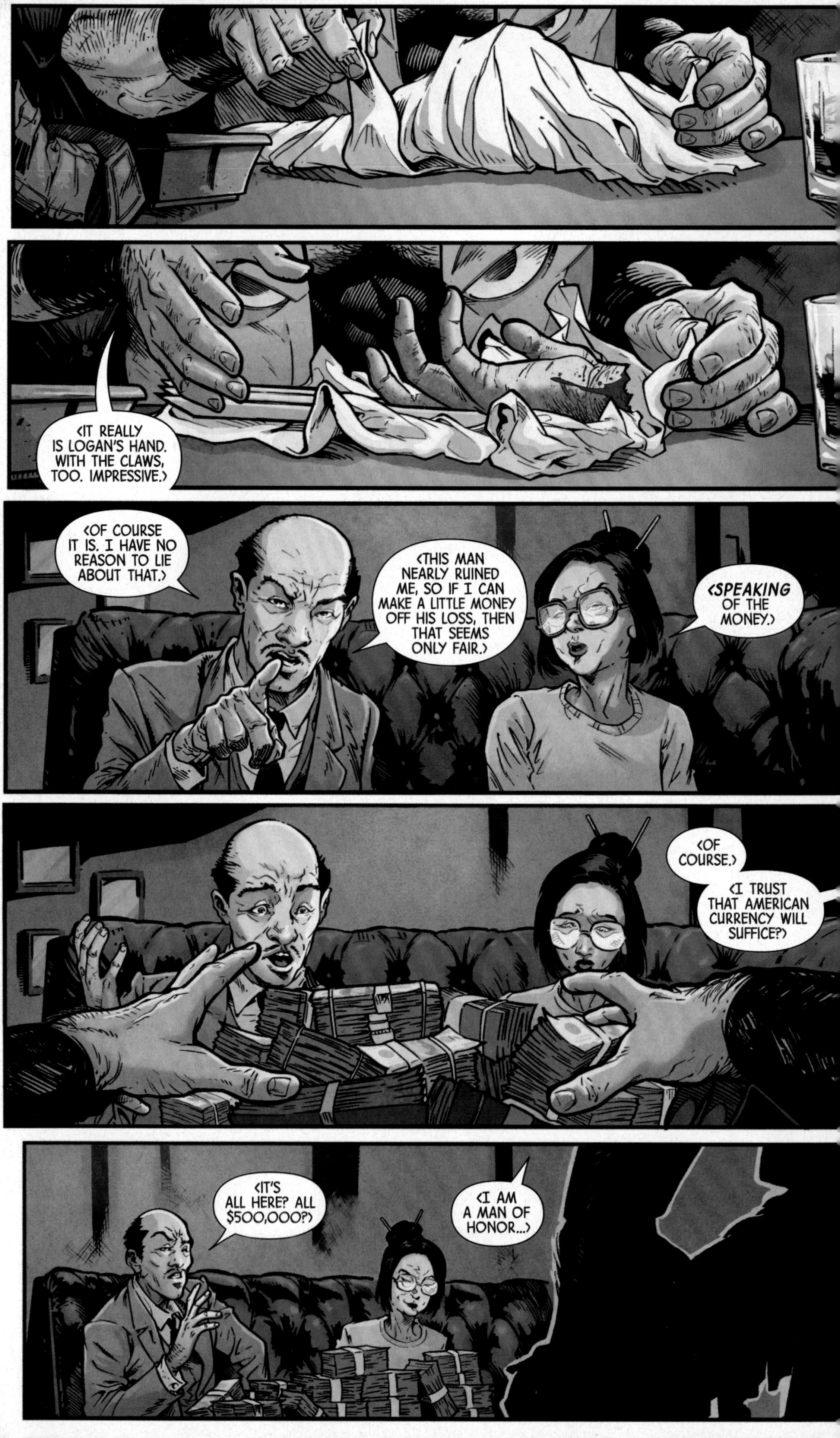

<IT REALLY IS LOGAN'S HAND. WITH THE CLAWS, TOO. IMPRESSIVE.>
<OF COURSE IT IS. I HAVE NO REASON TO LIE ABOUT THAT.>
<THIS MAN NEARLY RUINED ME, SO IF I CAN MAKE A LITTLE MONEY OFF HIS LOSS, THEN THAT SEEMS ONLY FAIR.>
<*SPEAKING* OF THE MONEY.>
<OF COURSE.>
<I TRUST THAT AMERICAN CURRENCY WILL SUFFICE?>
<IT'S ALL HERE? ALL $500,000?>
<I AM A MAN OF HONOR...>

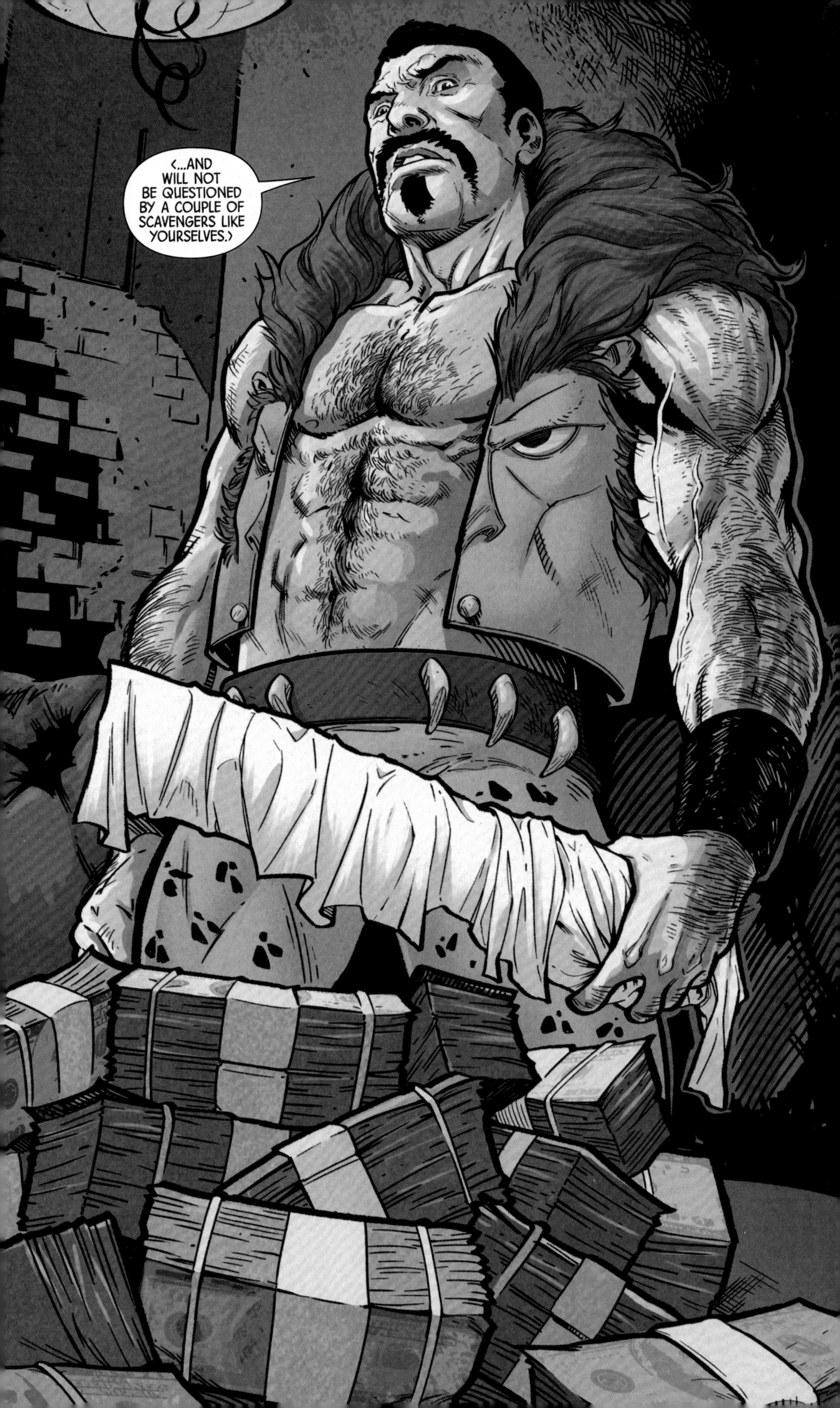
‹...AND WILL NOT BE QUESTIONED BY A COUPLE OF SCAVENGERS LIKE YOURSELVES.›

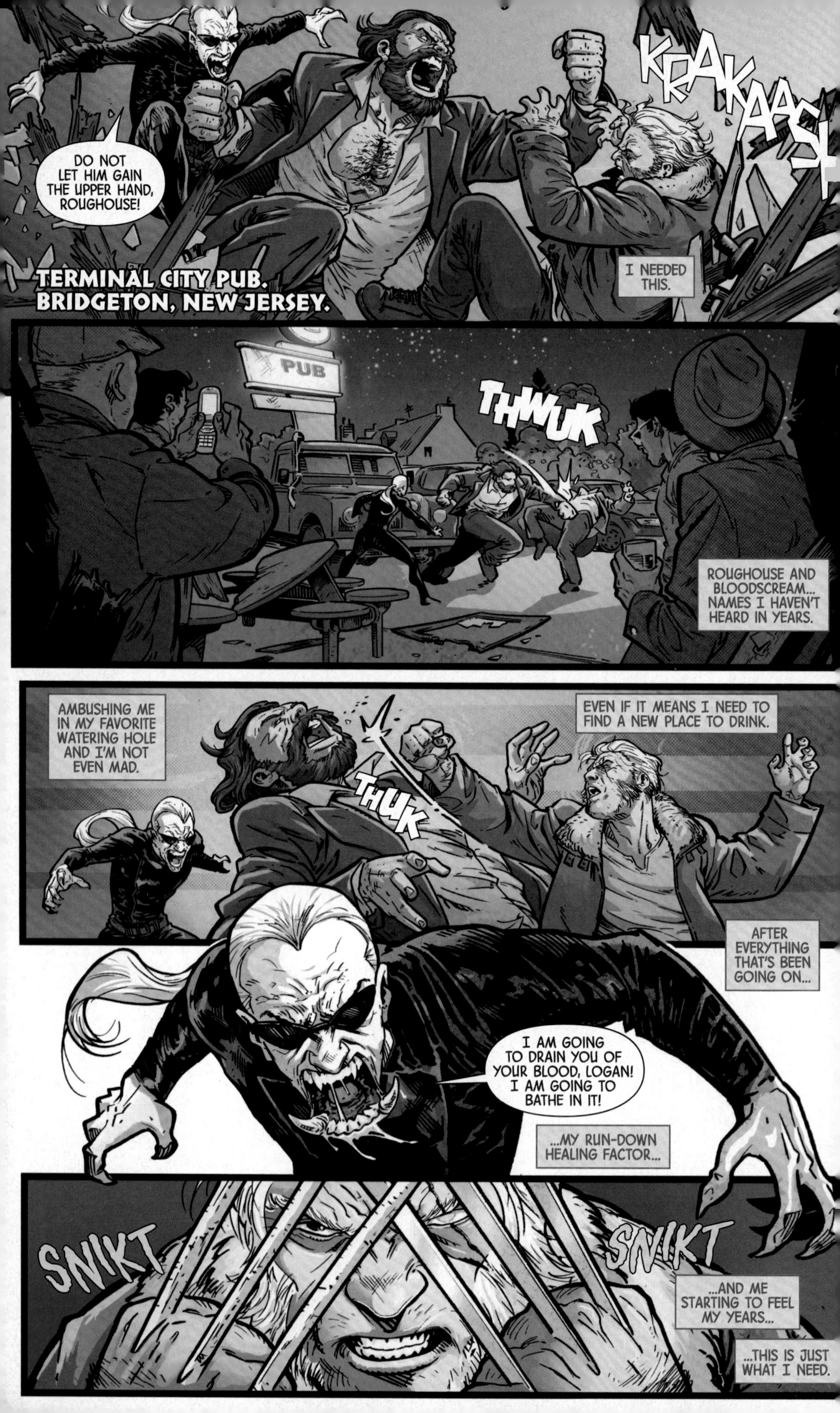
KRAKAASH
DO NOT LET HIM GAIN THE UPPER HAND, ROUGHOUSE!
TERMINAL CITY PUB. BRIDGETON, NEW JERSEY.
I NEEDED THIS.
PUB
THWUK
ROUGHOUSE AND BLOODSCREAM... NAMES I HAVEN'T HEARD IN YEARS.
AMBUSHING ME IN MY FAVORITE WATERING HOLE AND I'M NOT EVEN MAD.
EVEN IF IT MEANS I NEED TO FIND A NEW PLACE TO DRINK.
THUK
AFTER EVERYTHING THAT'S BEEN GOING ON...
I AM GOING TO DRAIN YOU OF YOUR BLOOD, LOGAN! I AM GOING TO BATHE IN IT!
...MY RUN-DOWN HEALING FACTOR...
SNIKT
SNIKT
...AND ME STARTING TO FEEL MY YEARS...
...THIS IS JUST WHAT I NEED.

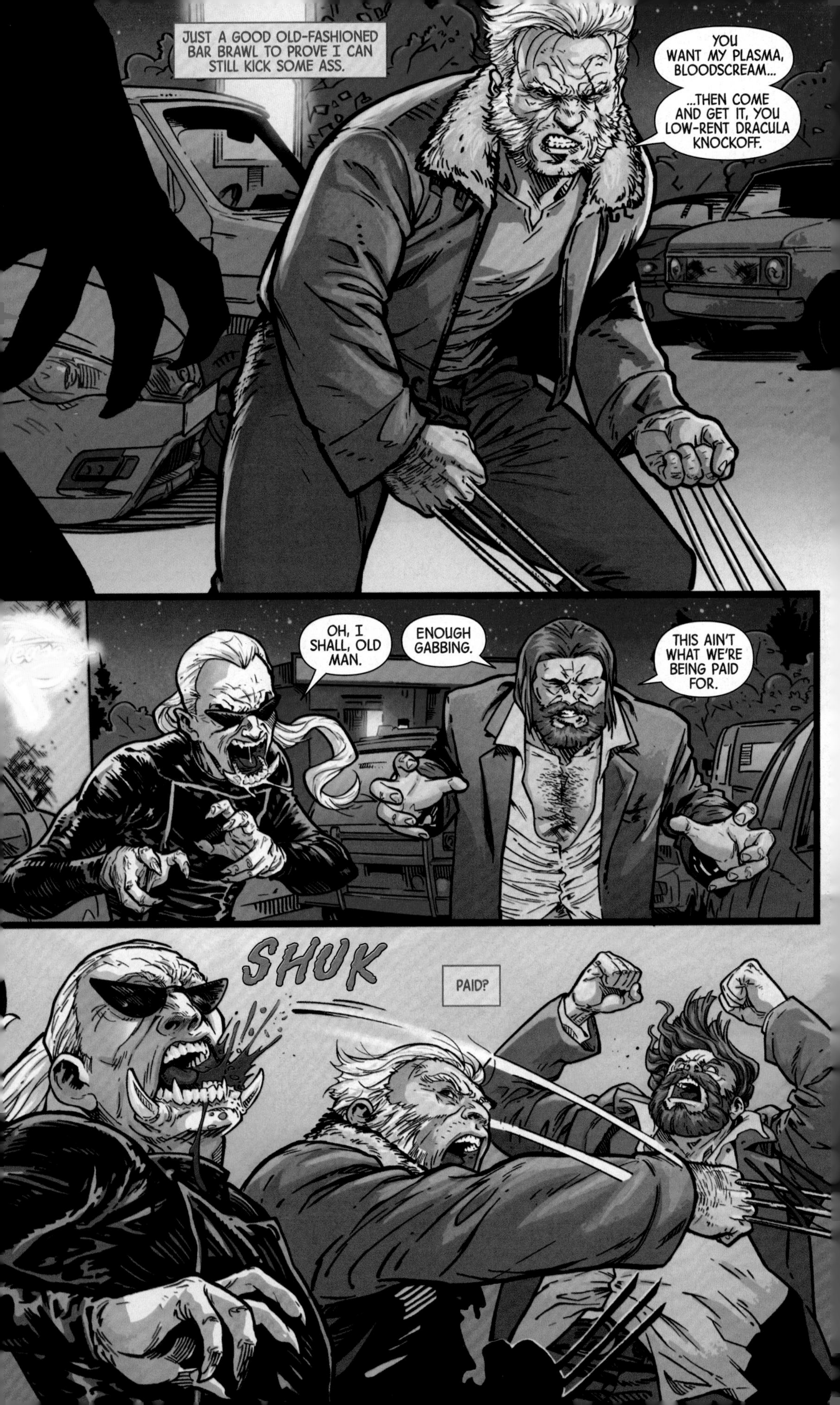

JUST A GOOD OLD-FASHIONED BAR BRAWL TO PROVE I CAN STILL KICK SOME ASS.
YOU WANT MY PLASMA, BLOODSCREAM...
...THEN COME AND GET IT, YOU LOW-RENT DRACULA KNOCKOFF.
OH, I SHALL, OLD MAN.
ENOUGH GABBING.
THIS AIN'T WHAT WE'RE BEING PAID FOR.
SHUK
PAID?

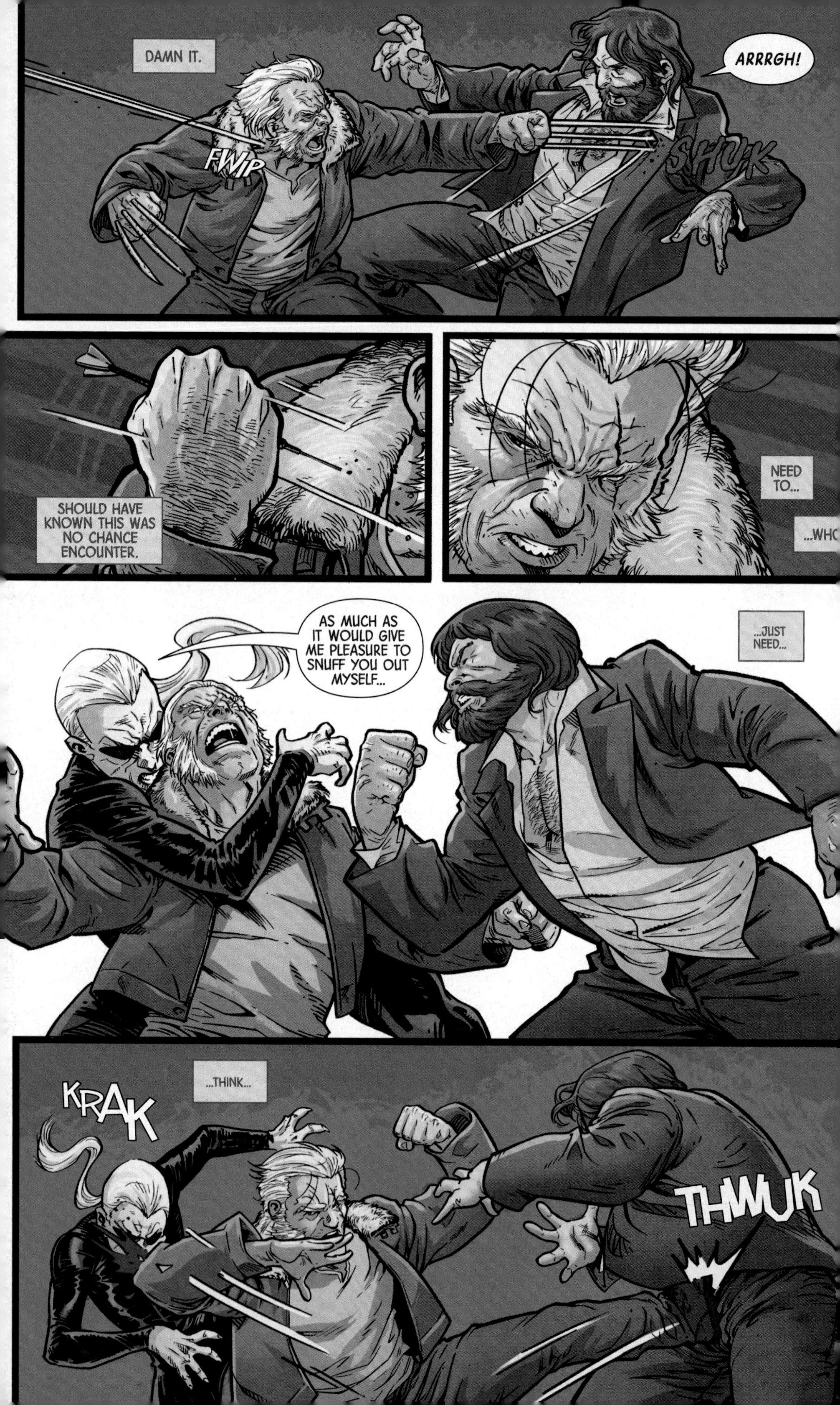

DAMN IT.
FWIP
ARRRGH!
SHUK
SHOULD HAVE KNOWN THIS WAS NO CHANCE ENCOUNTER.
NEED TO...
...WHO
AS MUCH AS IT WOULD GIVE ME PLEASURE TO SNUFF YOU OUT MYSELF...
...JUST NEED...
...THINK...
KRAK
THWUK

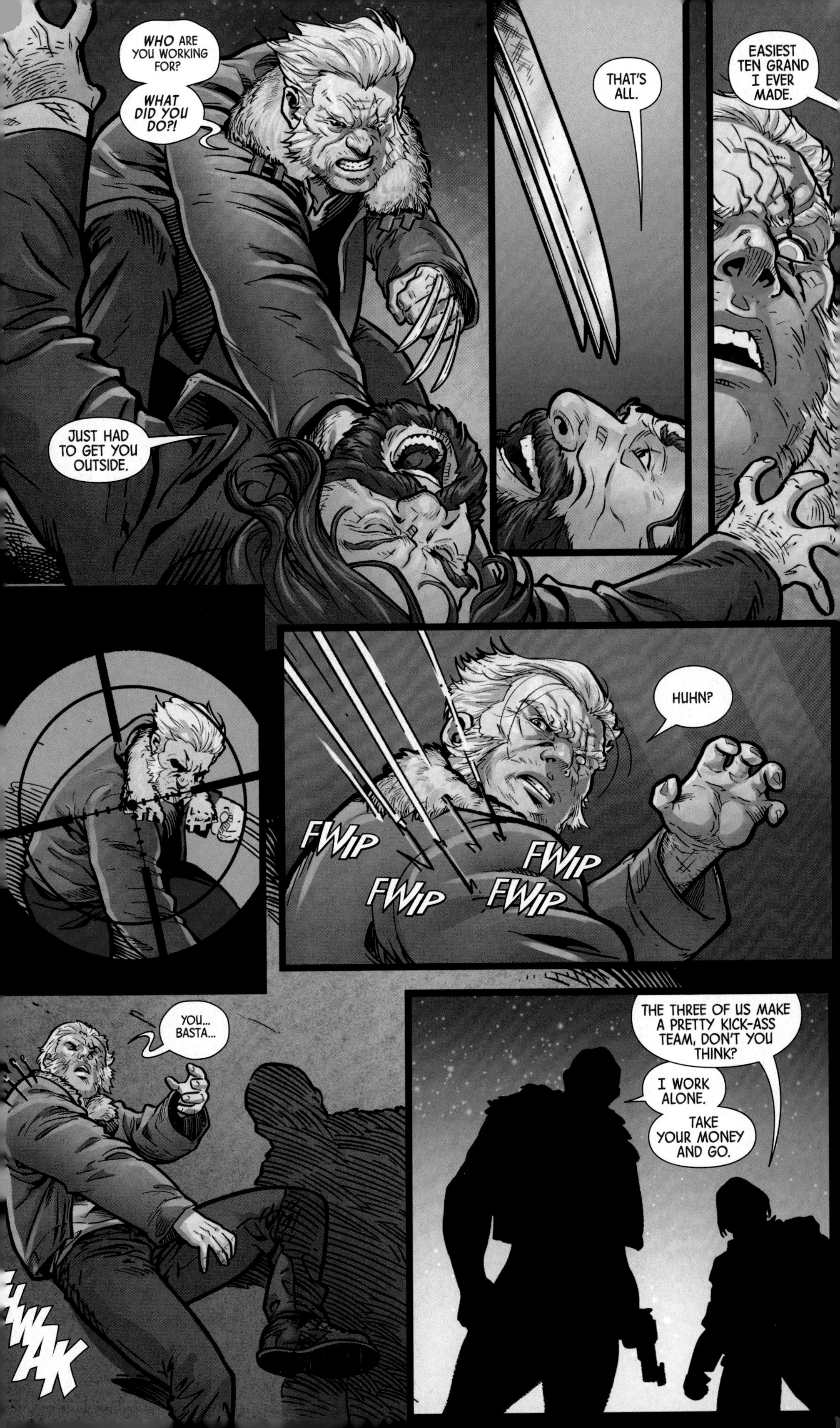
WHO ARE YOU WORKING FOR?
WHAT DID YOU DO?!
JUST HAD TO GET YOU OUTSIDE.
THAT'S ALL.
EASIEST TEN GRAND I EVER MADE.
HUHN?
FWIP
FWIP
FWIP
FWIP
YOU... BASTA...
THE THREE OF US MAKE A PRETTY KICK-ASS TEAM, DON'T YOU THINK?
I WORK ALONE.
TAKE YOUR MONEY AND GO.

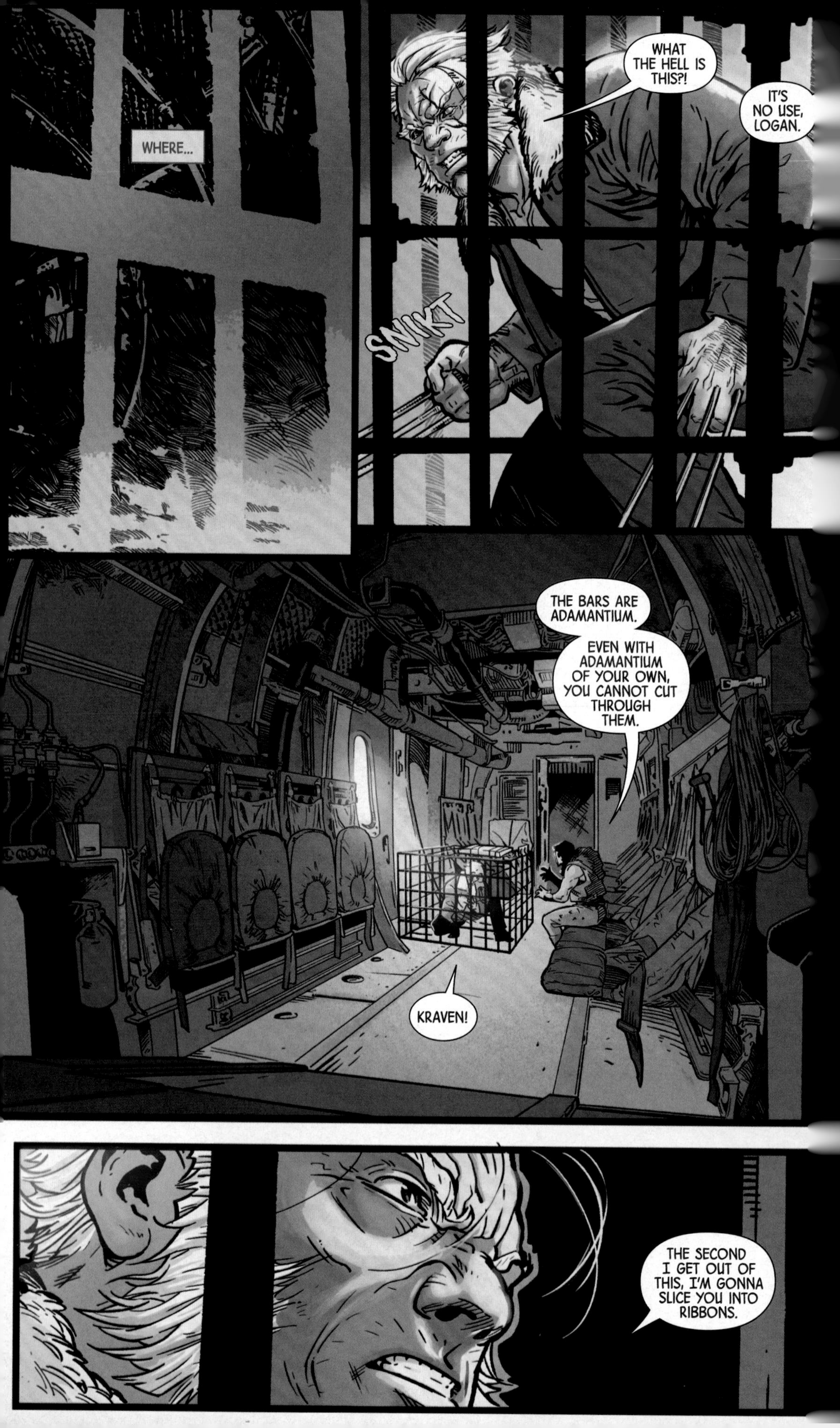
WHERE...
WHAT THE HELL IS THIS?!
IT'S NO USE, LOGAN.
SNIKT
THE BARS ARE ADAMANTIUM.
EVEN WITH ADAMANTIUM OF YOUR OWN, YOU CANNOT CUT THROUGH THEM.
KRAVEN!
THE SECOND I GET OUT OF THIS, I'M GONNA SLICE YOU INTO RIBBONS.

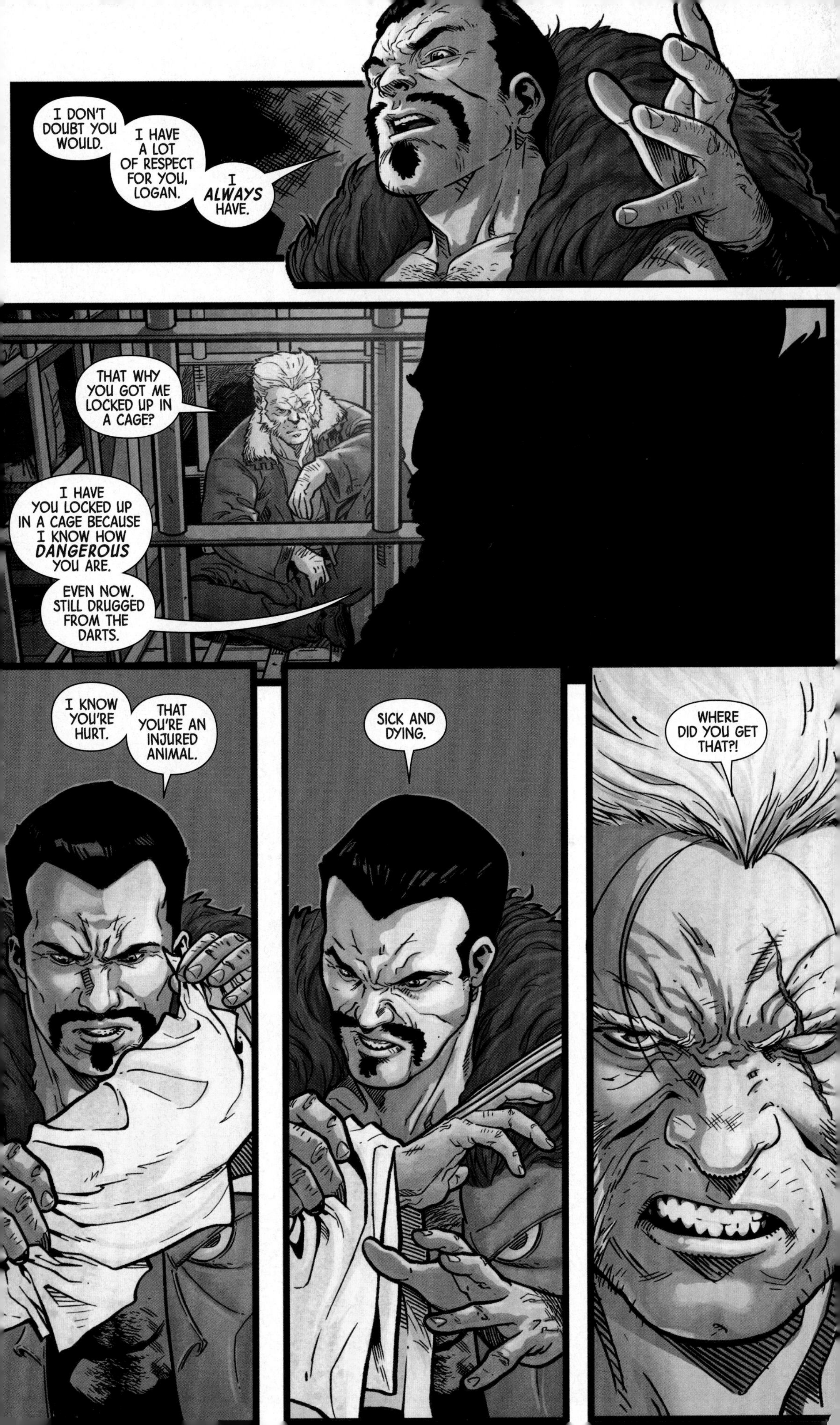
I DON'T DOUBT YOU WOULD.
I HAVE A LOT OF RESPECT FOR YOU, LOGAN.
I *ALWAYS* HAVE.
THAT WHY YOU GOT ME LOCKED UP IN A CAGE?
I HAVE YOU LOCKED UP IN A CAGE BECAUSE I KNOW HOW *DANGEROUS* YOU ARE.
EVEN NOW. STILL DRUGGED FROM THE DARTS.
I KNOW YOU'RE HURT.
THAT YOU'RE AN INJURED ANIMAL.
SICK AND DYING.
WHERE DID YOU GET THAT?!

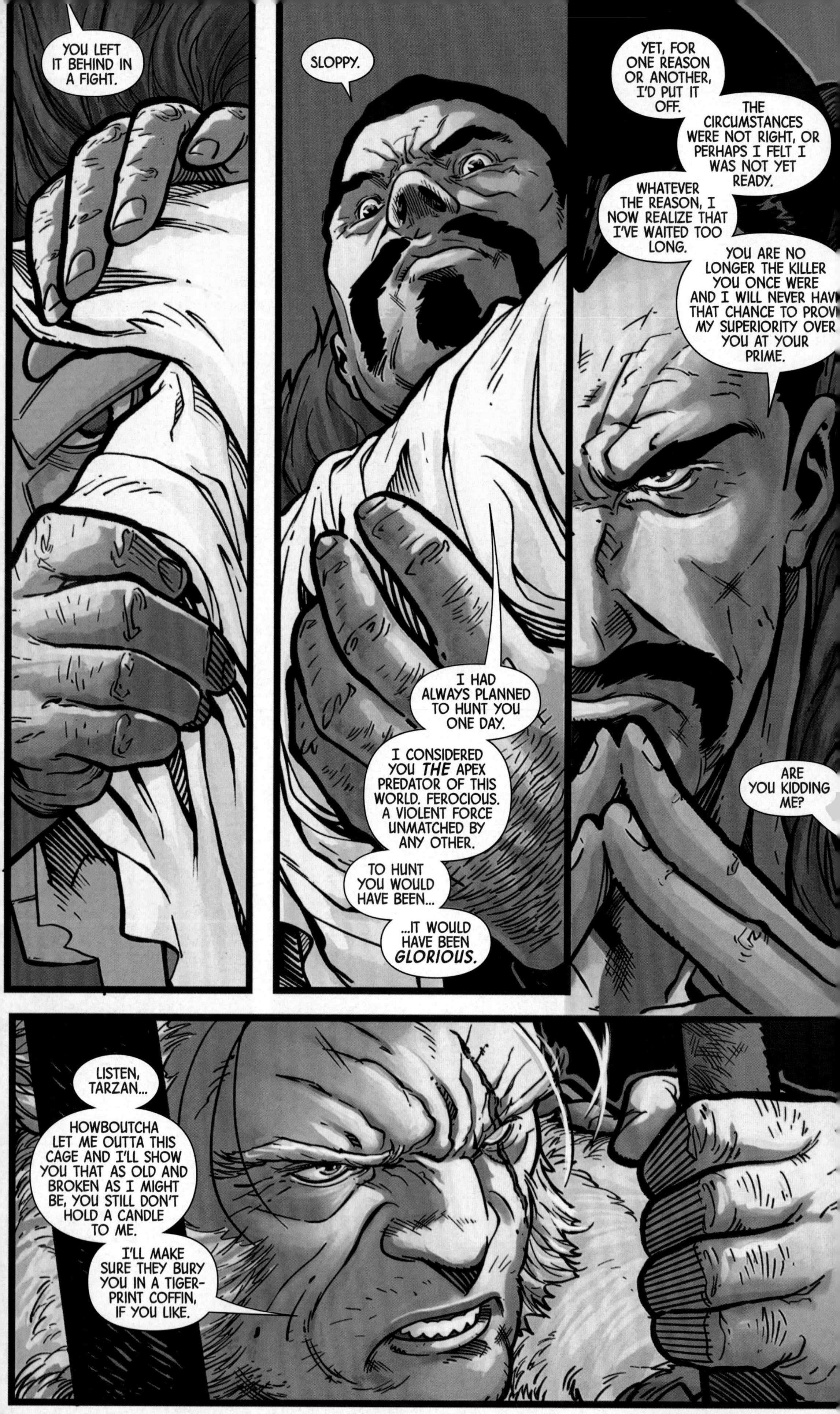
YOU LEFT IT BEHIND IN A FIGHT.
SLOPPY.
I HAD ALWAYS PLANNED TO HUNT YOU ONE DAY.
I CONSIDERED YOU *THE* APEX PREDATOR OF THIS WORLD. FEROCIOUS. A VIOLENT FORCE UNMATCHED BY ANY OTHER.
TO HUNT YOU WOULD HAVE BEEN...
...IT WOULD HAVE BEEN *GLORIOUS.*
YET, FOR ONE REASON OR ANOTHER, I'D PUT IT OFF.
THE CIRCUMSTANCES WERE NOT RIGHT, OR PERHAPS I FELT I WAS NOT YET READY.
WHATEVER THE REASON, I NOW REALIZE THAT I'VE WAITED TOO LONG.
YOU ARE NO LONGER THE KILLER YOU ONCE WERE AND I WILL NEVER HAV THAT CHANCE TO PROV MY SUPERIORITY OVER YOU AT YOUR PRIME.
ARE YOU KIDDING ME?
LISTEN, TARZAN...
HOWBOUTCHA LET ME OUTTA THIS CAGE AND I'LL SHOW YOU THAT AS OLD AND BROKEN AS I MIGHT BE, YOU STILL DON'T HOLD A CANDLE TO ME.
I'LL MAKE SURE THEY BURY YOU IN A TIGER-PRINT COFFIN, IF YOU LIKE.

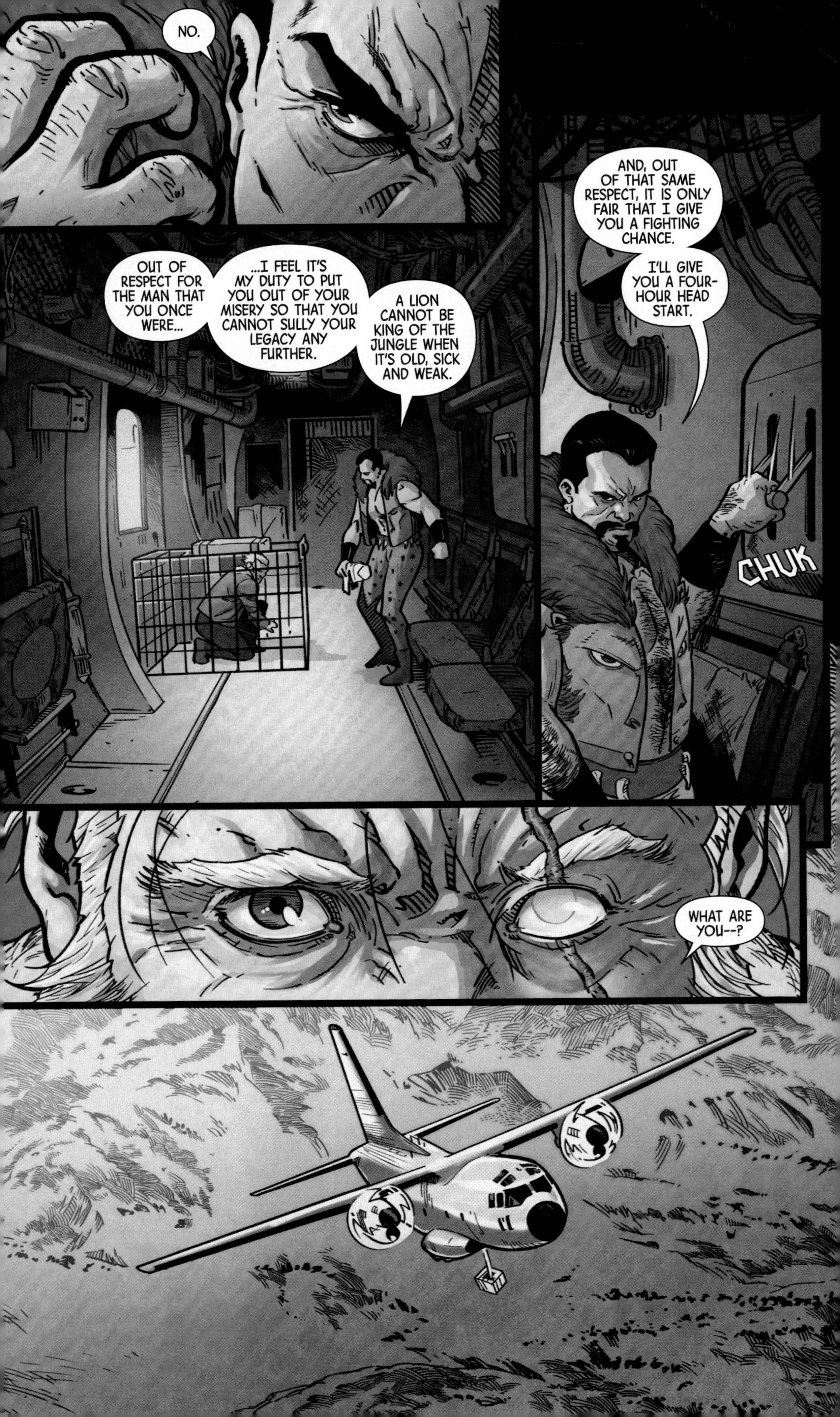
NO.
OUT OF RESPECT FOR THE MAN THAT YOU ONCE WERE...
...I FEEL IT'S MY DUTY TO PUT YOU OUT OF YOUR MISERY SO THAT YOU CANNOT SULLY YOUR LEGACY ANY FURTHER.
A LION CANNOT BE KING OF THE JUNGLE WHEN IT'S OLD, SICK AND WEAK.
AND, OUT OF THAT SAME RESPECT, IT IS ONLY FAIR THAT I GIVE YOU A FIGHTING CHANCE.
I'LL GIVE YOU A FOUR-HOUR HEAD START.
CHUK
WHAT ARE YOU--?

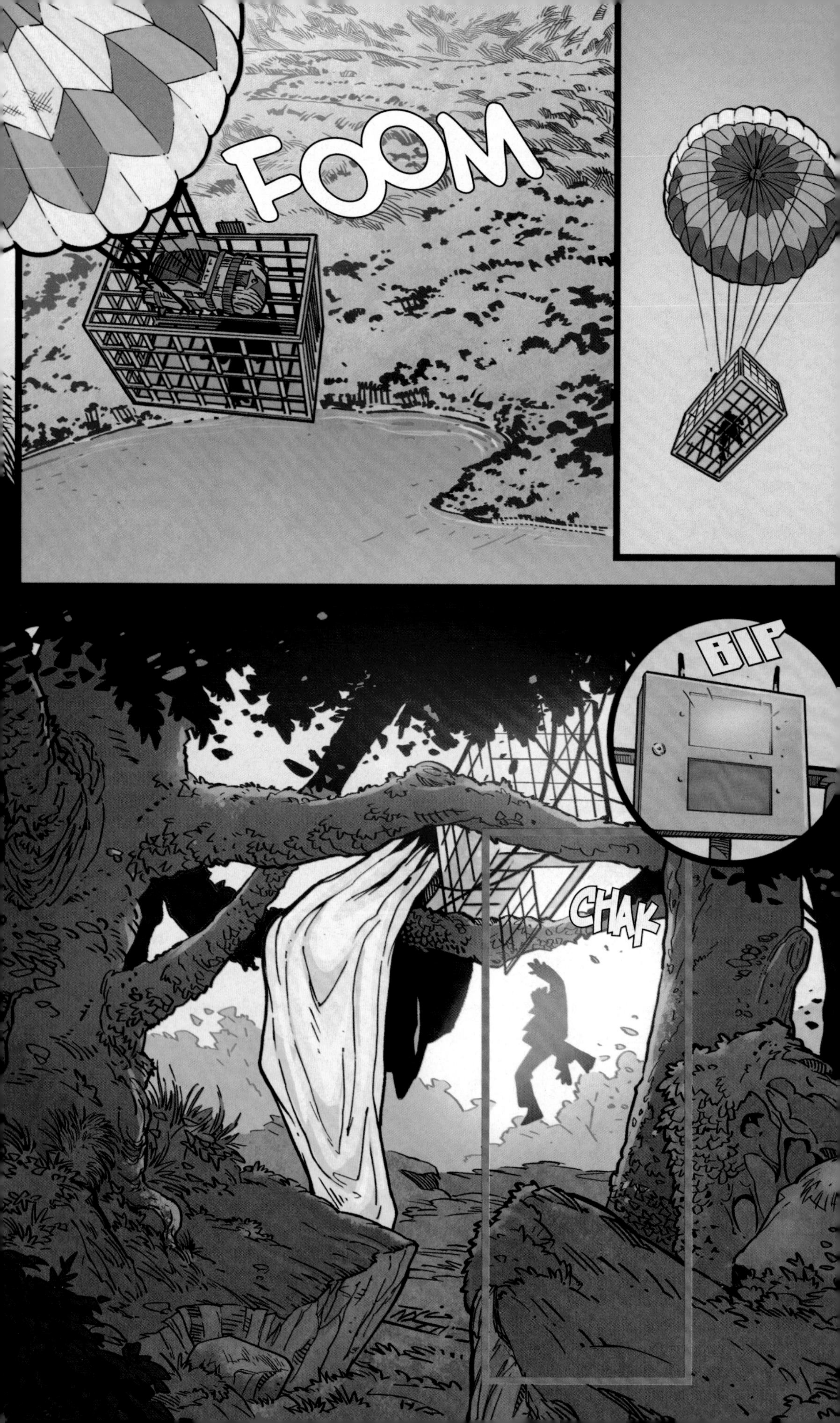
FOOM
BIP
CHAK

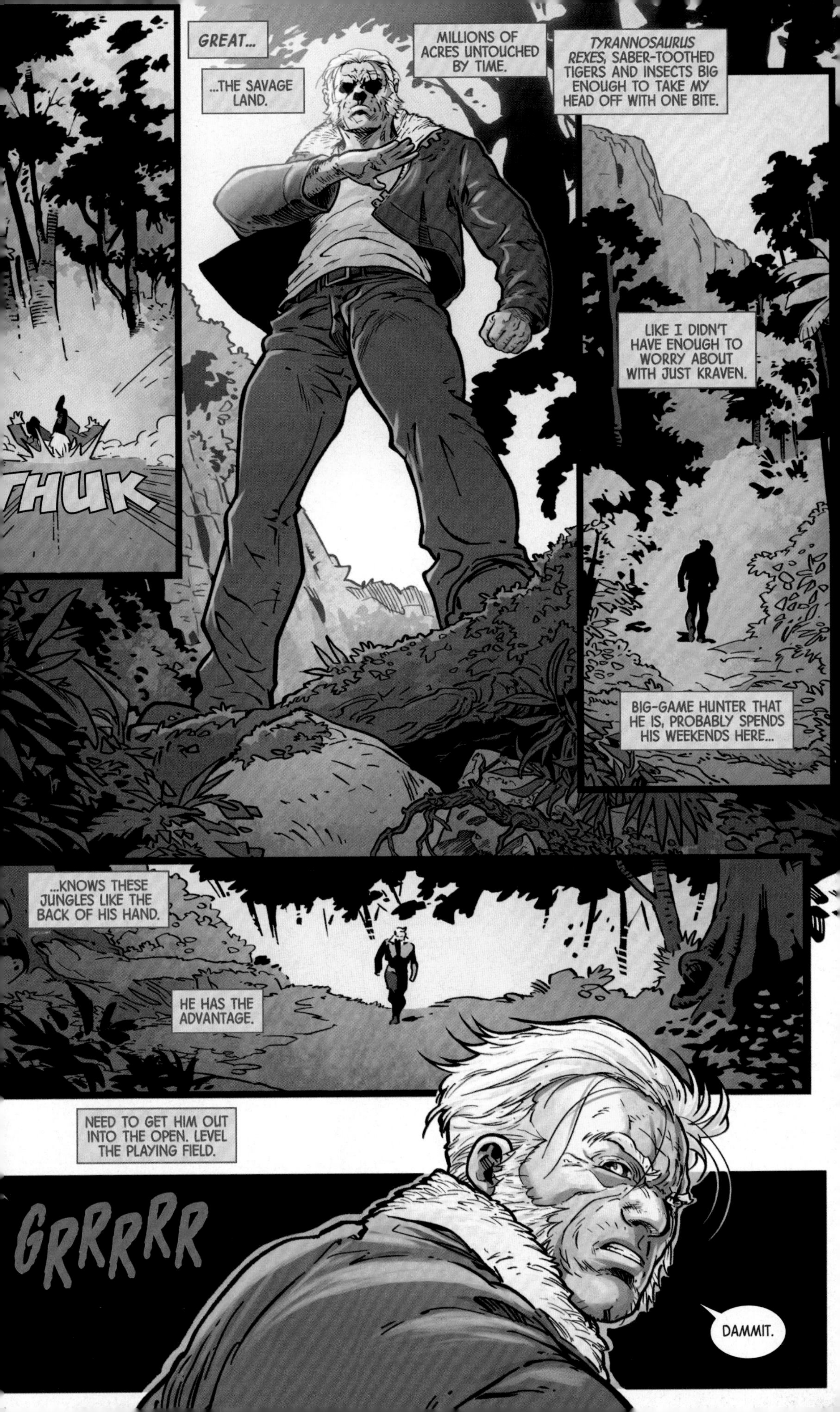
THUK
GREAT...
...THE SAVAGE LAND.
MILLIONS OF ACRES UNTOUCHED BY TIME.
TYRANNOSAURUS REXES, SABER-TOOTHED TIGERS AND INSECTS BIG ENOUGH TO TAKE MY HEAD OFF WITH ONE BITE.
LIKE I DIDN'T HAVE ENOUGH TO WORRY ABOUT WITH JUST KRAVEN.
BIG-GAME HUNTER THAT HE IS, PROBABLY SPENDS HIS WEEKENDS HERE...
...KNOWS THESE JUNGLES LIKE THE BACK OF HIS HAND.
HE HAS THE ADVANTAGE.
NEED TO GET HIM OUT INTO THE OPEN. LEVEL THE PLAYING FIELD.
GRRRRR
DAMMIT.

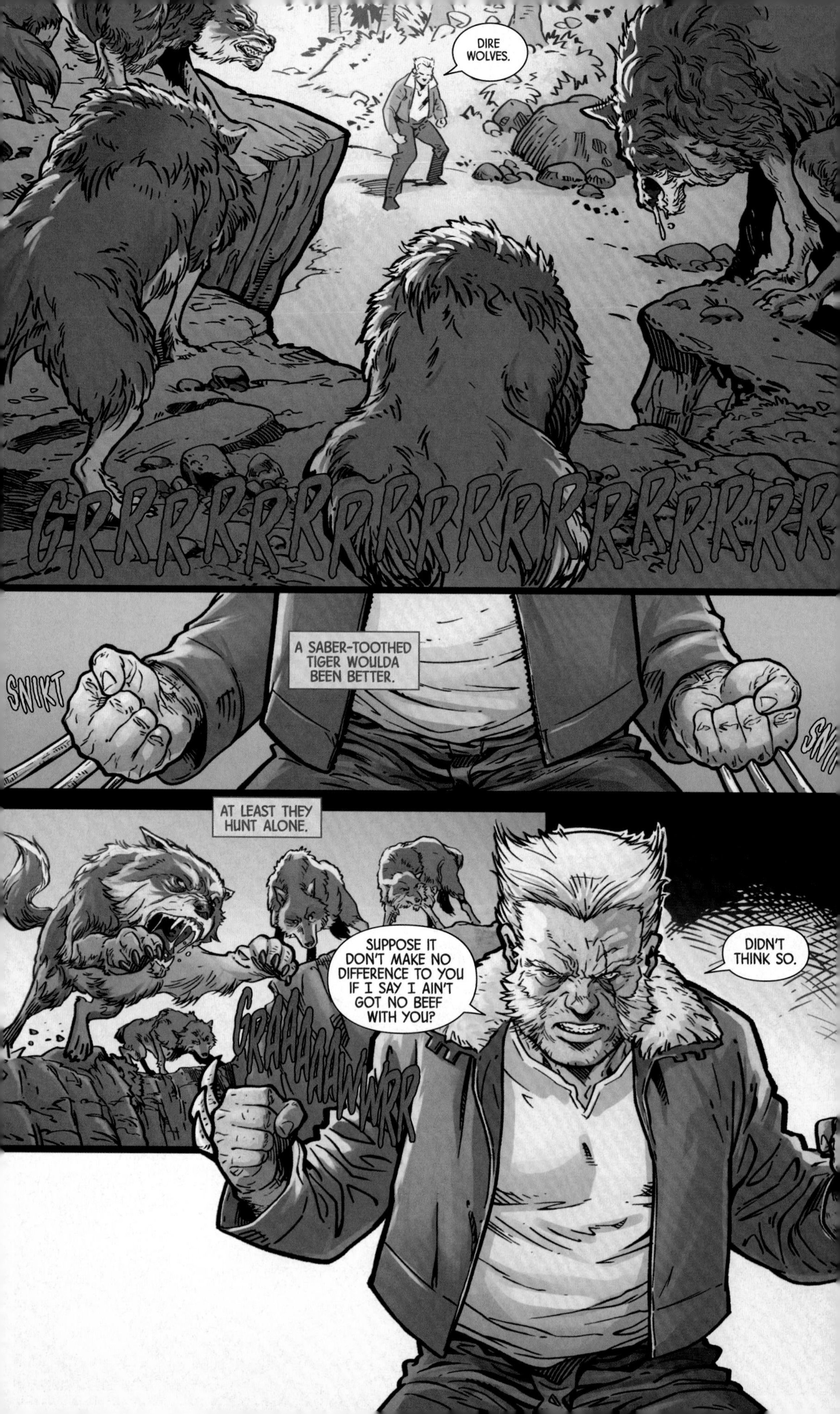
DIRE WOLVES.
GRRRRRRRRRRRRRRRR
A SABER-TOOTHED TIGER WOULDA BEEN BETTER.
SNIKT
SNI
AT LEAST THEY HUNT ALONE.
SUPPOSE IT DON'T MAKE NO DIFFERENCE TO YOU IF I SAY I AIN'T GOT NO BEEF WITH YOU?
GRAAAAAAWWRR
DIDN'T THINK SO.

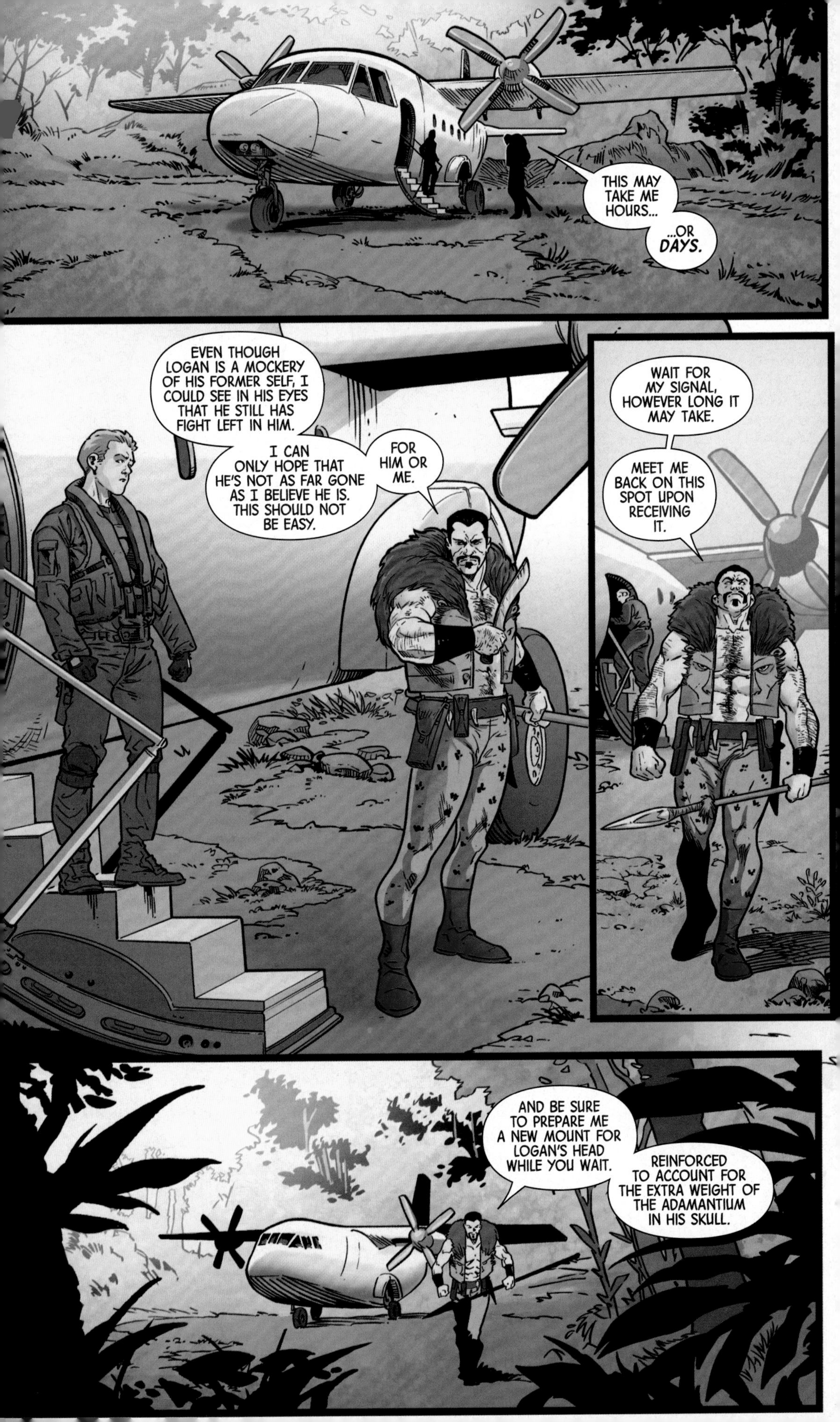
THIS MAY TAKE ME HOURS...
...OR DAYS.
EVEN THOUGH LOGAN IS A MOCKERY OF HIS FORMER SELF, I COULD SEE IN HIS EYES THAT HE STILL HAS FIGHT LEFT IN HIM.
I CAN ONLY HOPE THAT HE'S NOT AS FAR GONE AS I BELIEVE HE IS. THIS SHOULD NOT BE EASY.
FOR HIM OR ME.
WAIT FOR MY SIGNAL, HOWEVER LONG IT MAY TAKE.
MEET ME BACK ON THIS SPOT UPON RECEIVING IT.
AND BE SURE TO PREPARE ME A NEW MOUNT FOR LOGAN'S HEAD WHILE YOU WAIT.
REINFORCED TO ACCOUNT FOR THE EXTRA WEIGHT OF THE ADAMANTIUM IN HIS SKULL.

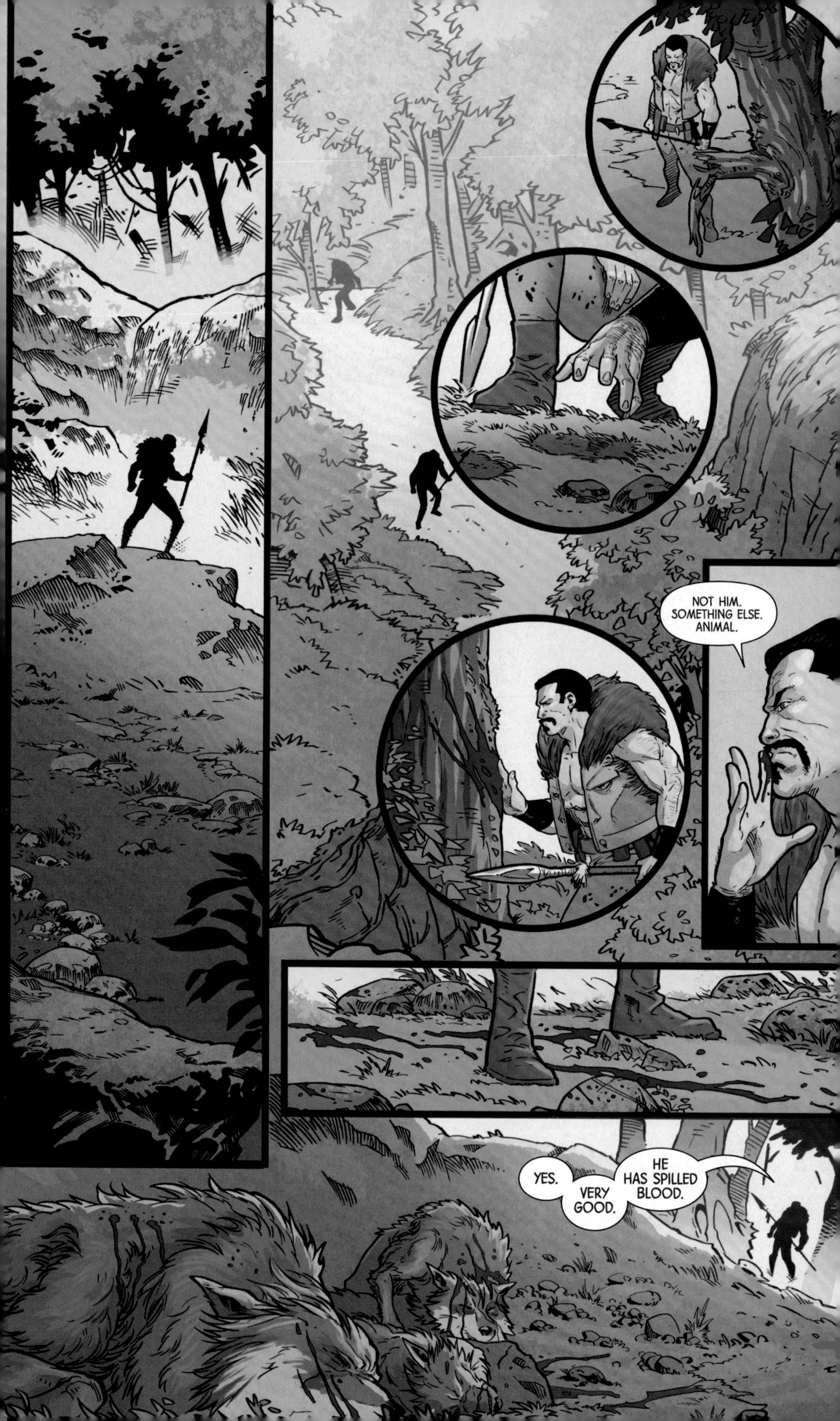
NOT HIM. SOMETHING ELSE. ANIMAL.
YES.
VERY GOOD.
HE HAS SPILLED BLOOD.

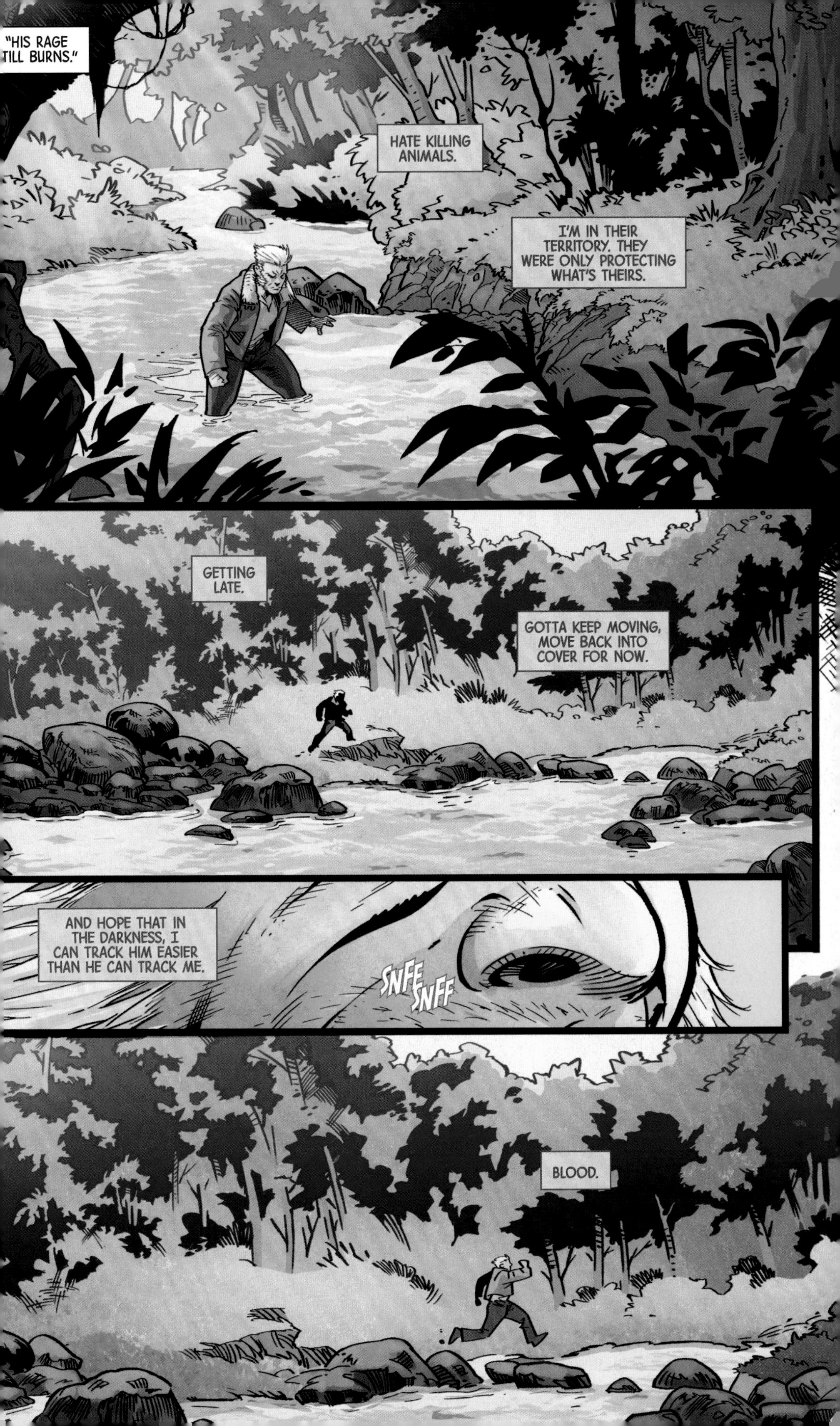
"HIS RAGE
TILL BURNS."
HATE KILLING ANIMALS.
I'M IN THEIR TERRITORY. THEY WERE ONLY PROTECTING WHAT'S THEIRS.
GETTING LATE.
GOTTA KEEP MOVING, MOVE BACK INTO COVER FOR NOW.
AND HOPE THAT IN THE DARKNESS, I CAN TRACK HIM EASIER THAN HE CAN TRACK ME.
SNFF SNFF
BLOOD.

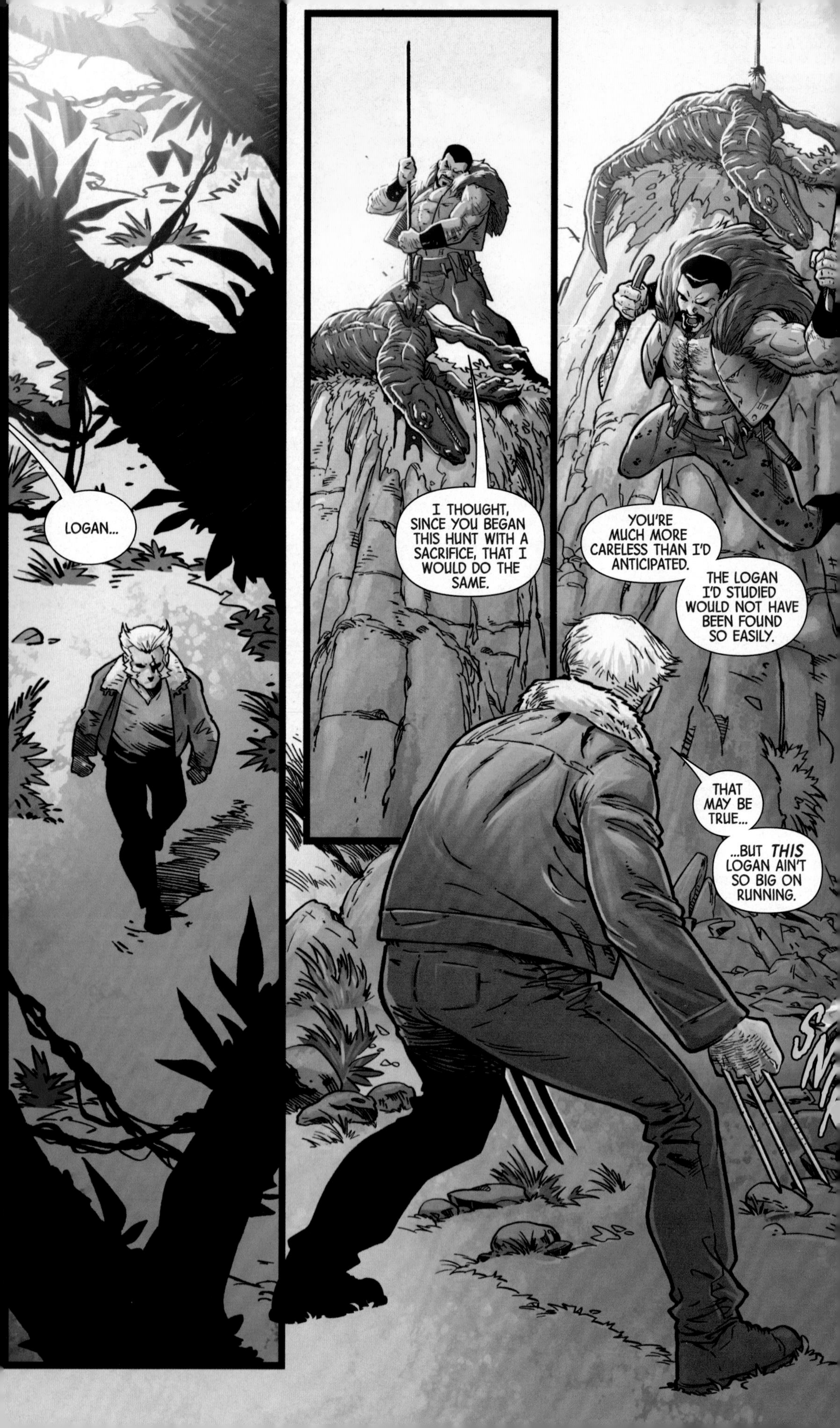
LOGAN...
I THOUGHT, SINCE YOU BEGAN THIS HUNT WITH A SACRIFICE, THAT I WOULD DO THE SAME.
YOU'RE MUCH MORE CARELESS THAN I'D ANTICIPATED.
THE LOGAN I'D STUDIED WOULD NOT HAVE BEEN FOUND SO EASILY.
THAT MAY BE TRUE...
...BUT *THIS* LOGAN AIN'T SO BIG ON RUNNING.

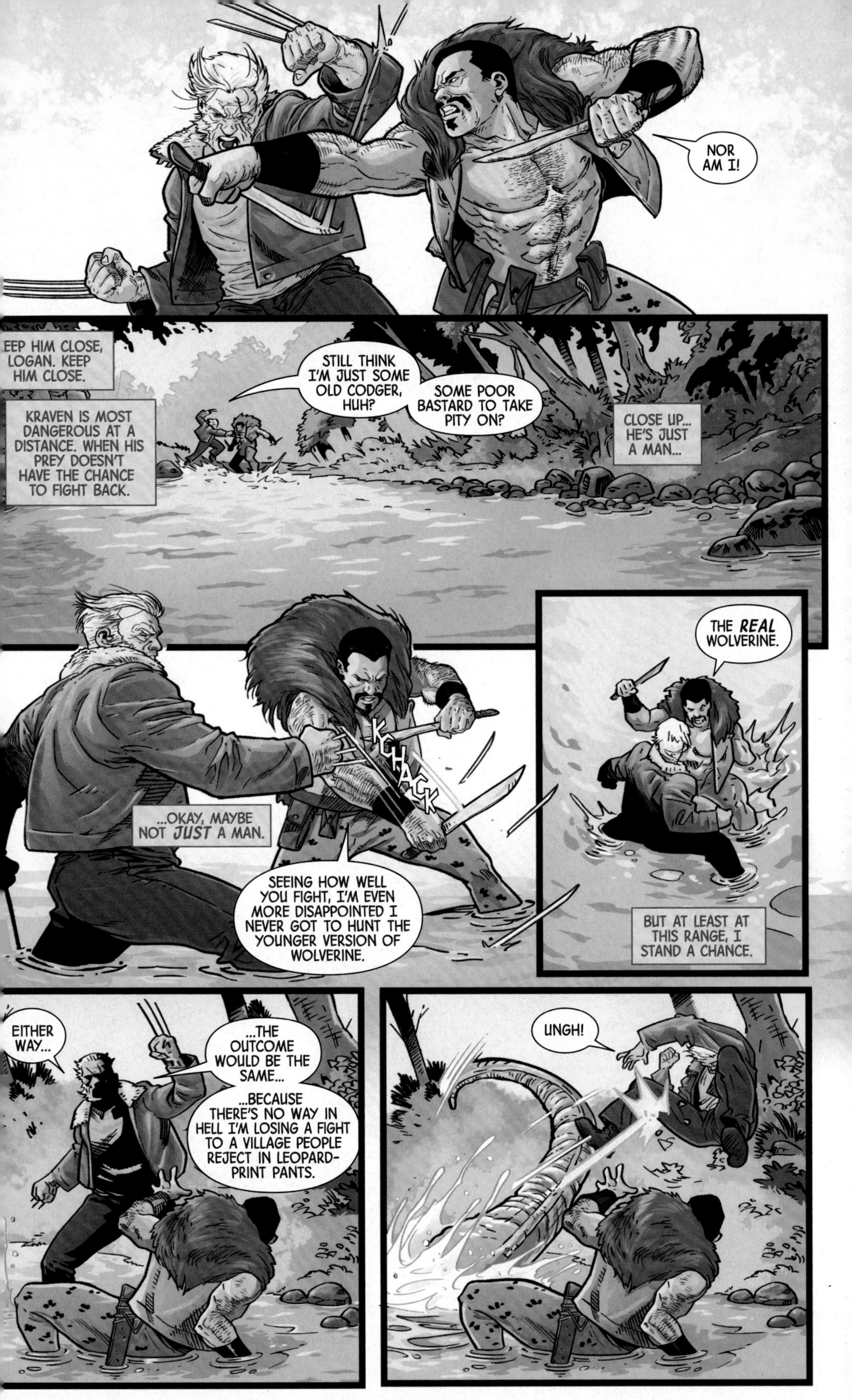
NOR AM I!
EEP HIM CLOSE, LOGAN. KEEP HIM CLOSE.
KRAVEN IS MOST DANGEROUS AT A DISTANCE. WHEN HIS PREY DOESN'T HAVE THE CHANCE TO FIGHT BACK.
STILL THINK I'M JUST SOME OLD CODGER, HUH?
SOME POOR BASTARD TO TAKE PITY ON?
CLOSE UP... HE'S JUST A MAN...
KCHACK
...OKAY, MAYBE NOT JUST A MAN.
SEEING HOW WELL YOU FIGHT, I'M EVEN MORE DISAPPOINTED I NEVER GOT TO HUNT THE YOUNGER VERSION OF WOLVERINE.
THE REAL WOLVERINE.
BUT AT LEAST AT THIS RANGE, I STAND A CHANCE.
EITHER WAY...
...THE OUTCOME WOULD BE THE SAME...
...BECAUSE THERE'S NO WAY IN HELL I'M LOSING A FIGHT TO A VILLAGE PEOPLE REJECT IN LEOPARD-PRINT PANTS.
UNGH!

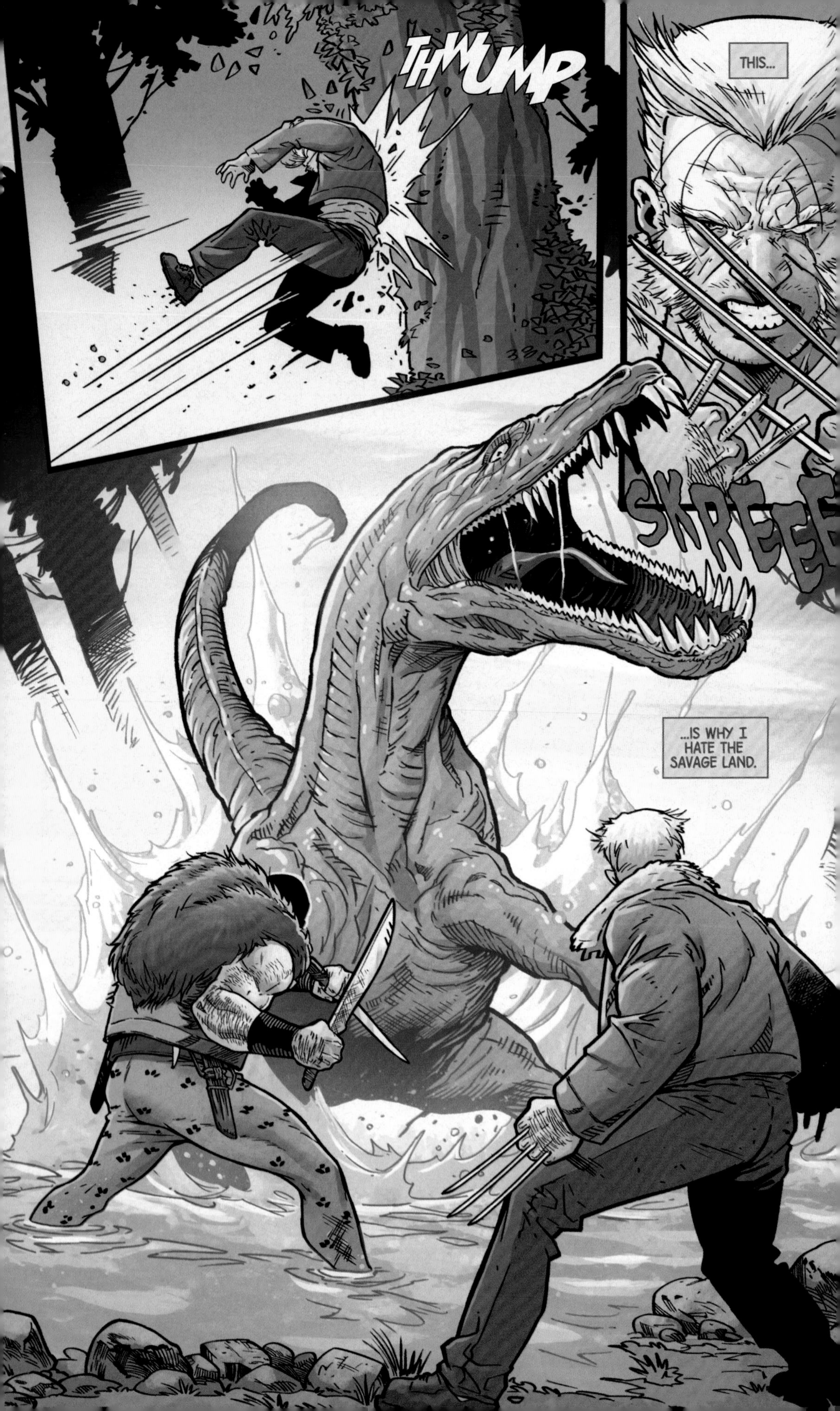
THWUMP
THIS...
SKREEE
...IS WHY I HATE THE SAVAGE LAND.

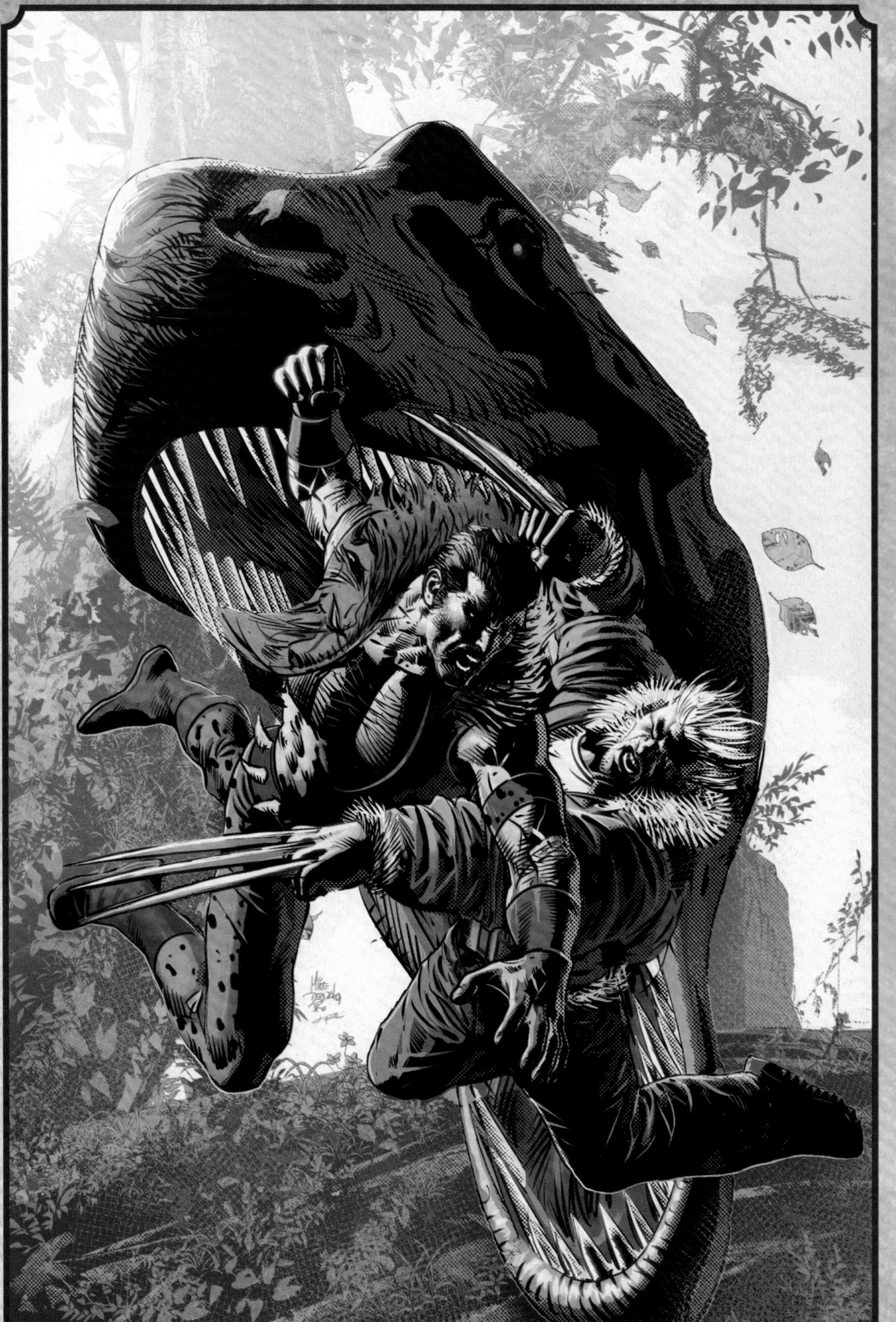

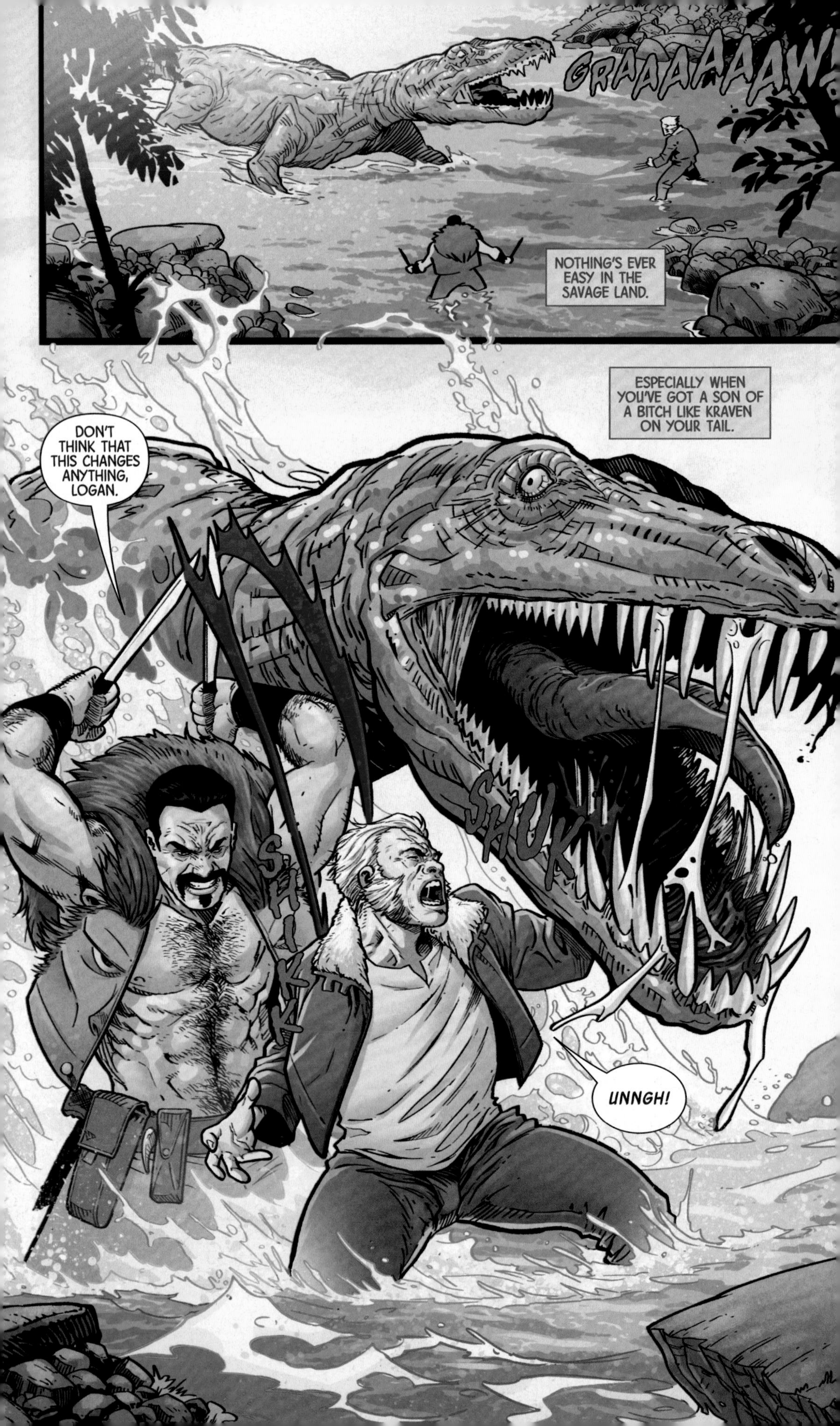
GRAAAAAAAW!
NOTHING'S EVER EASY IN THE SAVAGE LAND.
ESPECIALLY WHEN YOU'VE GOT A SON OF A BITCH LIKE KRAVEN ON YOUR TAIL.
DON'T THINK THAT THIS CHANGES ANYTHING, LOGAN.
SHIKT
SHUK
UNNGH!

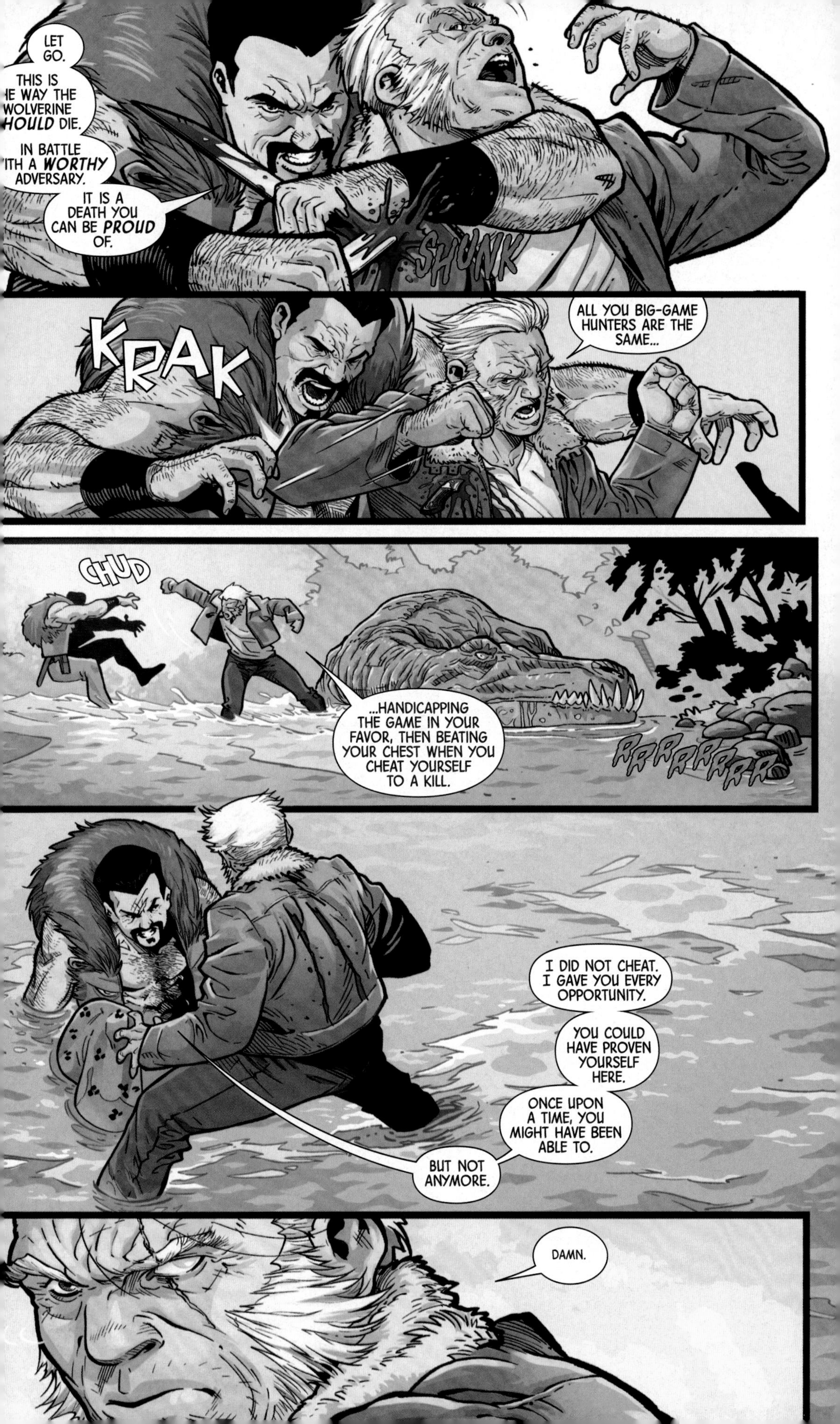
LET GO.
THIS IS
IE WAY THE
WOLVERINE
HOULD DIE.
IN BATTLE
ITH A WORTHY ADVERSARY.
IT IS A DEATH YOU CAN BE PROUD OF.
SHUNK
KRAK
ALL YOU BIG-GAME HUNTERS ARE THE SAME...
CHUD
...HANDICAPPING THE GAME IN YOUR FAVOR, THEN BEATING YOUR CHEST WHEN YOU CHEAT YOURSELF TO A KILL.
RRRRRRRRR
I DID NOT CHEAT. I GAVE YOU EVERY OPPORTUNITY.
YOU COULD HAVE PROVEN YOURSELF HERE.
ONCE UPON A TIME, YOU MIGHT HAVE BEEN ABLE TO.
BUT NOT ANYMORE.
DAMN.

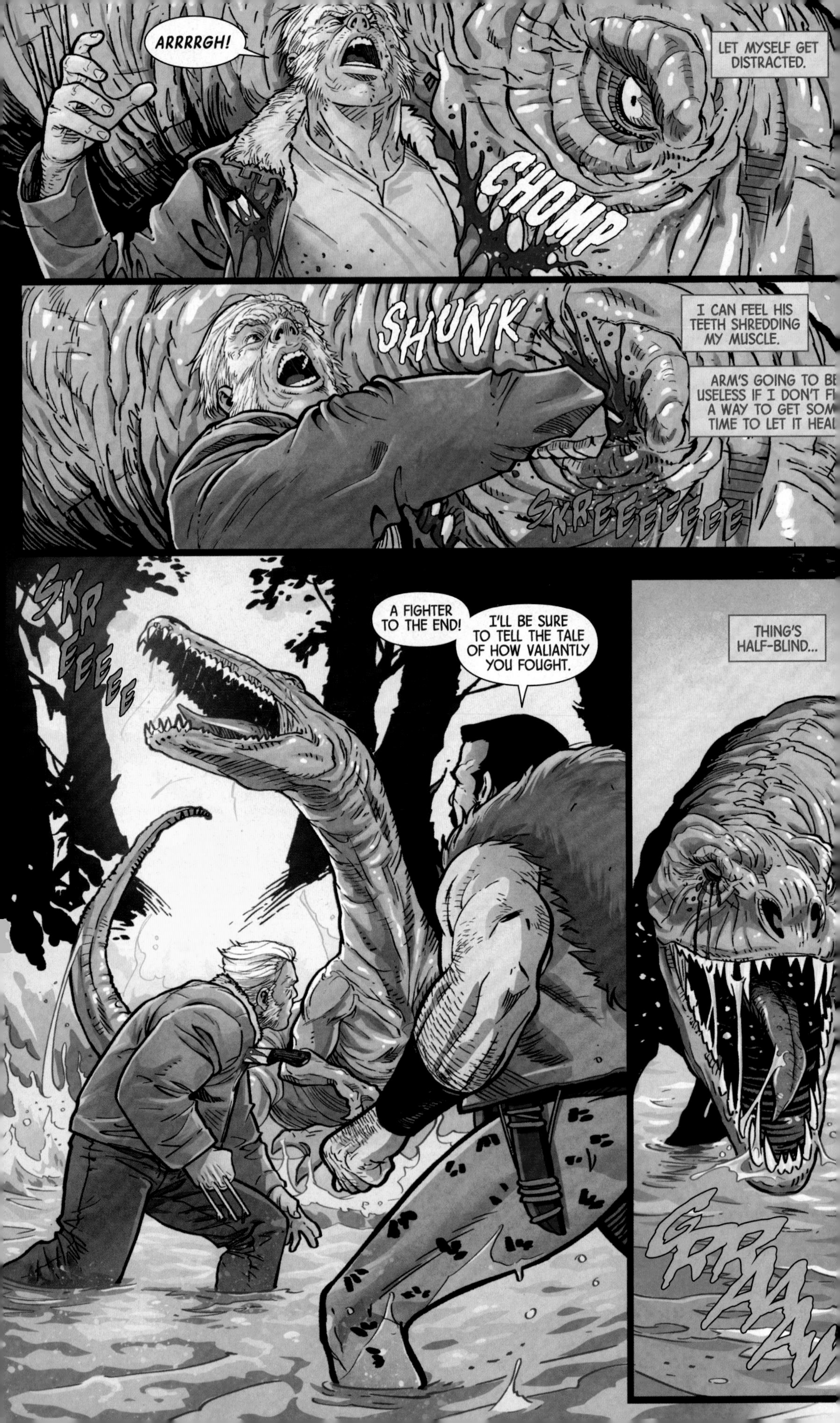
ARRRRGH!
LET MYSELF GET DISTRACTED.
CHOMP
SHUNK
I CAN FEEL HIS TEETH SHREDDING MY MUSCLE.
SKREEEEEEEE
A FIGHTER TO THE END!
I'LL BE SURE TO TELL THE TALE OF HOW VALIANTLY YOU FOUGHT.
SKREEEEE
THING'S HALF-BLIND...

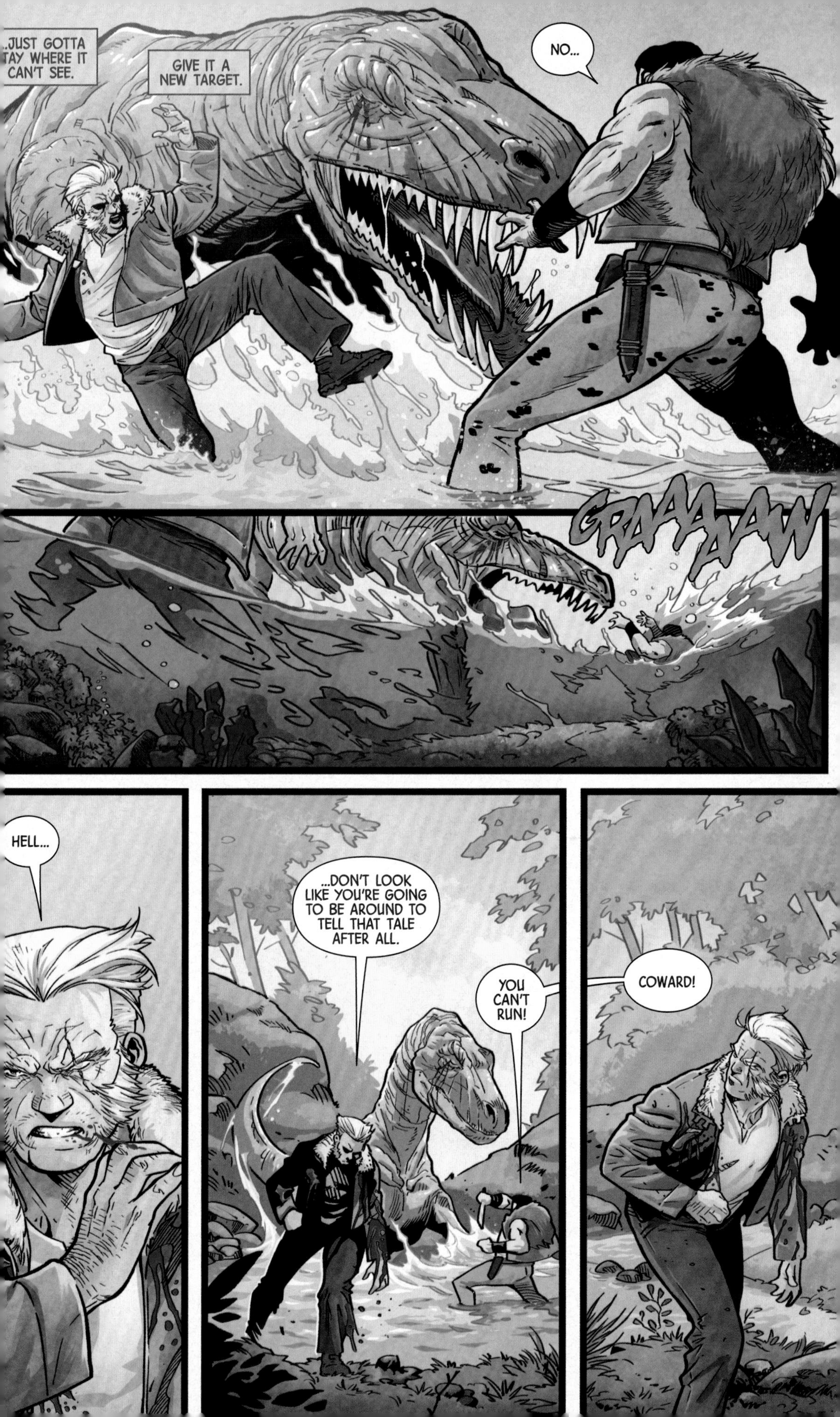
...JUST GOTTA
STAY WHERE IT
CAN'T SEE.
GIVE IT A
NEW TARGET.
NO...
GRAAAAAW
HELL...
...DON'T LOOK LIKE YOU'RE GOING TO BE AROUND TO TELL THAT TALE AFTER ALL.
YOU CAN'T RUN!
COWARD!

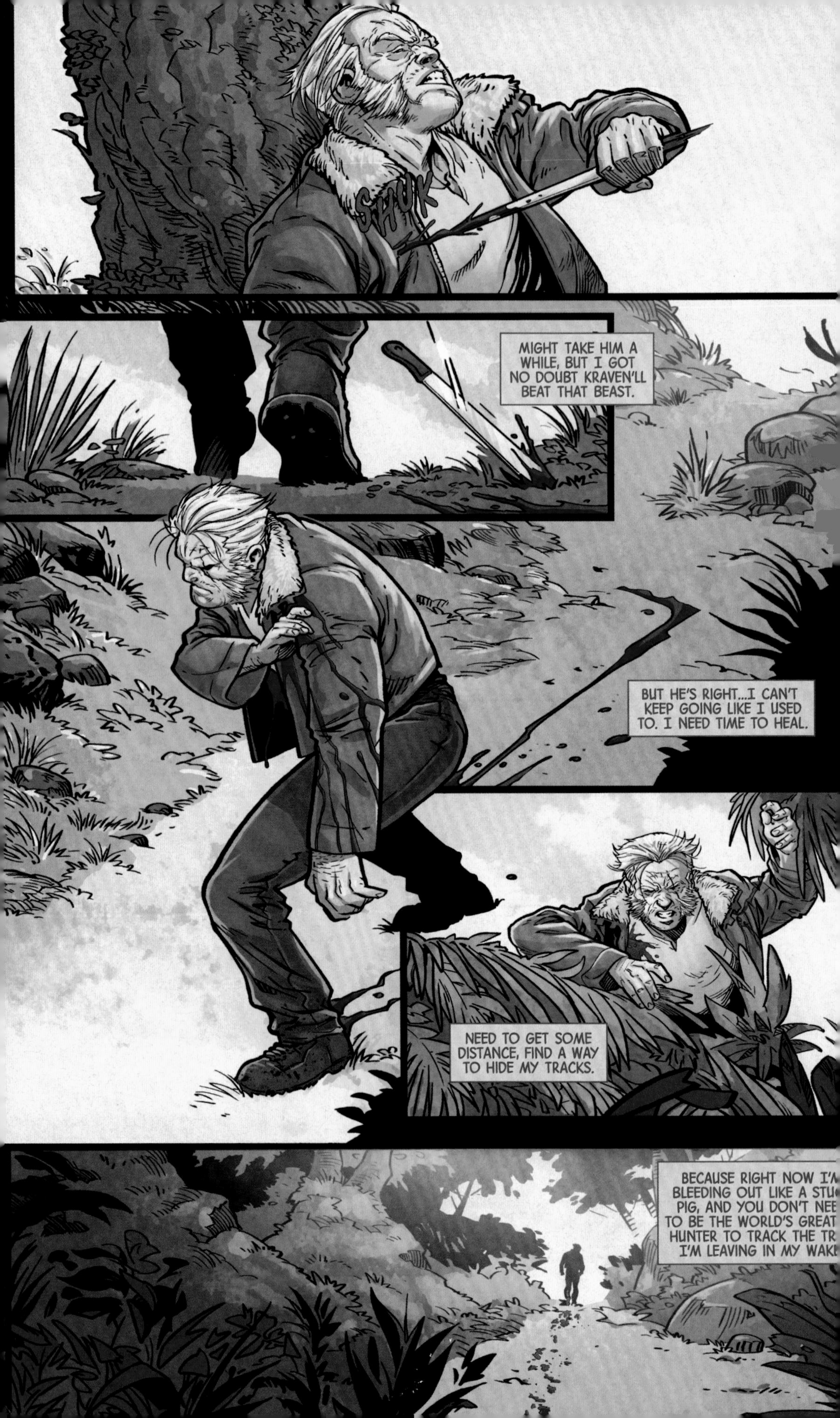
SHUK
MIGHT TAKE HIM A WHILE, BUT I GOT NO DOUBT KRAVEN'LL BEAT THAT BEAST.
BUT HE'S RIGHT...I CAN'T KEEP GOING LIKE I USED TO. I NEED TIME TO HEAL.
NEED TO GET SOME DISTANCE, FIND A WAY TO HIDE MY TRACKS.
BECAUSE RIGHT NOW I'M BLEEDING OUT LIKE A STU PIG, AND YOU DON'T NEE TO BE THE WORLD'S GREAT HUNTER TO TRACK THE TR I'M LEAVING IN MY WAK

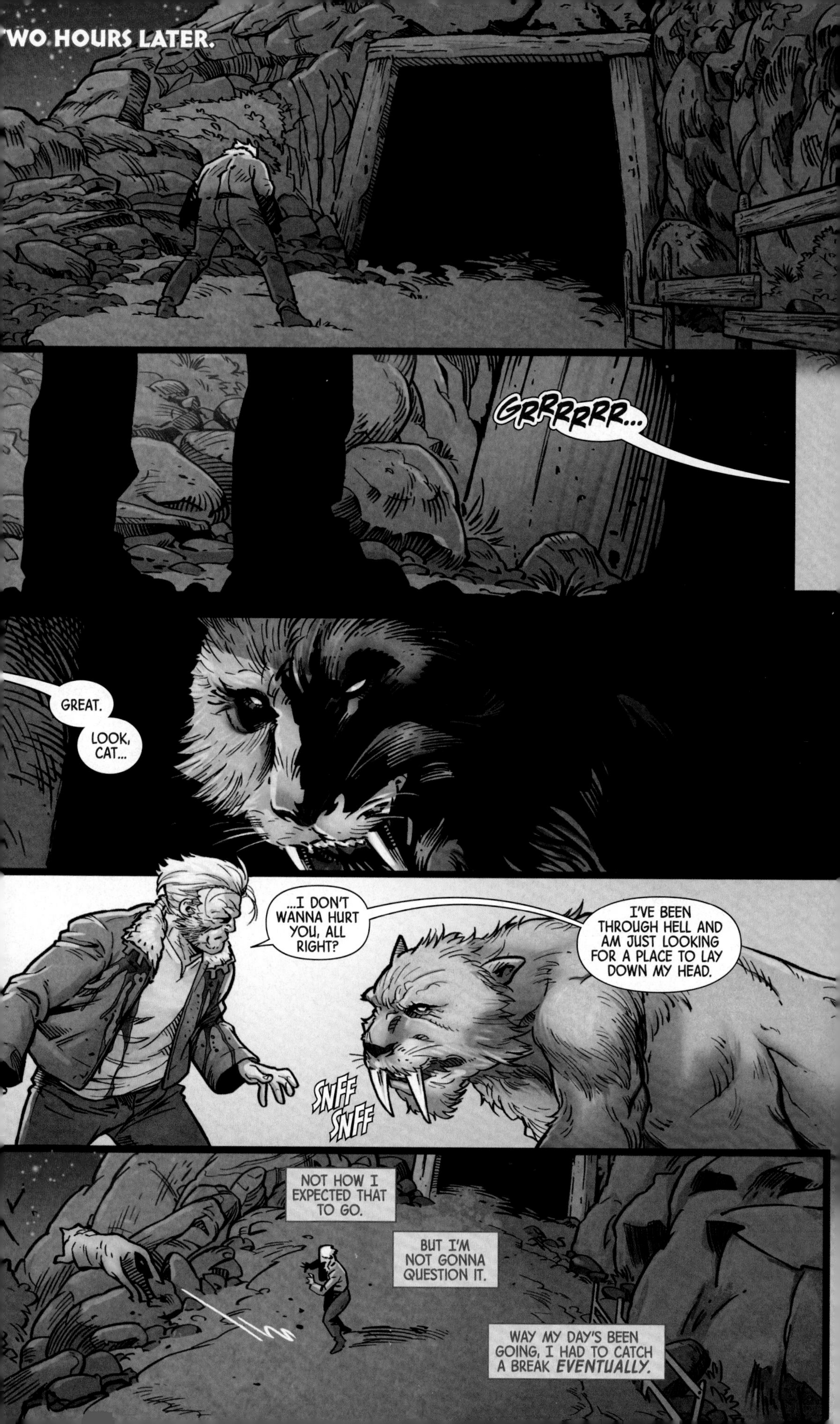

WO HOURS LATER.
GRRRRRR...
GREAT.
LOOK, CAT...
...I DON'T WANNA HURT YOU, ALL RIGHT?
I'VE BEEN THROUGH HELL AND AM JUST LOOKING FOR A PLACE TO LAY DOWN MY HEAD.
SNFF SNFF
NOT HOW I EXPECTED THAT TO GO.
BUT I'M NOT GONNA QUESTION IT.
WAY MY DAY'S BEEN GOING, I HAD TO CATCH A BREAK EVENTUALLY.

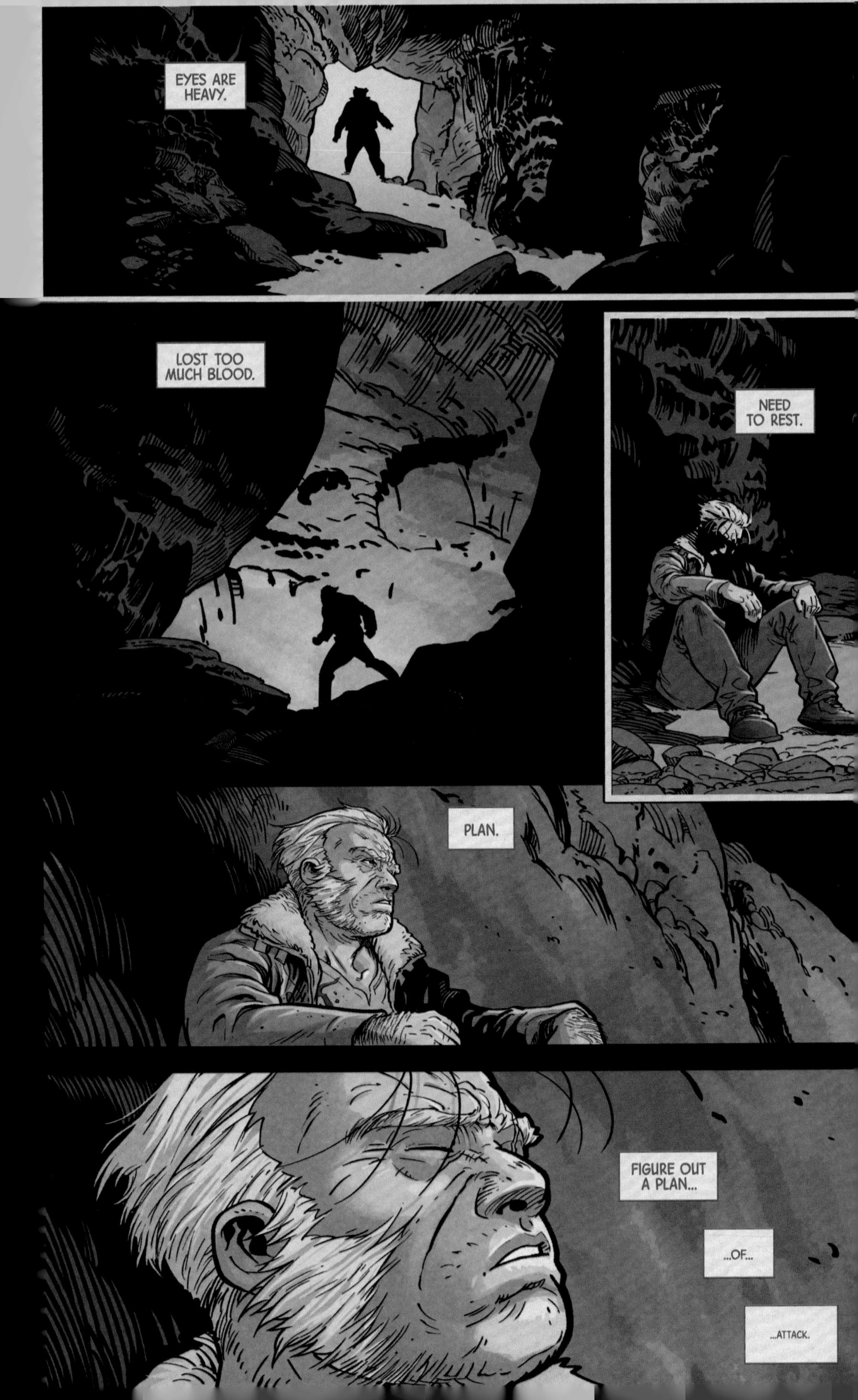
EYES ARE HEAVY.
LOST TOO MUCH BLOOD.
NEED TO REST.
PLAN.
FIGURE OUT A PLAN...
...OF...
...ATTACK.

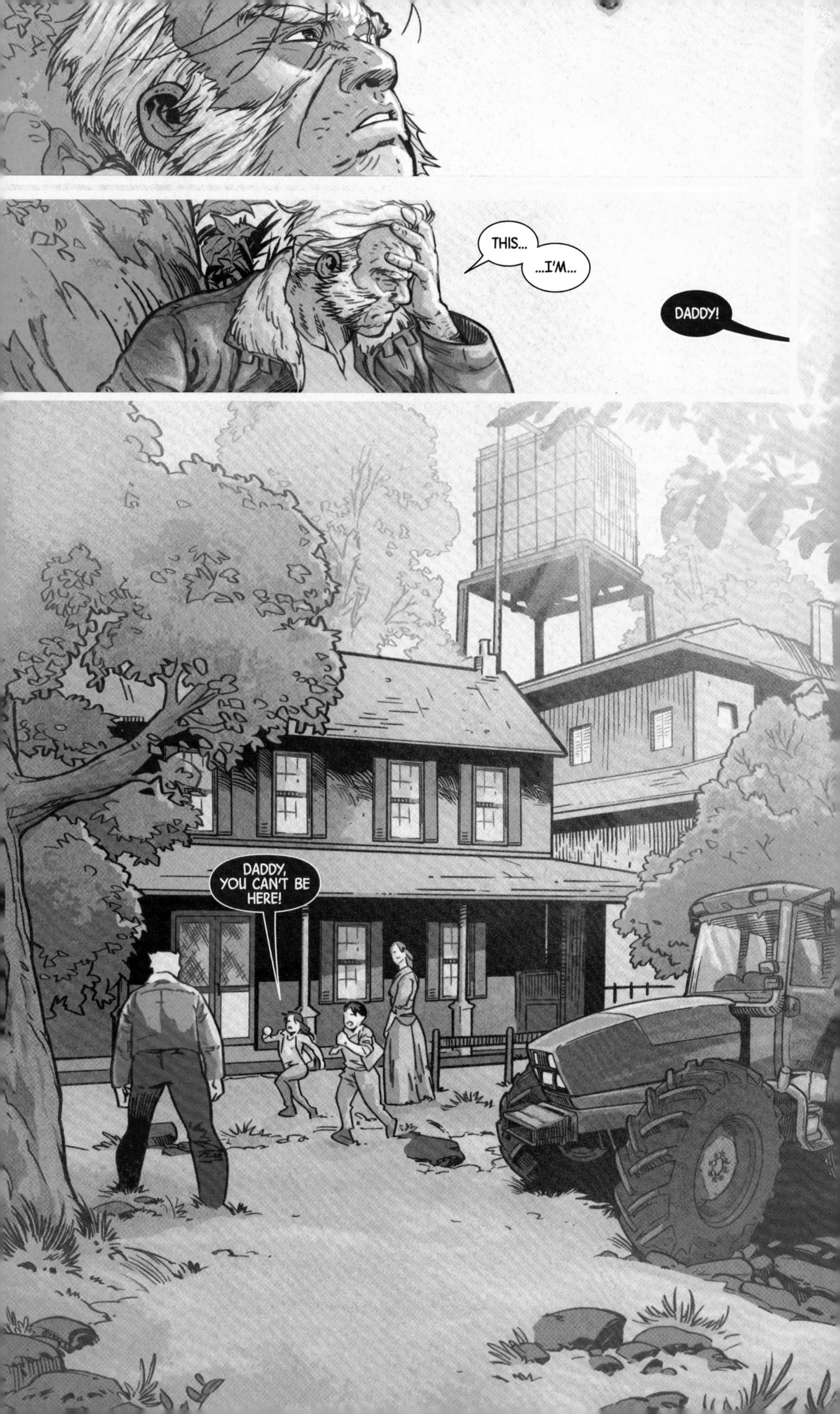
THIS...
...I'M...
DADDY!
DADDY, YOU CAN'T BE HERE!

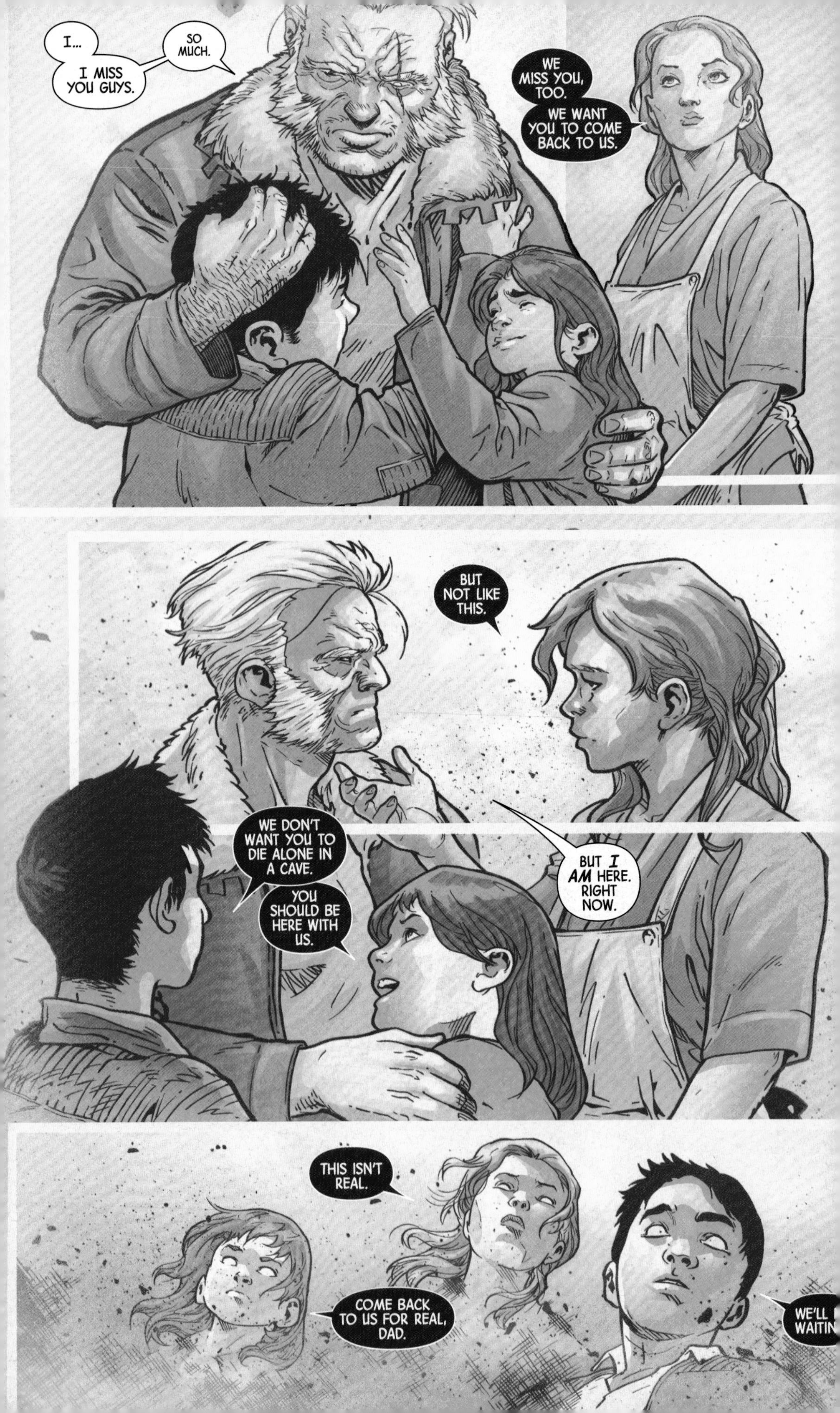
I...
I MISS YOU GUYS.
SO MUCH.
WE MISS YOU, TOO.
WE WANT YOU TO COME BACK TO US.
BUT NOT LIKE THIS.
WE DON'T WANT YOU TO DIE ALONE IN A CAVE.
YOU SHOULD BE HERE WITH US.
BUT I AM HERE. RIGHT NOW.
THIS ISN'T REAL.
COME BACK TO US FOR REAL, DAD.
WE'LL WAITIN

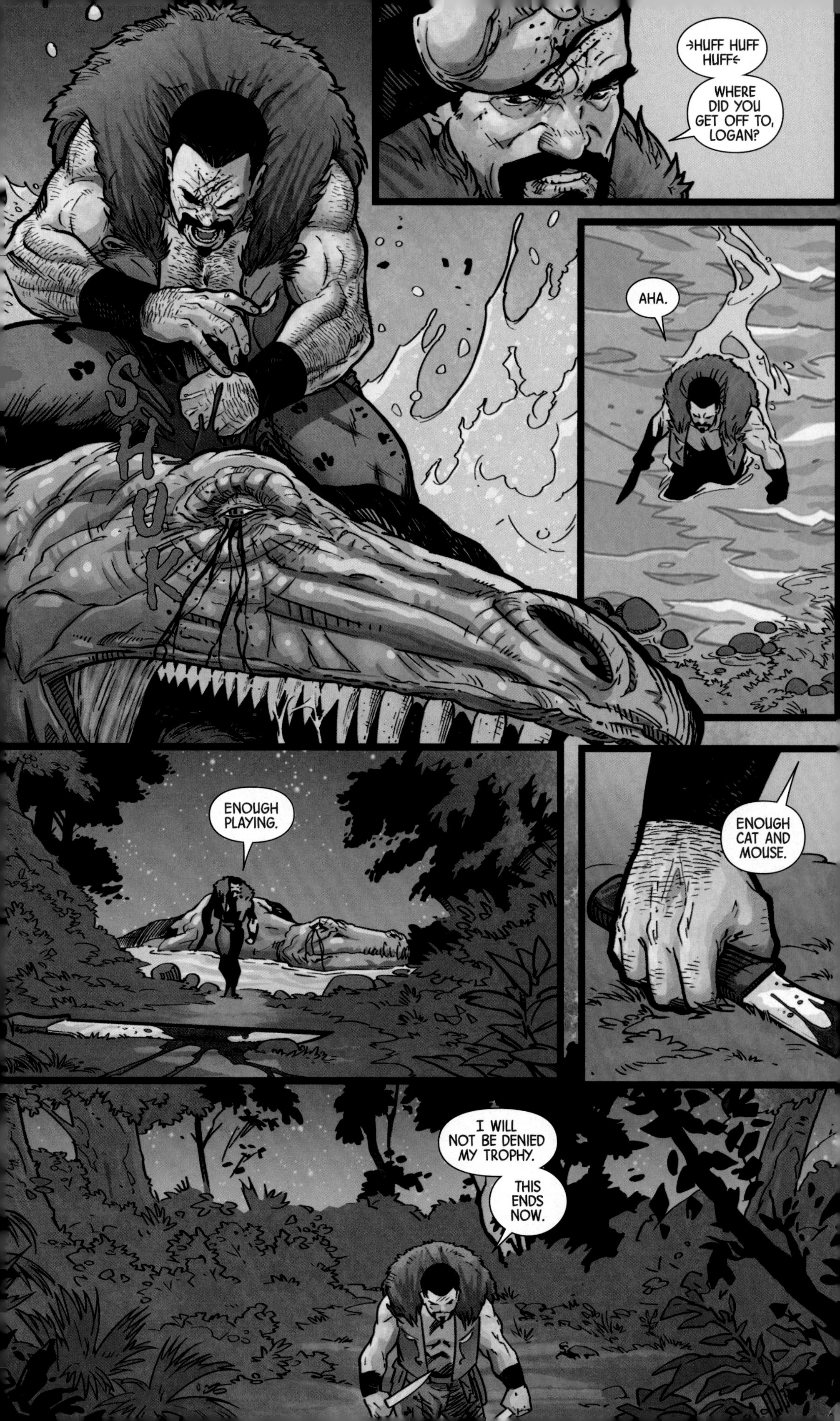

SHUK
>HUFF HUFF HUFF<
WHERE DID YOU GET OFF TO, LOGAN?
AHA.
ENOUGH PLAYING.
ENOUGH CAT AND MOUSE.
I WILL NOT BE DENIED MY TROPHY.
THIS ENDS NOW.

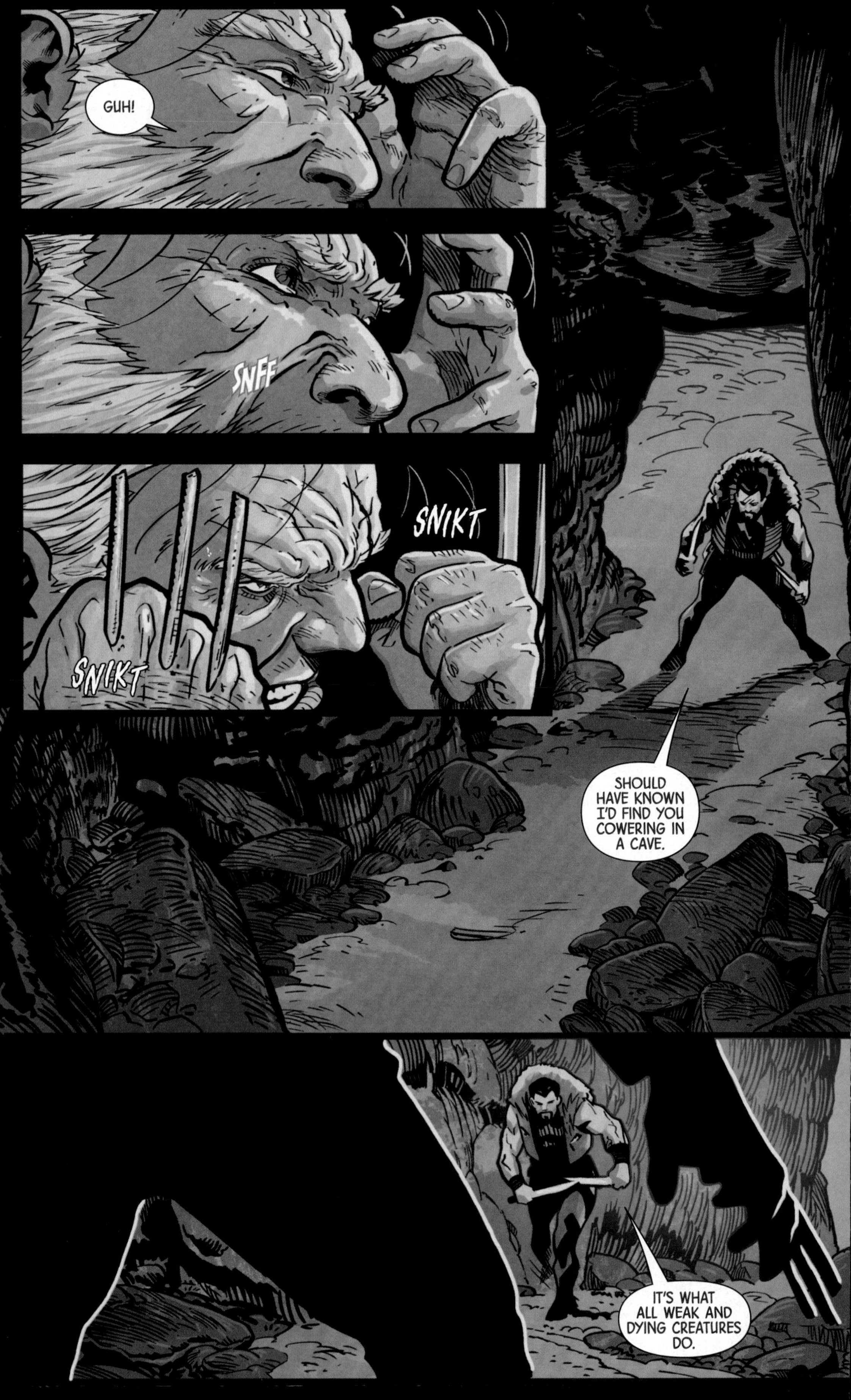
GUH!
SNFF
SNIKT
SNIKT
SHOULD HAVE KNOWN I'D FIND YOU COWERING IN A CAVE.
IT'S WHAT ALL WEAK AND DYING CREATURES DO.

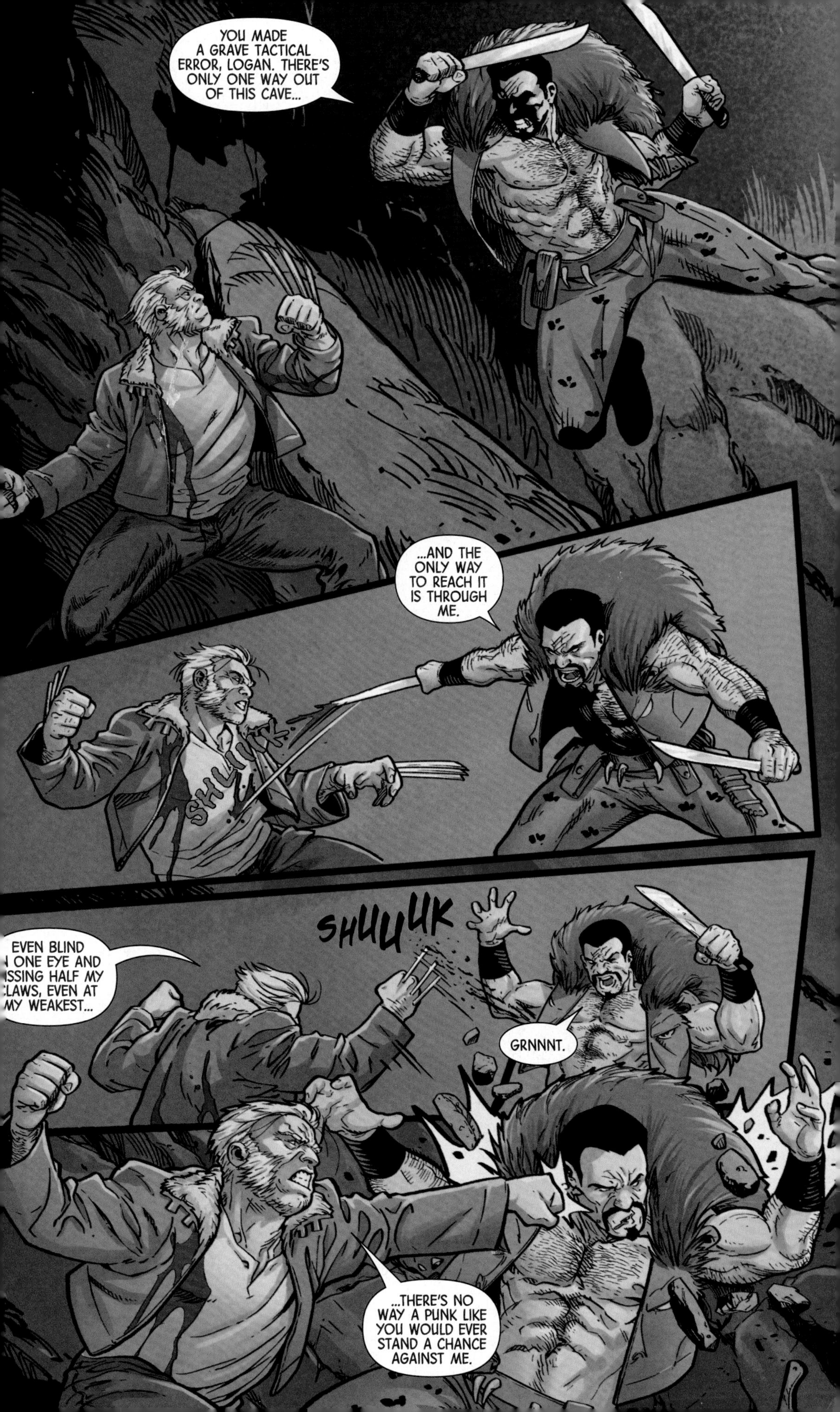
YOU MADE A GRAVE TACTICAL ERROR, LOGAN. THERE'S ONLY ONE WAY OUT OF THIS CAVE...
...AND THE ONLY WAY TO REACH IT IS THROUGH ME.
SHUUK
EVEN BLIND IN ONE EYE AND MISSING HALF MY CLAWS, EVEN AT MY WEAKEST...
SHUUUK
GRNNNT.
...THERE'S NO WAY A PUNK LIKE YOU WOULD EVER STAND A CHANCE AGAINST ME.

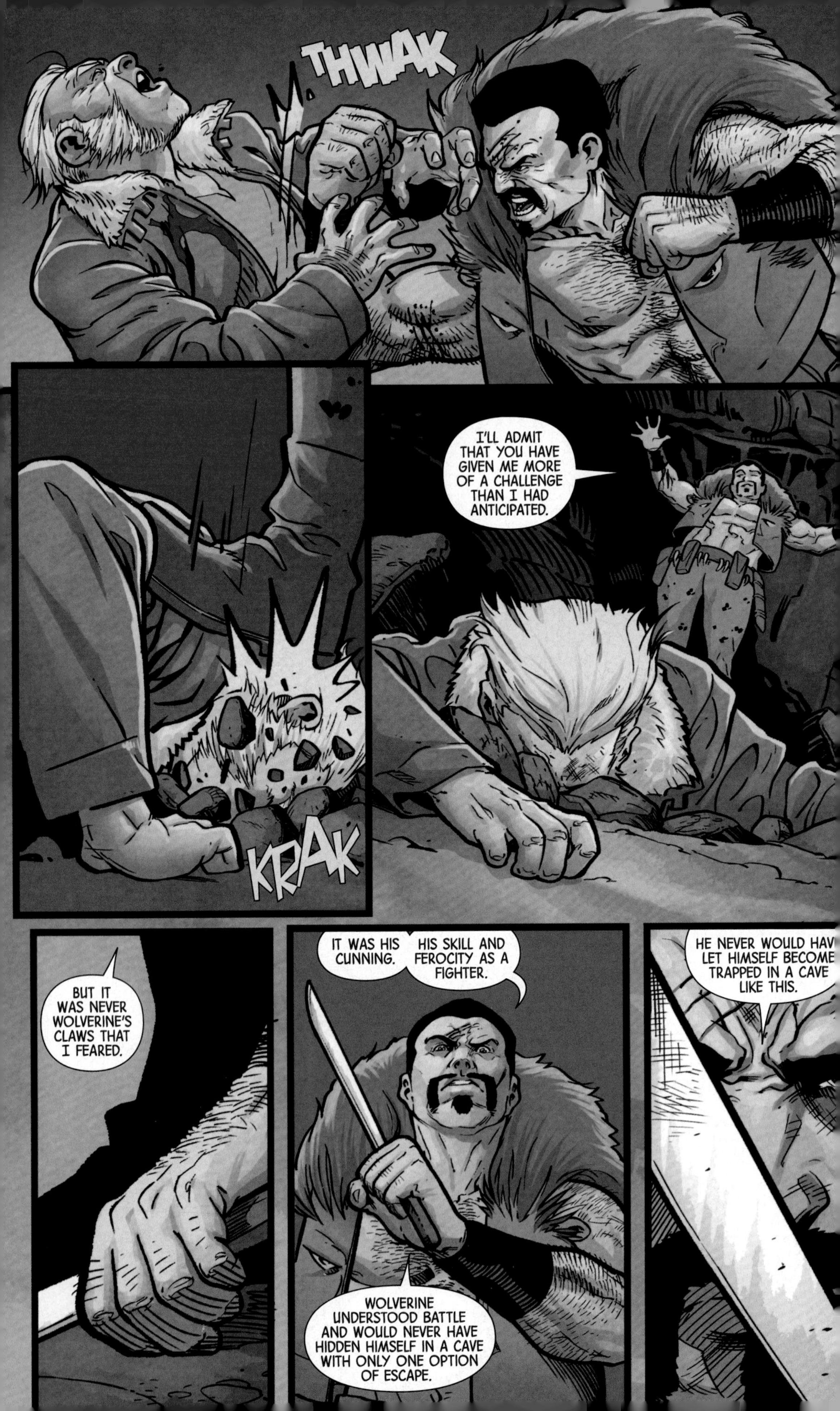
THWAK
KRAK
I'LL ADMIT THAT YOU HAVE GIVEN ME MORE OF A CHALLENGE THAN I HAD ANTICIPATED.
BUT IT WAS NEVER WOLVERINE'S CLAWS THAT I FEARED.
IT WAS HIS CUNNING.
HIS SKILL AND FEROCITY AS A FIGHTER.
WOLVERINE UNDERSTOOD BATTLE AND WOULD NEVER HAVE HIDDEN HIMSELF IN A CAVE WITH ONLY ONE OPTION OF ESCAPE.
HE NEVER WOULD HAV LET HIMSELF BECOME TRAPPED IN A CAVE LIKE THIS.

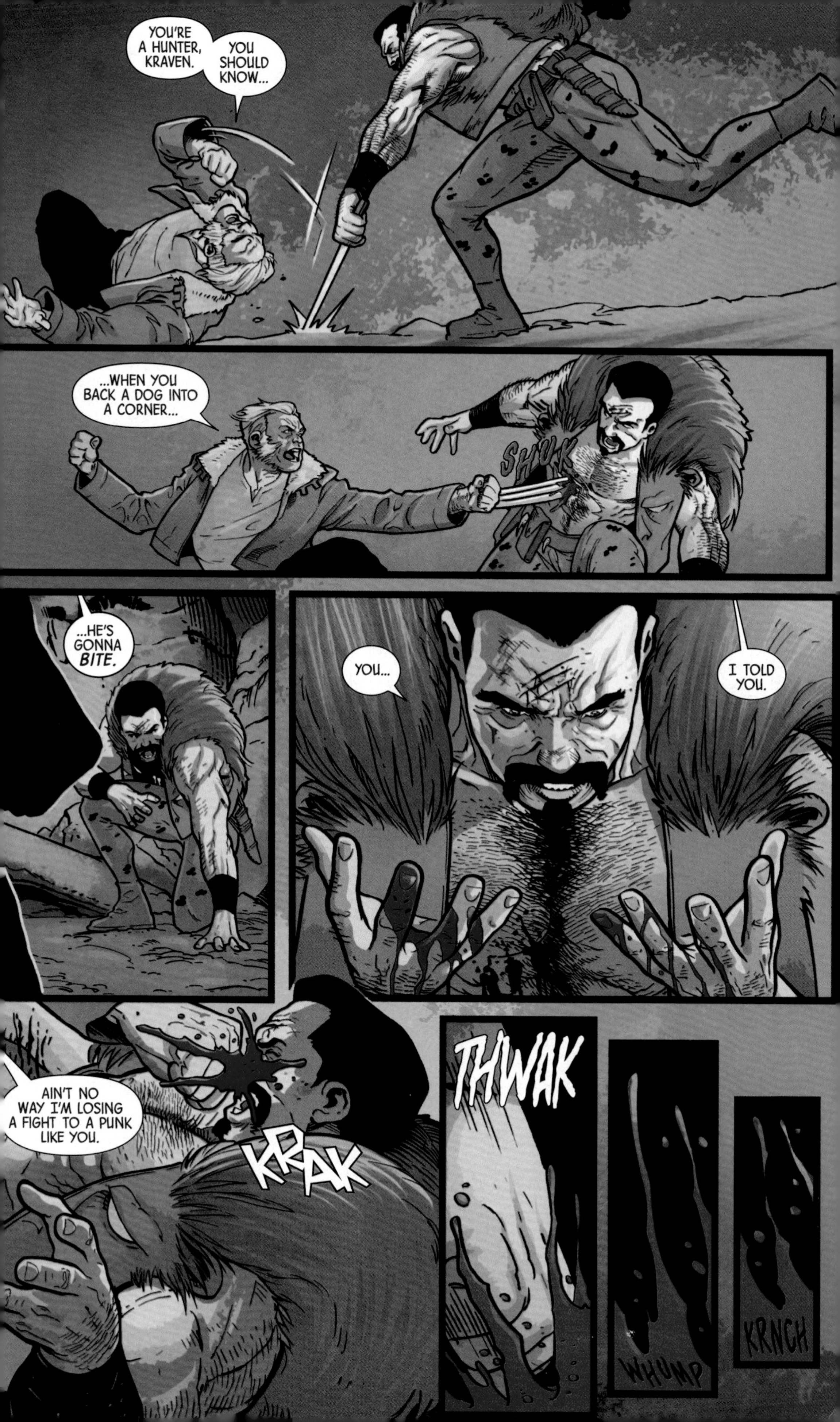

YOU'RE A HUNTER, KRAVEN.
YOU SHOULD KNOW...
...WHEN YOU BACK A DOG INTO A CORNER...
SHUK
...HE'S GONNA *BITE.*
YOU...
I TOLD YOU.
AIN'T NO WAY I'M LOSING A FIGHT TO A PUNK LIKE YOU.
KRAK
THWAK
WHUMP
KRNCH

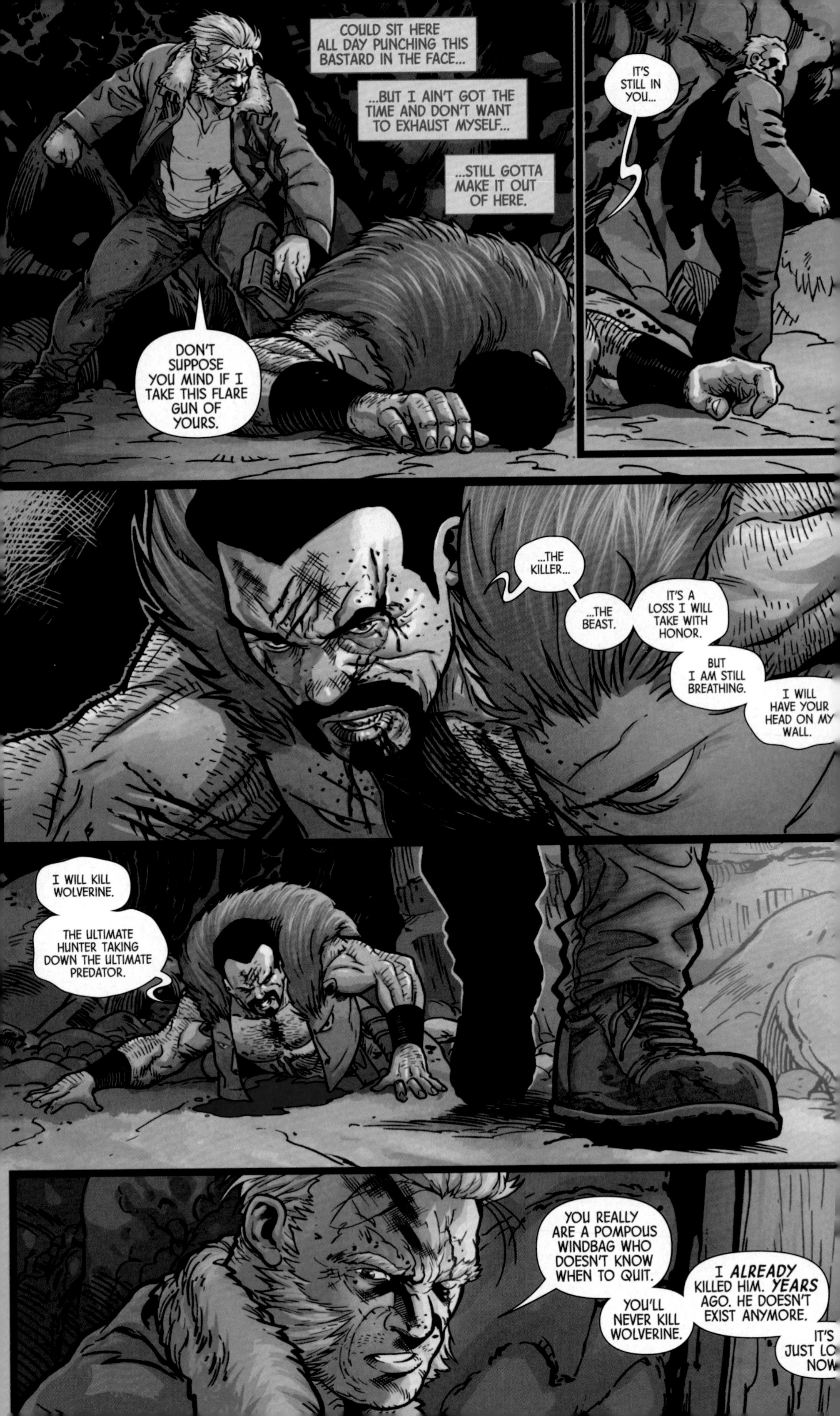
COULD SIT HERE ALL DAY PUNCHING THIS BASTARD IN THE FACE...
...BUT I AIN'T GOT THE TIME AND DON'T WANT TO EXHAUST MYSELF...
...STILL GOTTA MAKE IT OUT OF HERE.
DON'T SUPPOSE YOU MIND IF I TAKE THIS FLARE GUN OF YOURS.
IT'S STILL IN YOU...
...THE KILLER...
...THE BEAST.
IT'S A LOSS I WILL TAKE WITH HONOR.
BUT I AM STILL BREATHING.
I WILL HAVE YOUR HEAD ON MY WALL.
I WILL KILL WOLVERINE.
THE ULTIMATE HUNTER TAKING DOWN THE ULTIMATE PREDATOR.
YOU REALLY ARE A POMPOUS WINDBAG WHO DOESN'T KNOW WHEN TO QUIT.
YOU'LL NEVER KILL WOLVERINE.
I *ALREADY* KILLED HIM. *YEARS* AGO. HE DOESN'T EXIST ANYMORE.

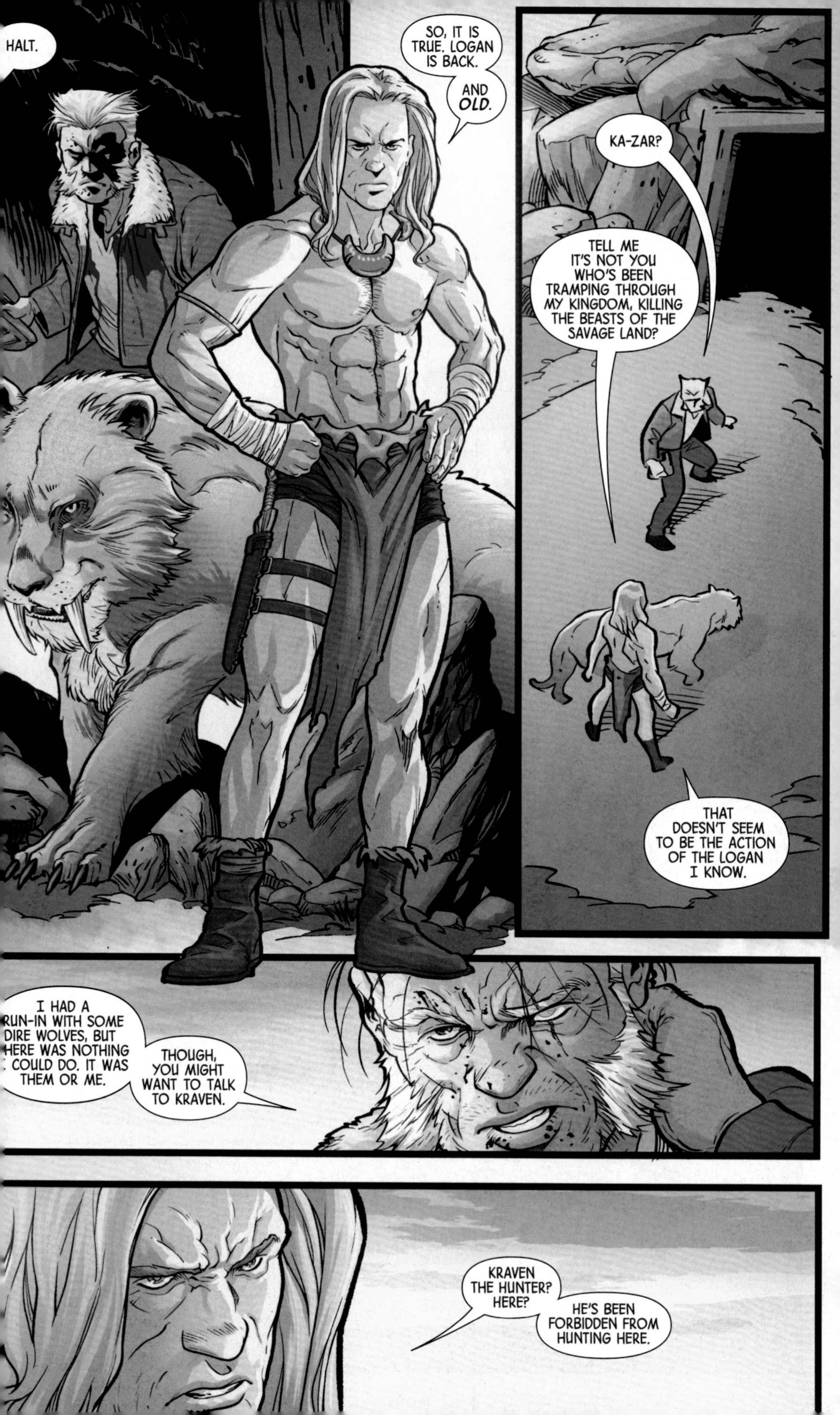

HALT.
SO, IT IS TRUE. LOGAN IS BACK.
AND *OLD.*
KA-ZAR?
TELL ME IT'S NOT YOU WHO'S BEEN TRAMPING THROUGH MY KINGDOM, KILLING THE BEASTS OF THE SAVAGE LAND?
THAT DOESN'T SEEM TO BE THE ACTION OF THE LOGAN I KNOW.
I HAD A RUN-IN WITH SOME DIRE WOLVES, BUT HERE WAS NOTHING COULD DO. IT WAS THEM OR ME.
THOUGH, YOU MIGHT WANT TO TALK TO KRAVEN.
KRAVEN THE HUNTER? HERE?
HE'S BEEN FORBIDDEN FROM HUNTING HERE.

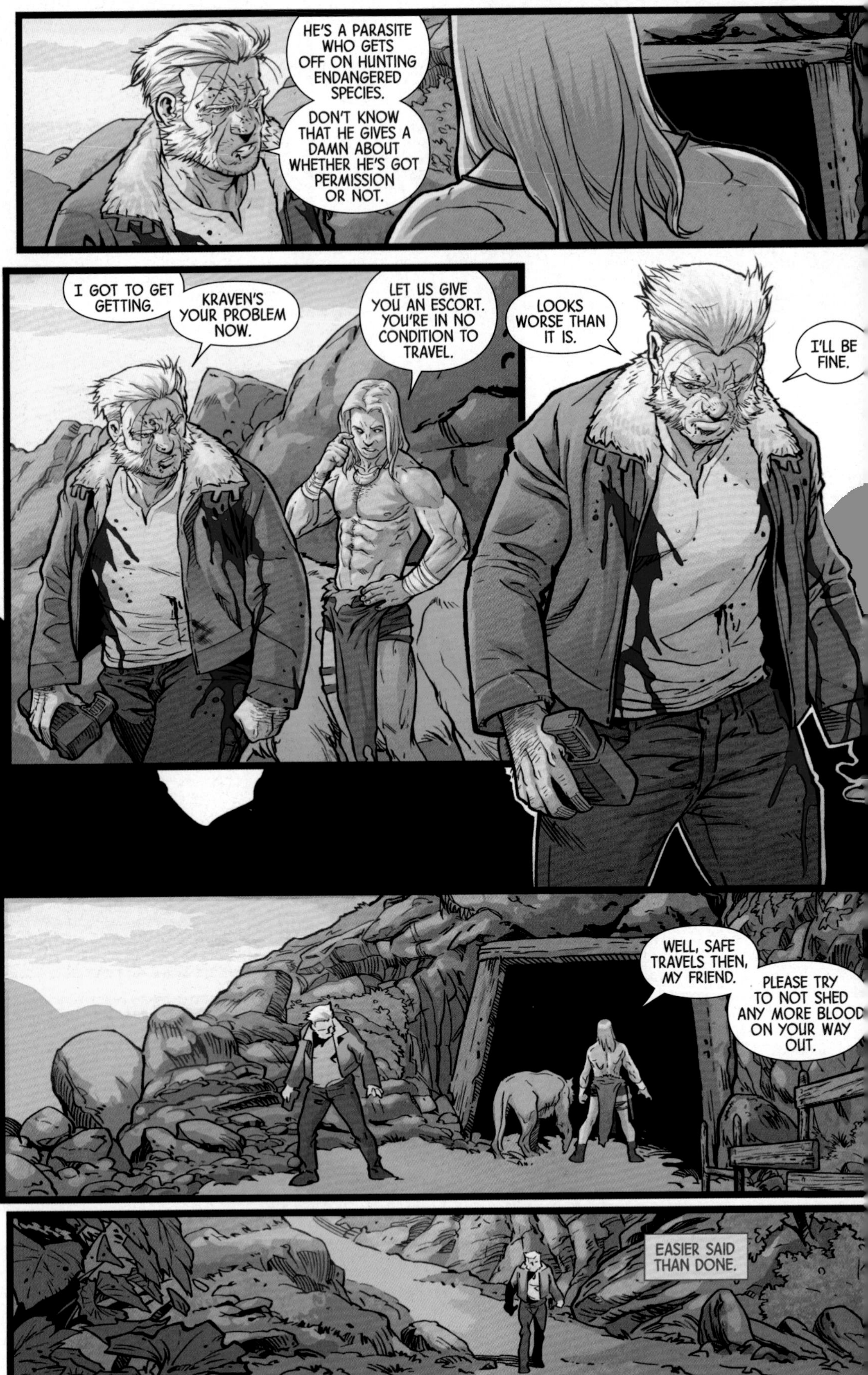

HE'S A PARASITE WHO GETS OFF ON HUNTING ENDANGERED SPECIES.
DON'T KNOW THAT HE GIVES A DAMN ABOUT WHETHER HE'S GOT PERMISSION OR NOT.
I GOT TO GET GETTING.
KRAVEN'S YOUR PROBLEM NOW.
LET US GIVE YOU AN ESCORT. YOU'RE IN NO CONDITION TO TRAVEL.
LOOKS WORSE THAN IT IS.
I'LL BE FINE.
WELL, SAFE TRAVELS THEN, MY FRIEND.
PLEASE TRY TO NOT SHED ANY MORE BLOOD ON YOUR WAY OUT.
EASIER SAID THAN DONE.

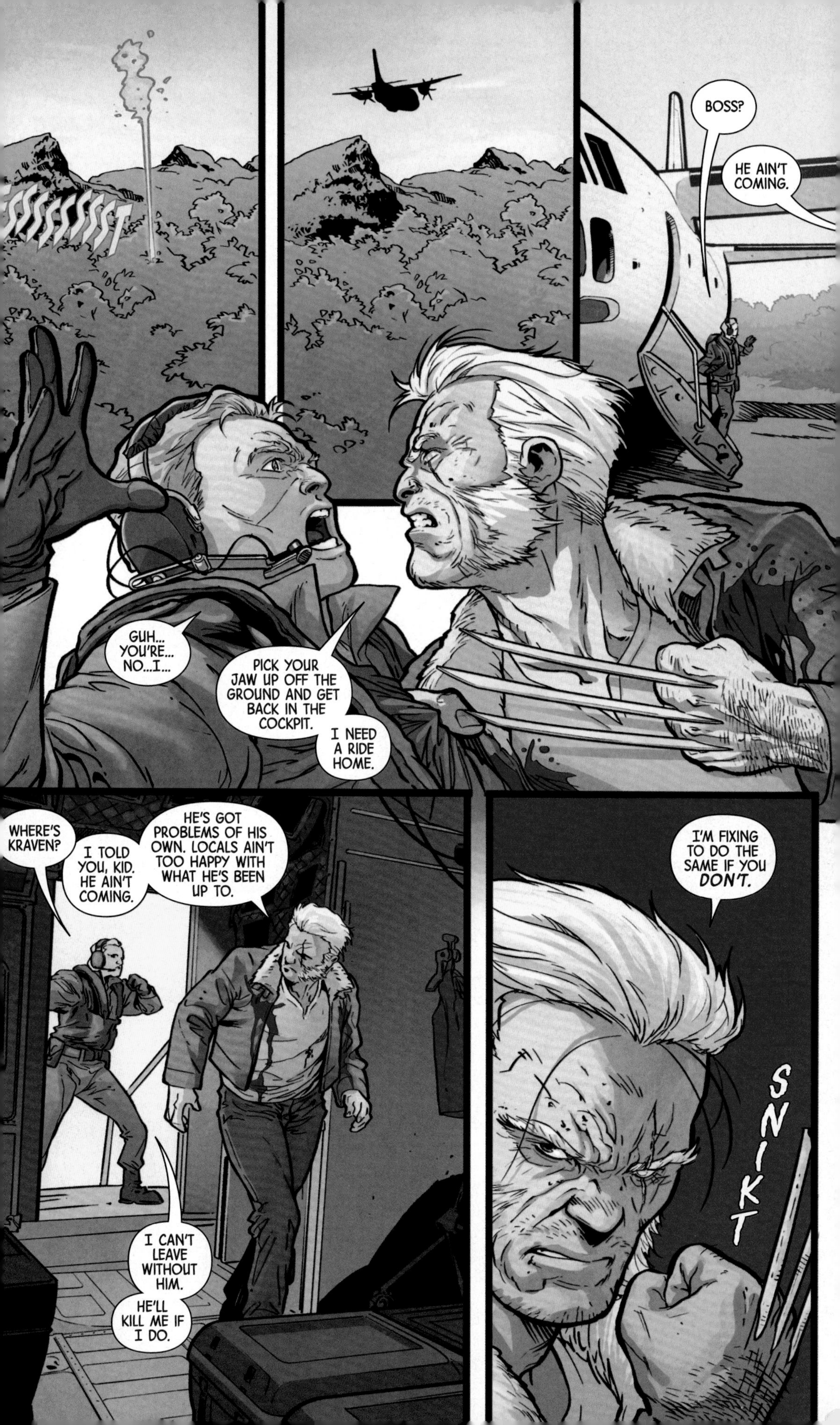
SSSSSSSSST
BOSS?
HE AIN'T COMING.
GUH... YOU'RE... NO...I...
PICK YOUR JAW UP OFF THE GROUND AND GET BACK IN THE COCKPIT.
I NEED A RIDE HOME.
WHERE'S KRAVEN?
I TOLD YOU, KID. HE AIN'T COMING.
HE'S GOT PROBLEMS OF HIS OWN. LOCALS AIN'T TOO HAPPY WITH WHAT HE'S BEEN UP TO.
I CAN'T LEAVE WITHOUT HIM.
HE'LL KILL ME IF I DO.
I'M FIXING TO DO THE SAME IF YOU *DON'T.*
SNIKT

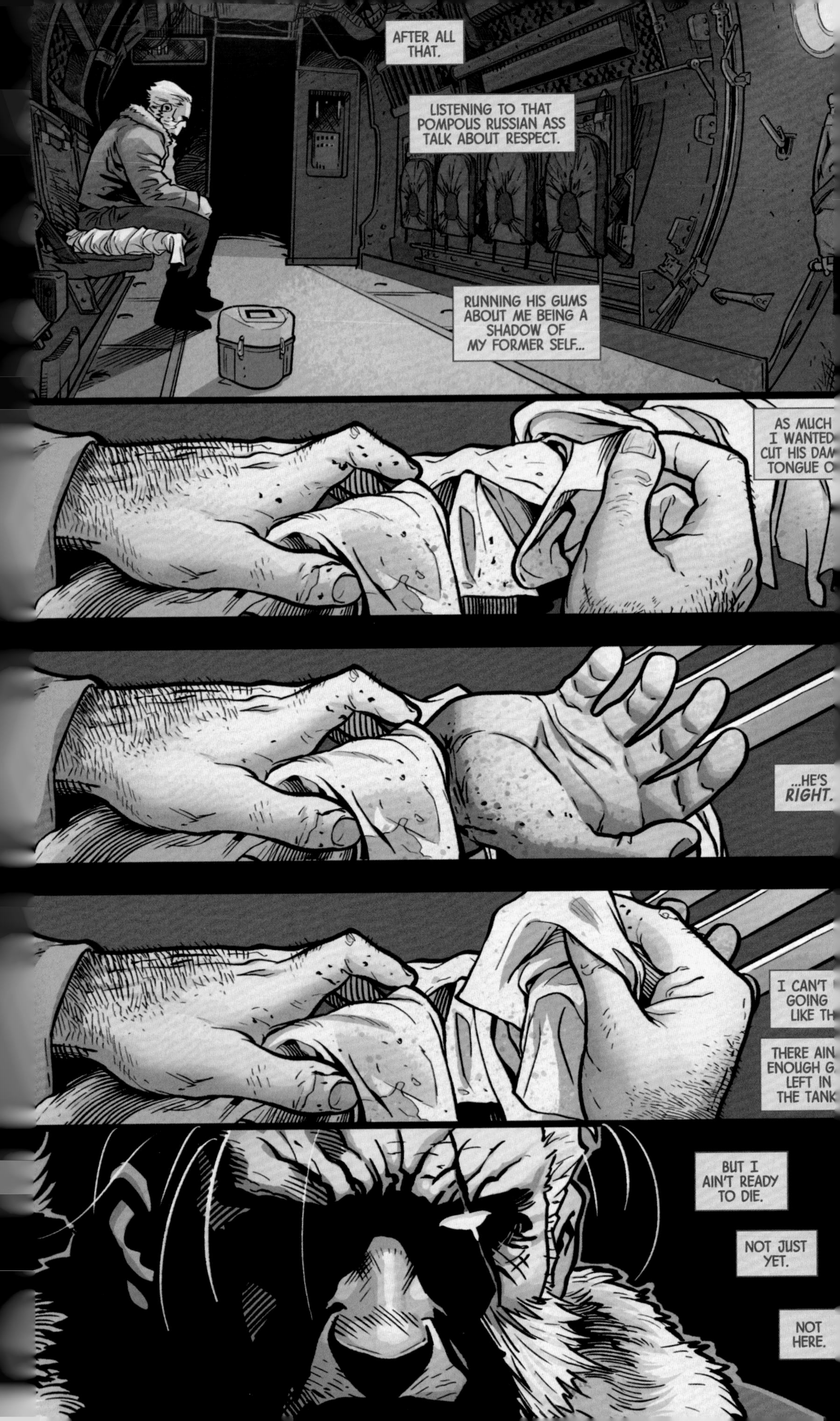

AFTER ALL THAT.
LISTENING TO THAT POMPOUS RUSSIAN ASS TALK ABOUT RESPECT.
RUNNING HIS GUMS ABOUT ME BEING A SHADOW OF MY FORMER SELF...
AS MUCH I WANTED CUT HIS DAM TONGUE O
...HE'S *RIGHT.*
I CAN'T GOING LIKE TH
THERE AIN ENOUGH G LEFT IN THE TANK
BUT I AIN'T READY TO DIE.
NOT JUST YET.
NOT HERE.

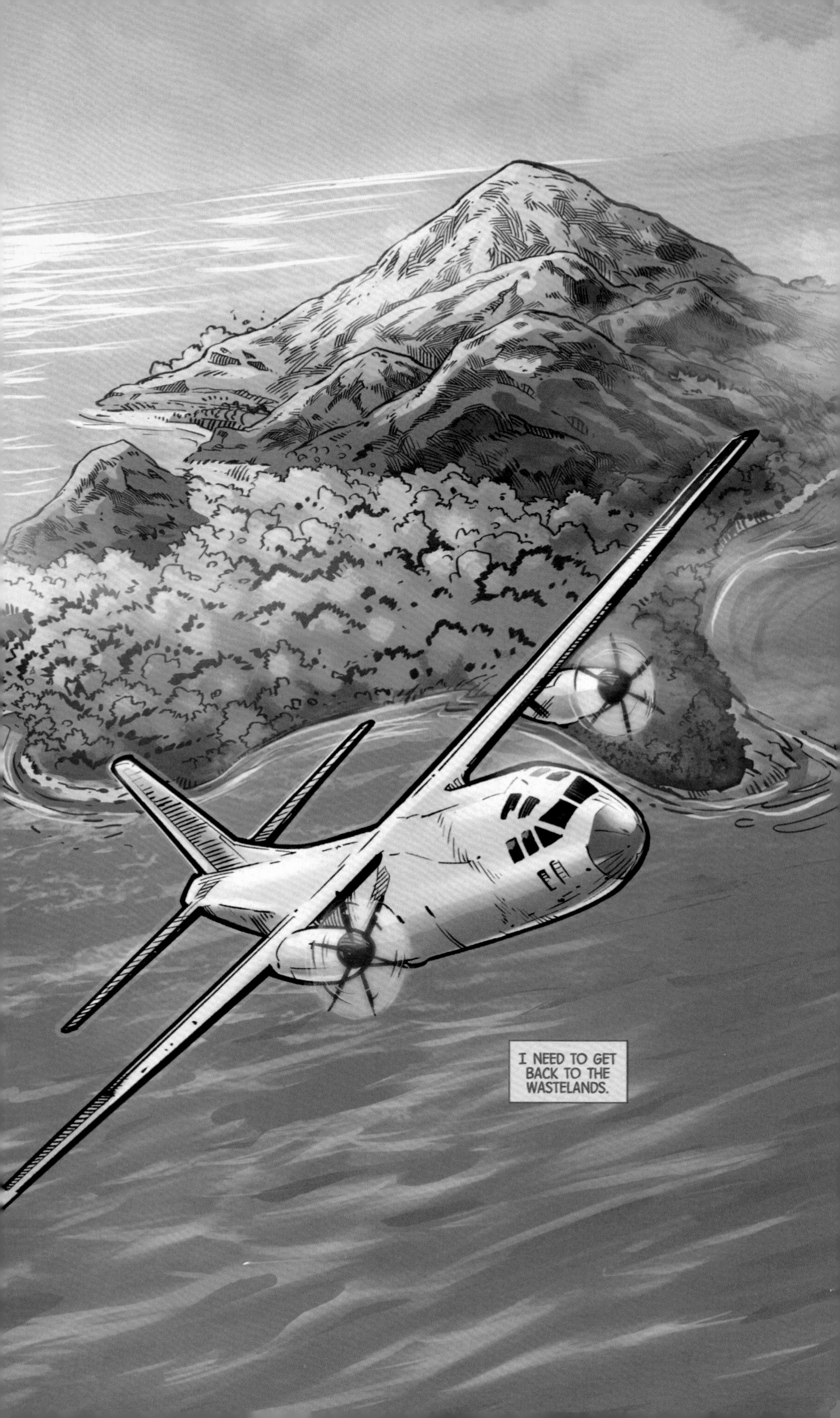
I NEED TO GET BACK TO THE WASTELANDS.

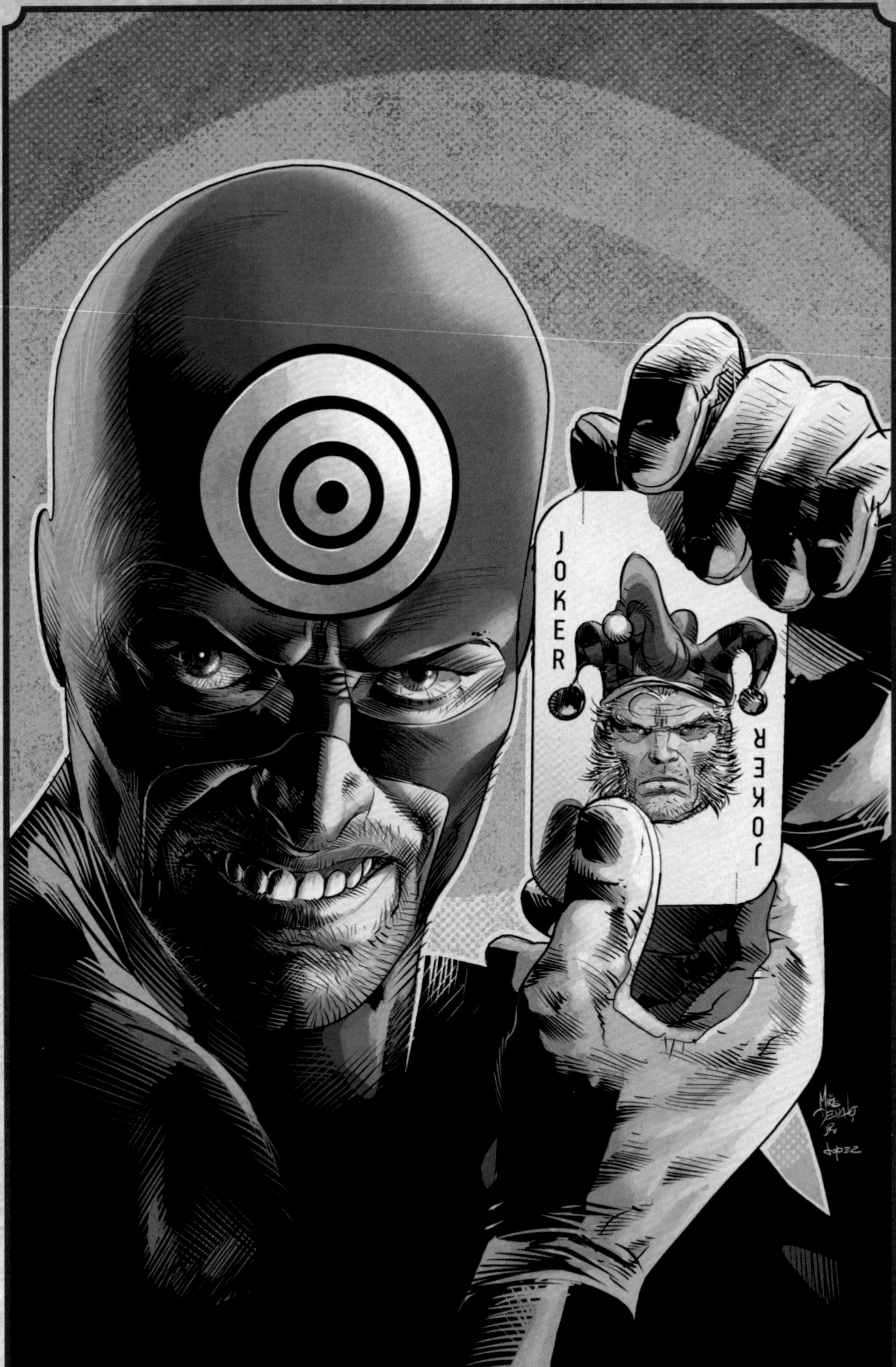
JOKER
JOKER

43

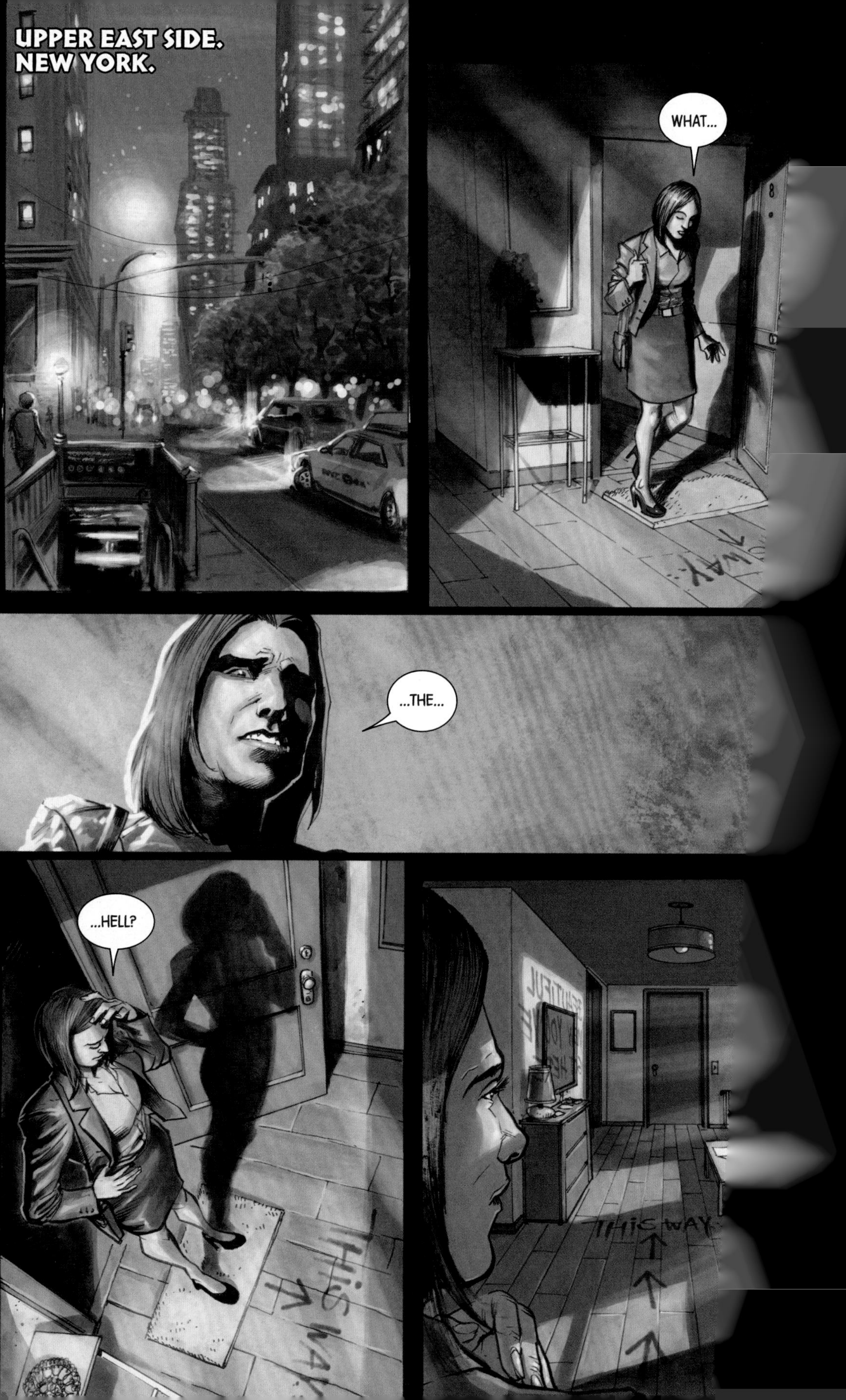
UPPER EAST SIDE.
NEW YORK.
WHAT...
...THE...
...HELL?
THIS WAY

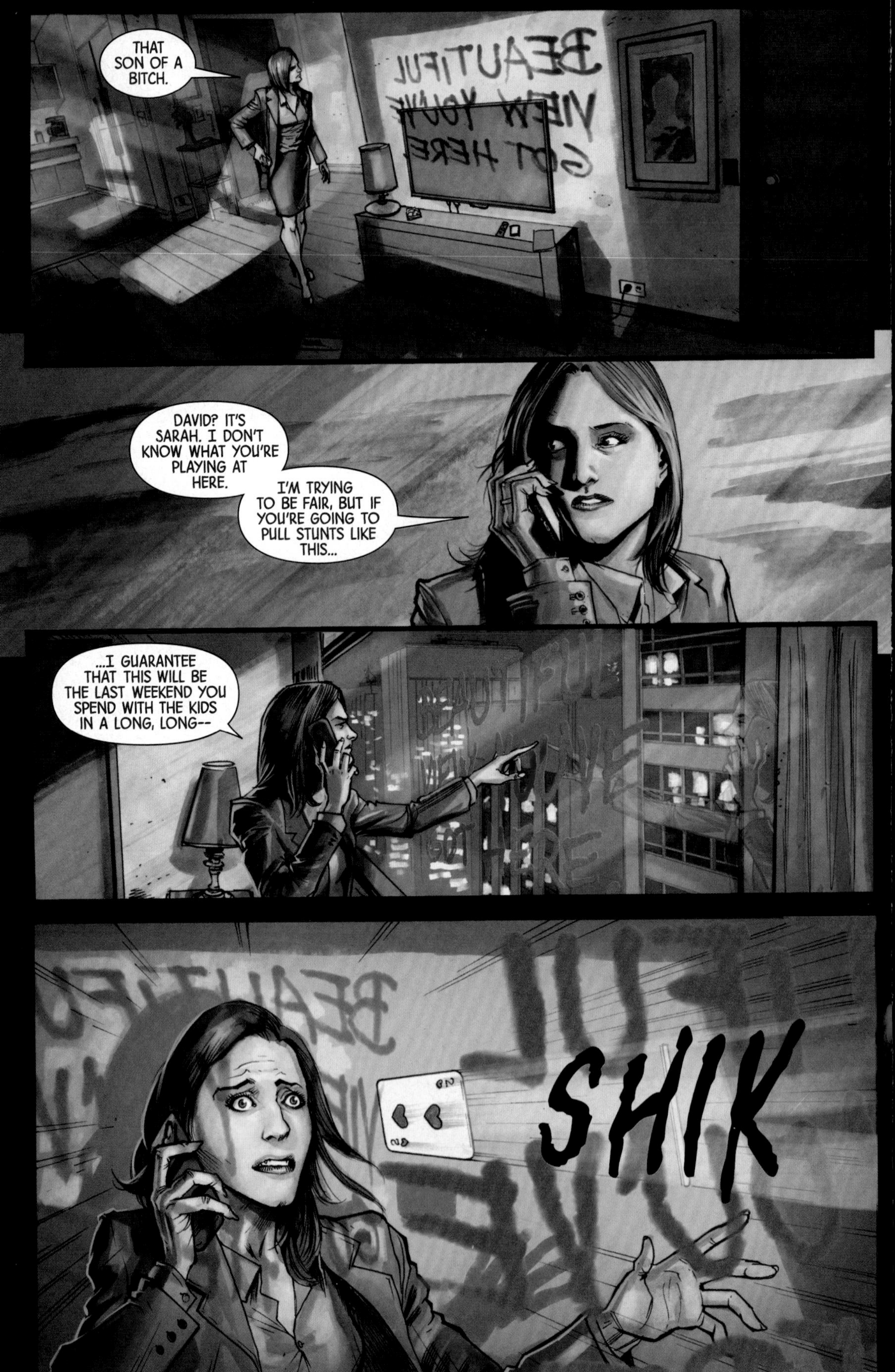
THAT SON OF A BITCH.
BEAUTIFUL VIEW YOU'VE GOT HERE
DAVID? IT'S SARAH. I DON'T KNOW WHAT YOU'RE PLAYING AT HERE.
I'M TRYING TO BE FAIR, BUT IF YOU'RE GOING TO PULL STUNTS LIKE THIS...
...I GUARANTEE THAT THIS WILL BE THE LAST WEEKEND YOU SPEND WITH THE KIDS IN A LONG, LONG--
SHIK

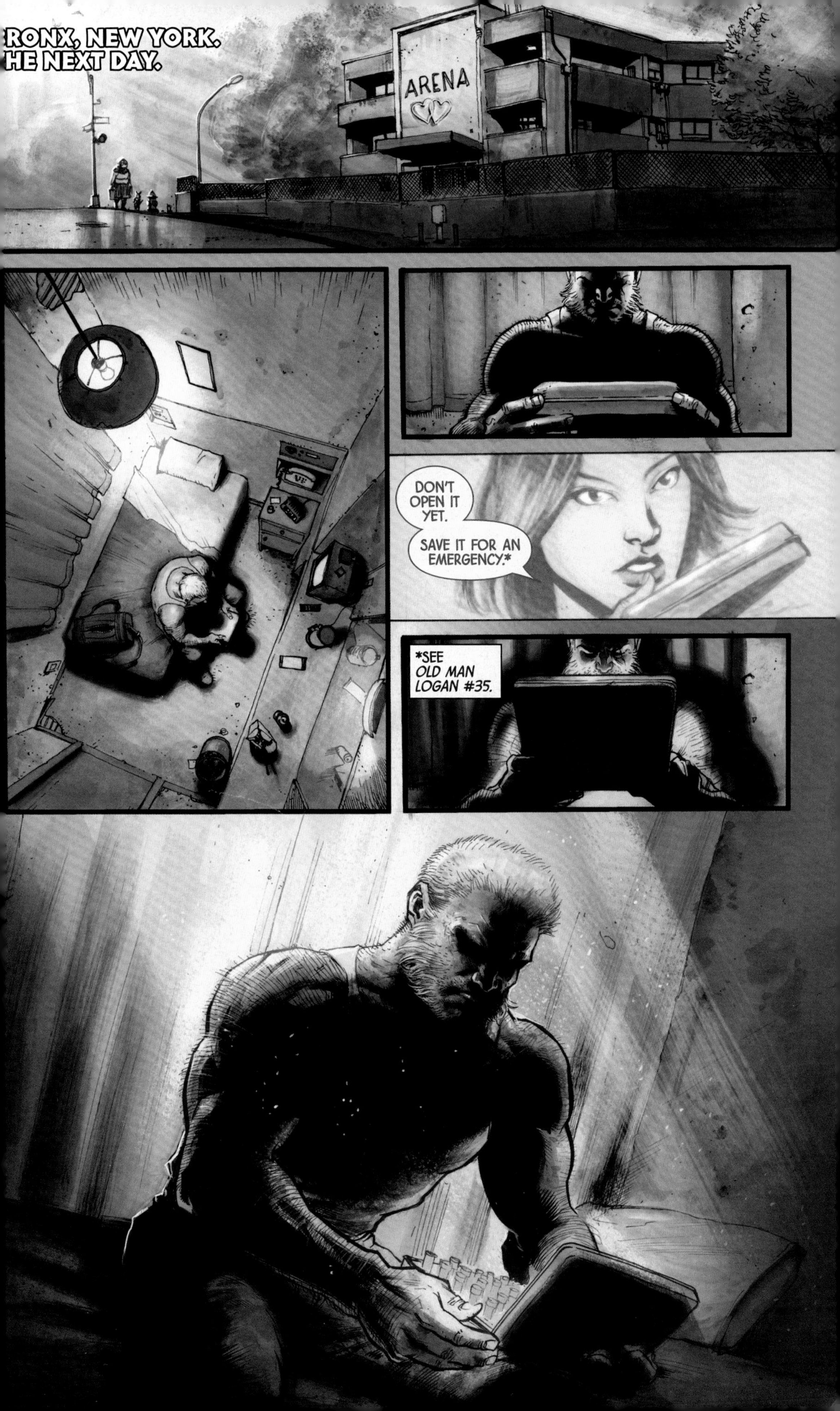
RONX, NEW YORK.
HE NEXT DAY.
ARENA
DON'T OPEN IT YET.
SAVE IT FOR AN EMERGENCY.*
*SEE OLD MAN LOGAN #35.

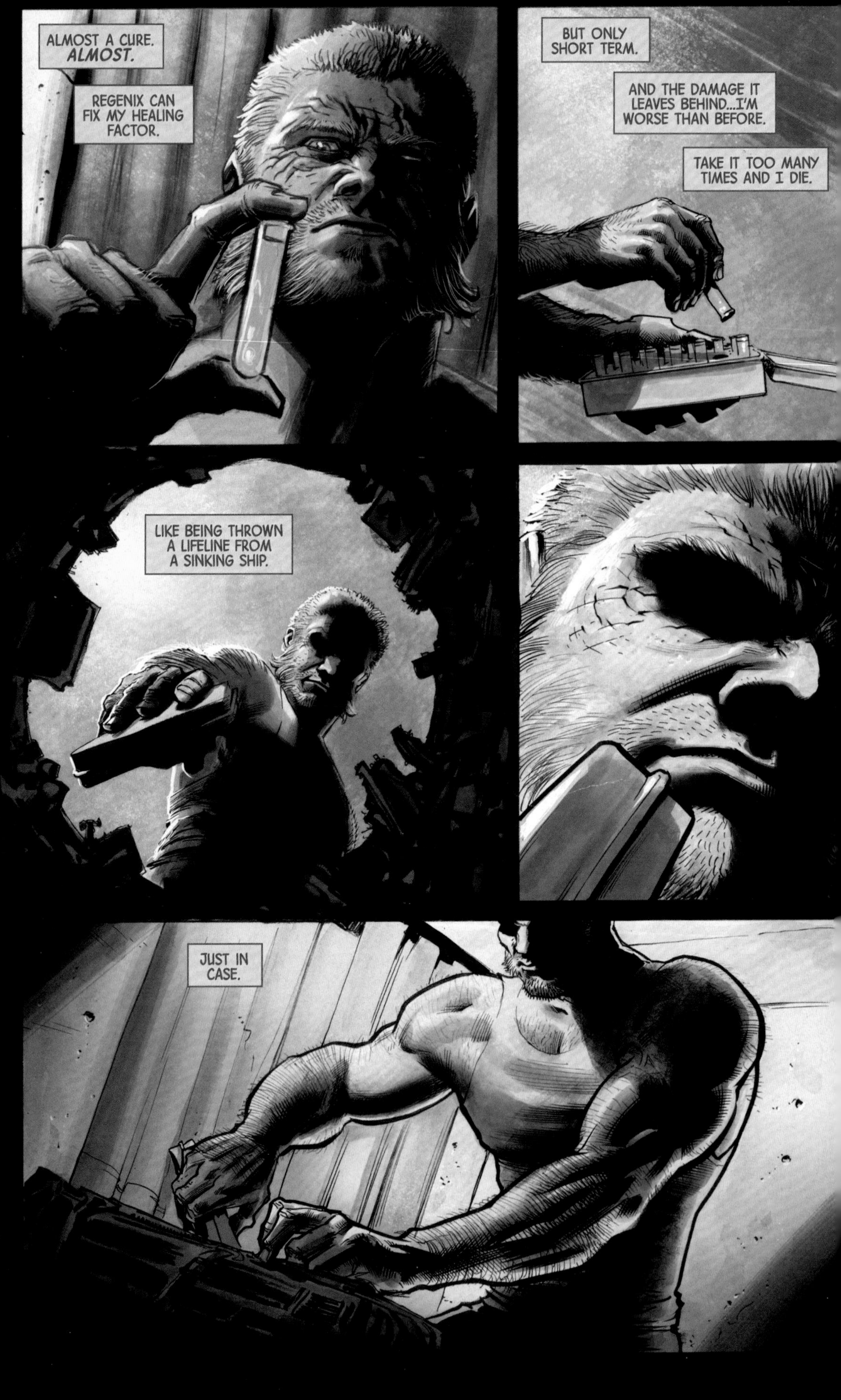
ALMOST A CURE. *ALMOST.*
REGENIX CAN FIX MY HEALING FACTOR.
BUT ONLY SHORT TERM.
AND THE DAMAGE IT LEAVES BEHIND...I'M WORSE THAN BEFORE.
TAKE IT TOO MANY TIMES AND I DIE.
LIKE BEING THROWN A LIFELINE FROM A SINKING SHIP.
JUST IN CASE.

DON'T KNOW WHERE I'M HEADED.

JUST AWAY FROM HERE.

CHECKING OUT.

ALL RIGHT.

I TELL YA, I'M SAD TO SEE YOU GO, OLD-TIMER.

YOU'RE THE ONLY ONE IN THIS RATHOLE WHO PAYS HIS RENT ON TIME AND DON'T GIVE ME NO HASSLES.

AWAY FROM NEW YORK.

...FOUND DEAD IN HER UPPER EAST SIDE APARTMENT. POLICE ARE NOT--

TURN THAT UP.

WHAT?

THE TV. TURN IT UP.

BREAKING NEWS
Upper East Side
MURDER
Benjamin Schimdt

--RELEASING FURTHER DETAILS AT THIS POINT.

ALL RIGHT, ALL RIGHT. CHILL YOUR LIP, MAN. I'M ON IT.

BREAKING
Upper East Side
MURDER
Benjamin Schimdt

SARAH DEWEY, A PULITZER PRIZE-WINNING JOURNALIST FOR HER COVERAGE OF THE CONFLICT IN AFGHANISTAN--

--FOUND HERSELF IN THE PUBLIC SPOTLIGHT RECENTLY AS THE CO-WRITER OF MAYOR WILSON FISK'S WILDLY SUCCESSFUL BIOGRAPHY, THE LIFE AND TIMES OF WILSON FISK.

SHE IS SURVIVED BY HER TWO CHILDREN.

LOOKS LIKE I'LL NEED THE ROOM FOR ANOTHER WEEK.

COMING UP, YOU WON'T BELIEVE WHAT THESE NEW YORK SANITATION WORKERS ARE GROWING IN THE SEWERS.

WHATEVER, MAN. YOU GOT THE MONEY, YOU CAN STAY FOR AS LONG AS YOU LIKE.

EVERY TIME.

I TRY TO LEAVE THIS LIFE AND FATE FINDS ONE MORE REASON FOR ME TO STICK AROUND.

LIKE A CRUEL JOKE.

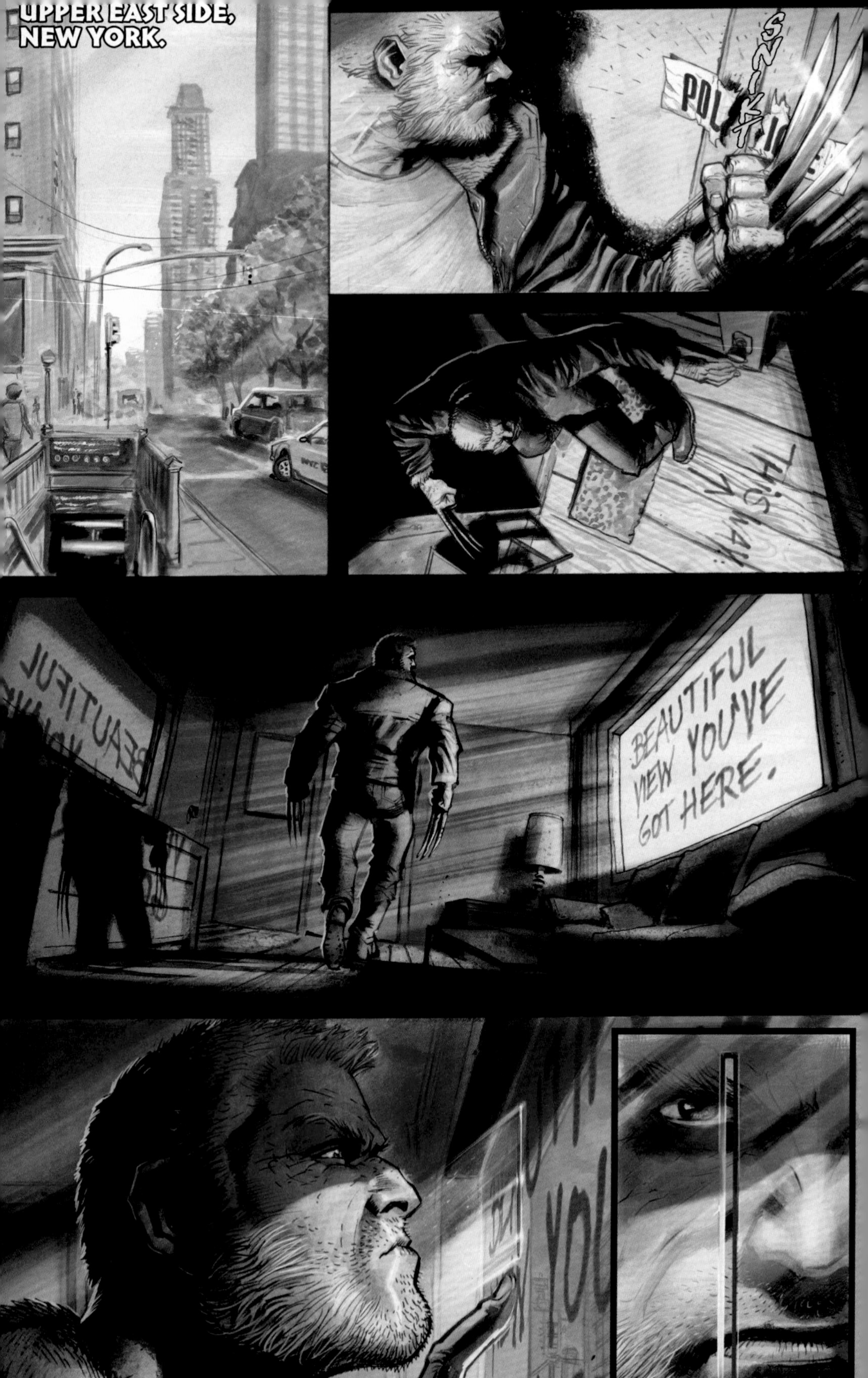
UPPER EAST SIDE,
NEW YORK.
SNIKT
THIS WAY!
BEAUTIFUL VIEW YOU'VE GOT HERE.

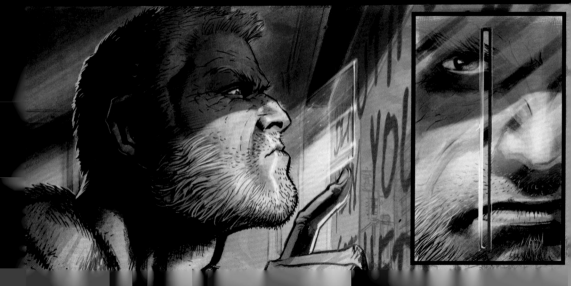

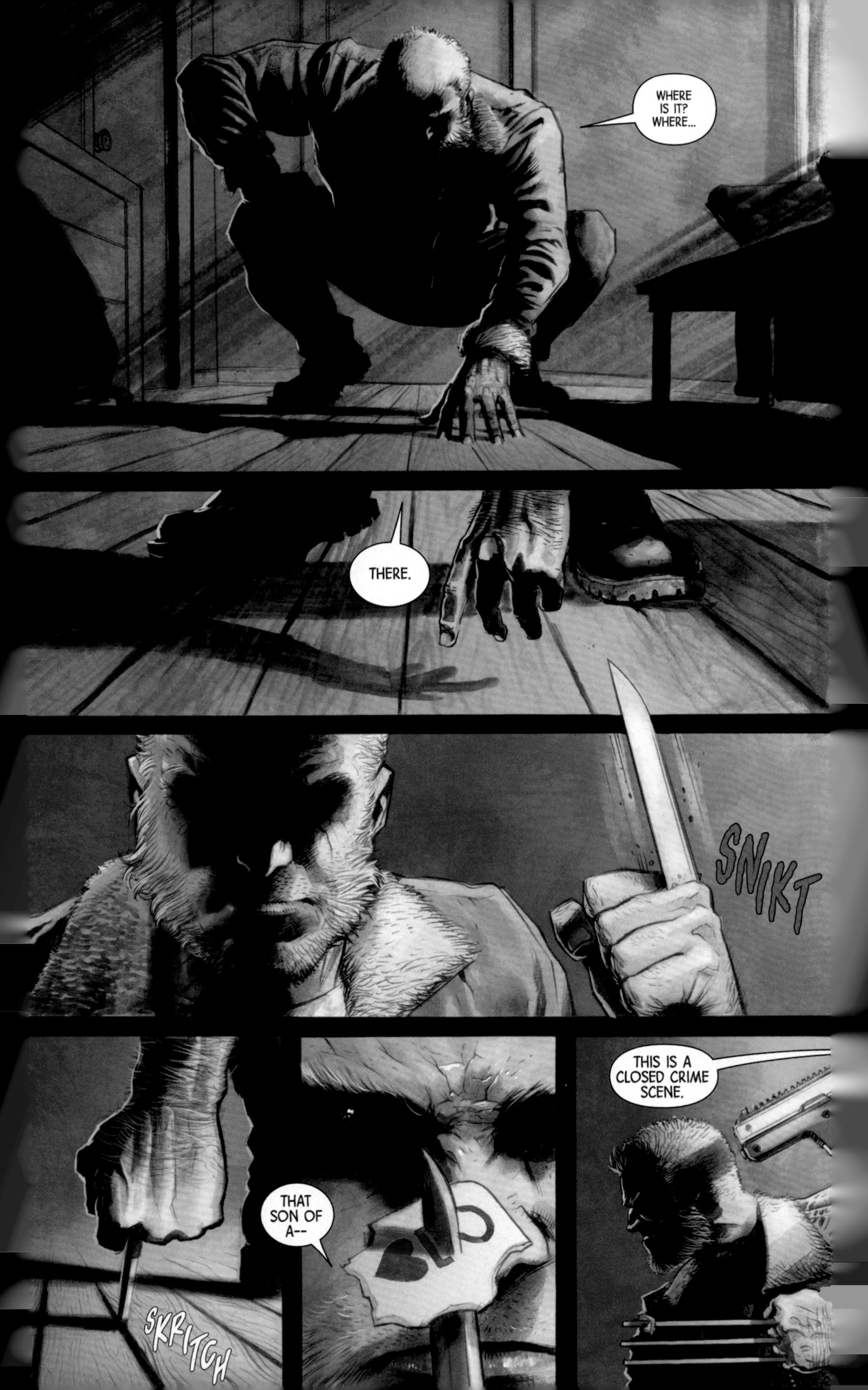
WHERE IS IT? WHERE...
THERE.
SNIKT
SKRITCH
THAT SON OF A--
THIS IS A CLOSED CRIME SCENE.

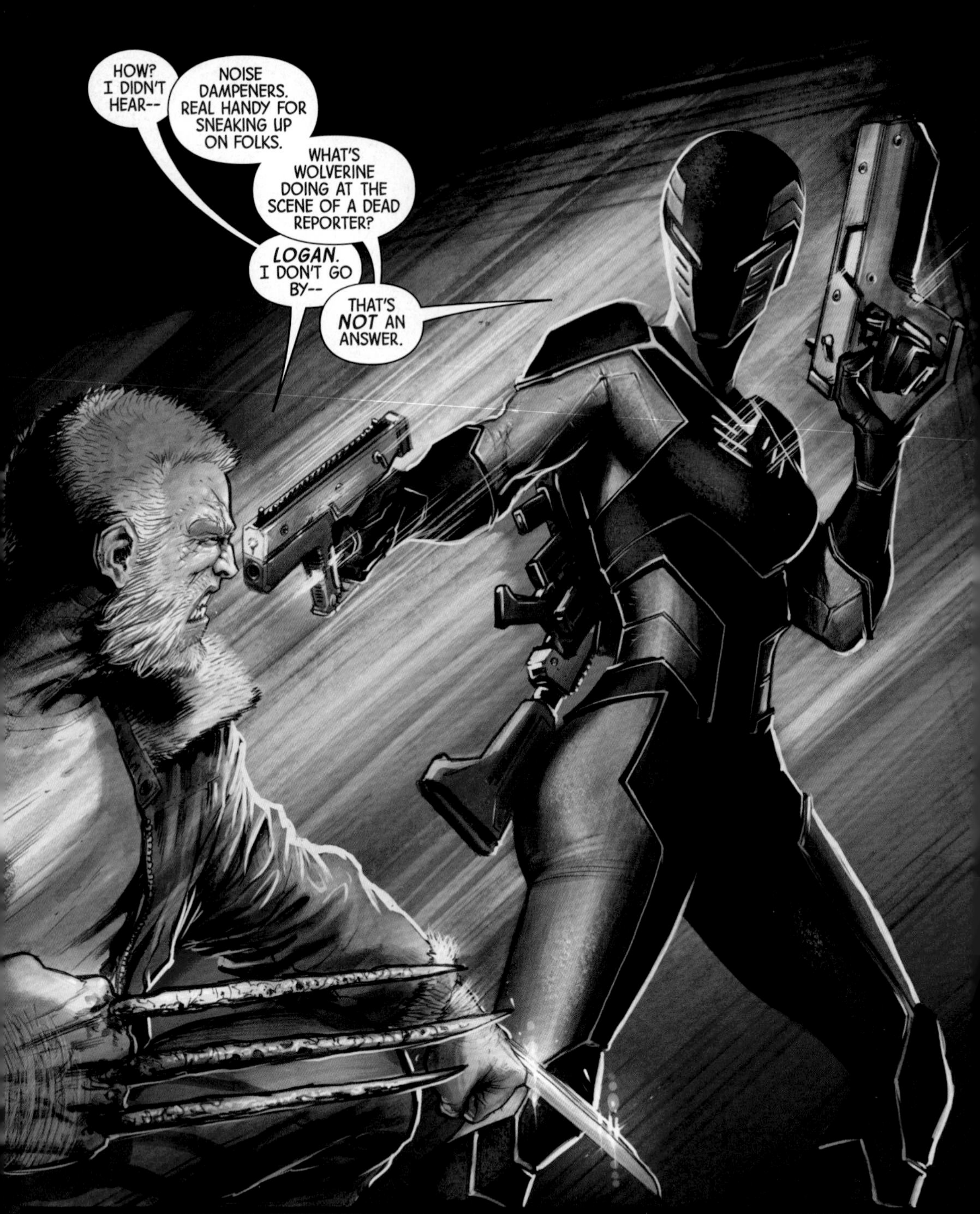
HOW? I DIDN'T HEAR--
NOISE DAMPENERS. REAL HANDY FOR SNEAKING UP ON FOLKS.
WHAT'S WOLVERINE DOING AT THE SCENE OF A DEAD REPORTER?
LOGAN. I DON'T GO BY--
THAT'S NOT AN ANSWER.
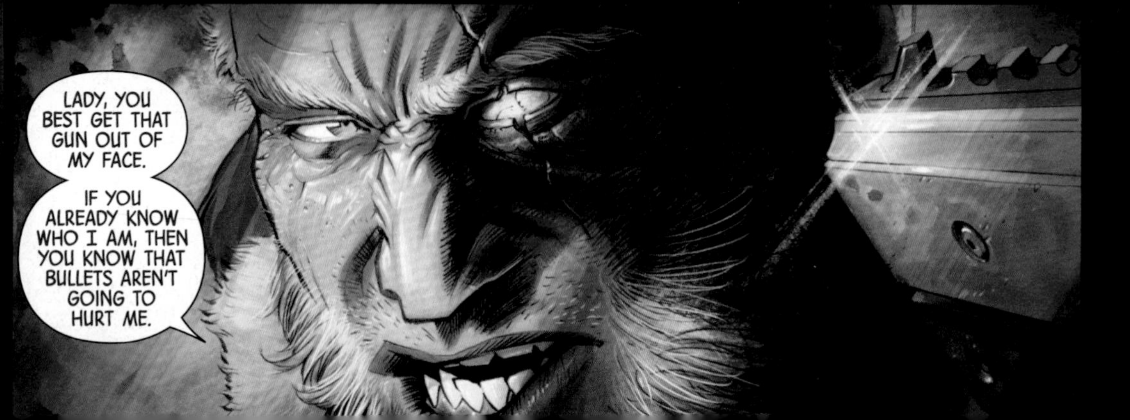
LADY, YOU BEST GET THAT GUN OUT OF MY FACE.
IF YOU ALREADY KNOW WHO I AM, THEN YOU KNOW THAT BULLETS AREN'T GOING TO HURT ME.

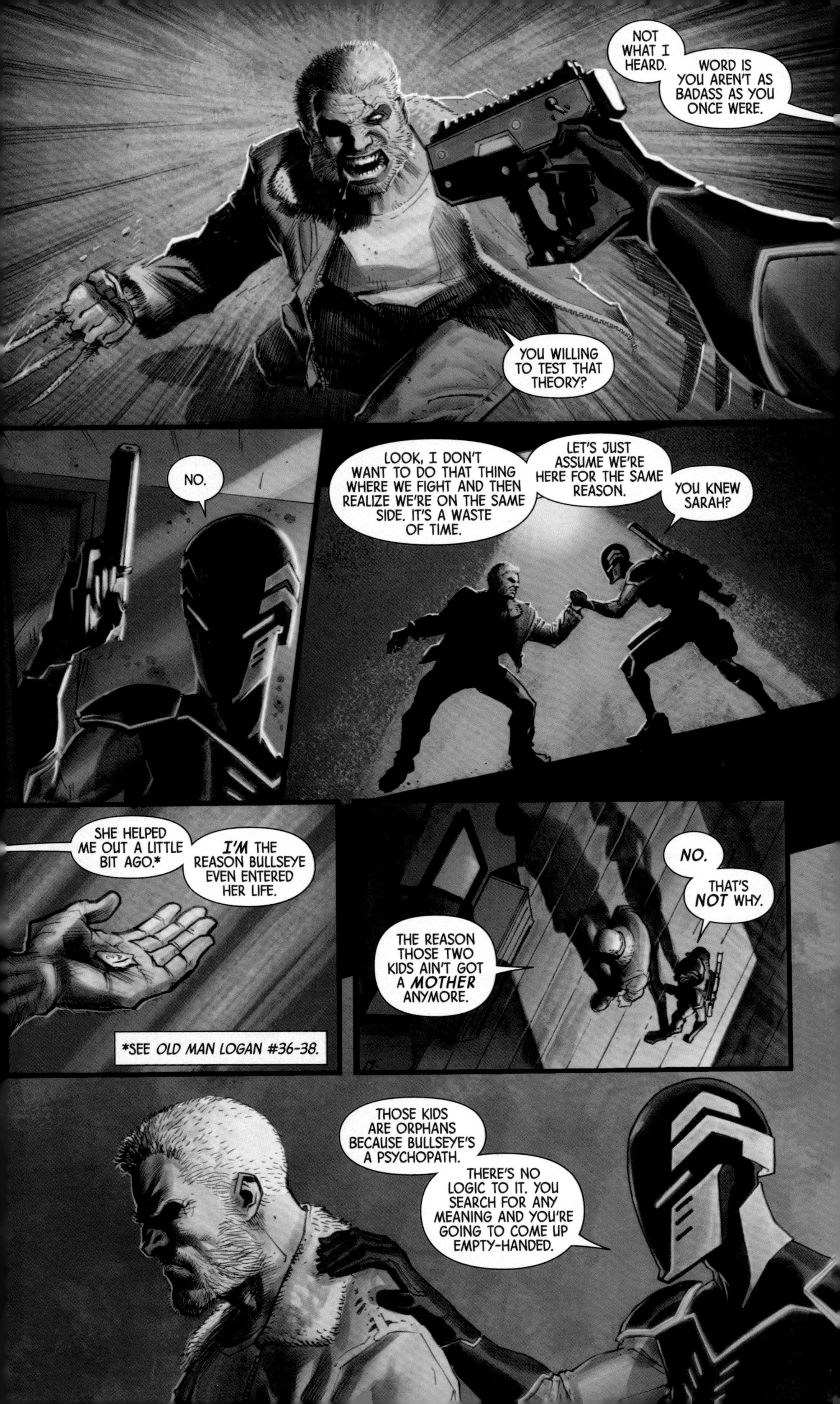
NOT WHAT I HEARD.
WORD IS YOU AREN'T AS BADASS AS YOU ONCE WERE.
YOU WILLING TO TEST THAT THEORY?
NO.
LOOK, I DON'T WANT TO DO THAT THING WHERE WE FIGHT AND THEN REALIZE WE'RE ON THE SAME SIDE. IT'S A WASTE OF TIME.
LET'S JUST ASSUME WE'RE HERE FOR THE SAME REASON.
YOU KNEW SARAH?
SHE HELPED ME OUT A LITTLE BIT AGO.*
I'M THE REASON BULLSEYE EVEN ENTERED HER LIFE.
*SEE *OLD MAN LOGAN #36-38.*
THE REASON THOSE TWO KIDS AIN'T GOT A ***MOTHER*** ANYMORE.
NO.
THAT'S ***NOT*** WHY.
THOSE KIDS ARE ORPHANS BECAUSE BULLSEYE'S A PSYCHOPATH.
THERE'S NO LOGIC TO IT. YOU SEARCH FOR ANY MEANING AND YOU'RE GOING TO COME UP EMPTY-HANDED.

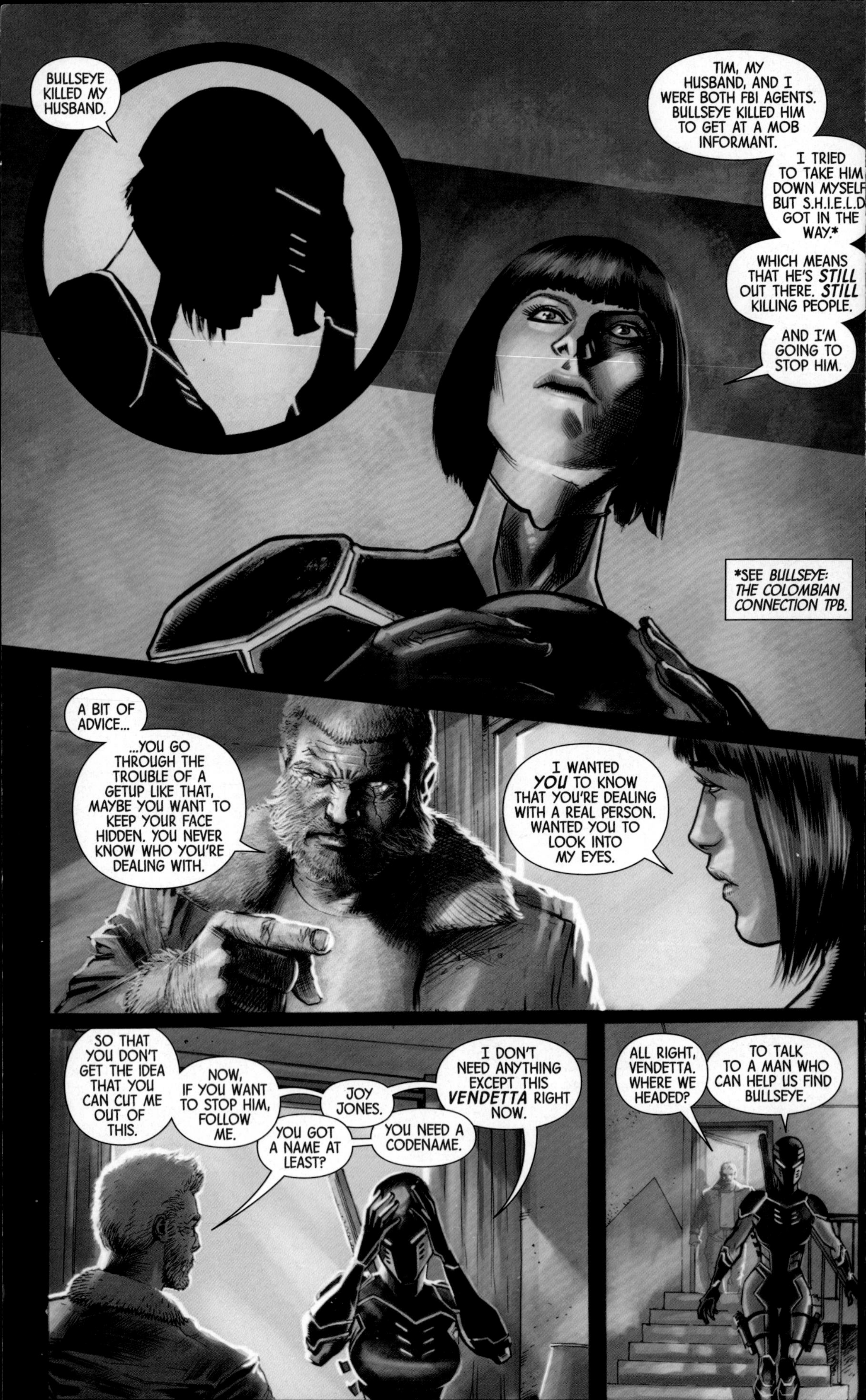
BULLSEYE KILLED MY HUSBAND.
TIM, MY HUSBAND, AND I WERE BOTH FBI AGENTS. BULLSEYE KILLED HIM TO GET AT A MOB INFORMANT.
I TRIED TO TAKE HIM DOWN MYSELF BUT S.H.I.E.L.D. GOT IN THE WAY.*
WHICH MEANS THAT HE'S STILL OUT THERE. STILL KILLING PEOPLE.
AND I'M GOING TO STOP HIM.
*SEE BULLSEYE: THE COLOMBIAN CONNECTION TPB.
A BIT OF ADVICE...
...YOU GO THROUGH THE TROUBLE OF A GETUP LIKE THAT, MAYBE YOU WANT TO KEEP YOUR FACE HIDDEN. YOU NEVER KNOW WHO YOU'RE DEALING WITH.
I WANTED YOU TO KNOW THAT YOU'RE DEALING WITH A REAL PERSON. WANTED YOU TO LOOK INTO MY EYES.
SO THAT YOU DON'T GET THE IDEA THAT YOU CAN CUT ME OUT OF THIS.
NOW, IF YOU WANT TO STOP HIM, FOLLOW ME.
YOU GOT A NAME AT LEAST?
JOY JONES.
YOU NEED A CODENAME.
I DON'T NEED ANYTHING EXCEPT THIS VENDETTA RIGHT NOW.
ALL RIGHT, VENDETTA. WHERE WE HEADED?
TO TALK TO A MAN WHO CAN HELP US FIND BULLSEYE.

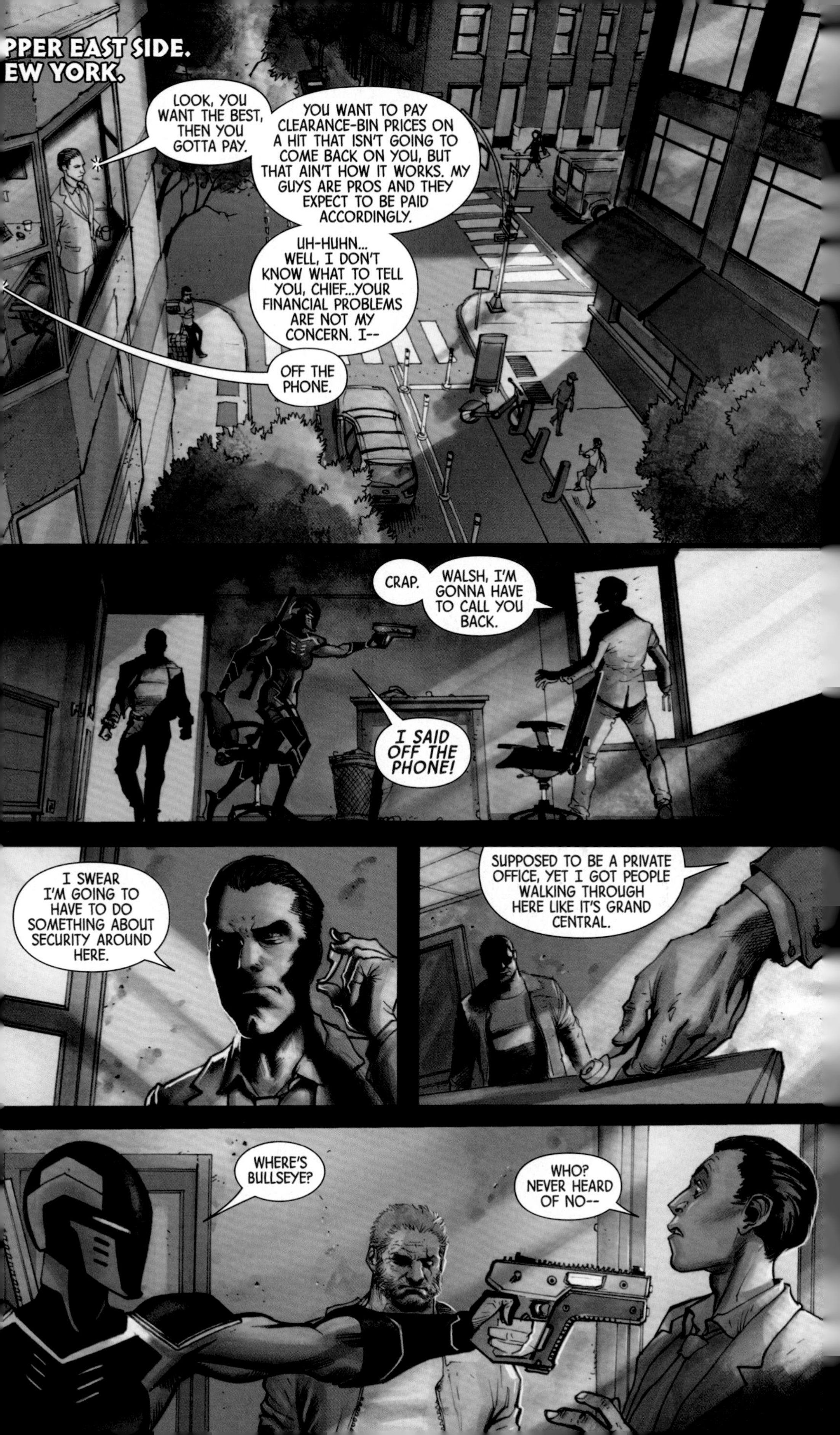
PPER EAST SIDE.
EW YORK.
LOOK, YOU WANT THE BEST, THEN YOU GOTTA PAY.
YOU WANT TO PAY CLEARANCE-BIN PRICES ON A HIT THAT ISN'T GOING TO COME BACK ON YOU, BUT THAT AIN'T HOW IT WORKS. MY GUYS ARE PROS AND THEY EXPECT TO BE PAID ACCORDINGLY.
UH-HUHN... WELL, I DON'T KNOW WHAT TO TELL YOU, CHIEF...YOUR FINANCIAL PROBLEMS ARE NOT MY CONCERN. I--
OFF THE PHONE.
CRAP.
WALSH, I'M GONNA HAVE TO CALL YOU BACK.
I SAID OFF THE PHONE!
I SWEAR I'M GOING TO HAVE TO DO SOMETHING ABOUT SECURITY AROUND HERE.
SUPPOSED TO BE A PRIVATE OFFICE, YET I GOT PEOPLE WALKING THROUGH HERE LIKE IT'S GRAND CENTRAL.
WHERE'S BULLSEYE?
WHO? NEVER HEARD OF NO--

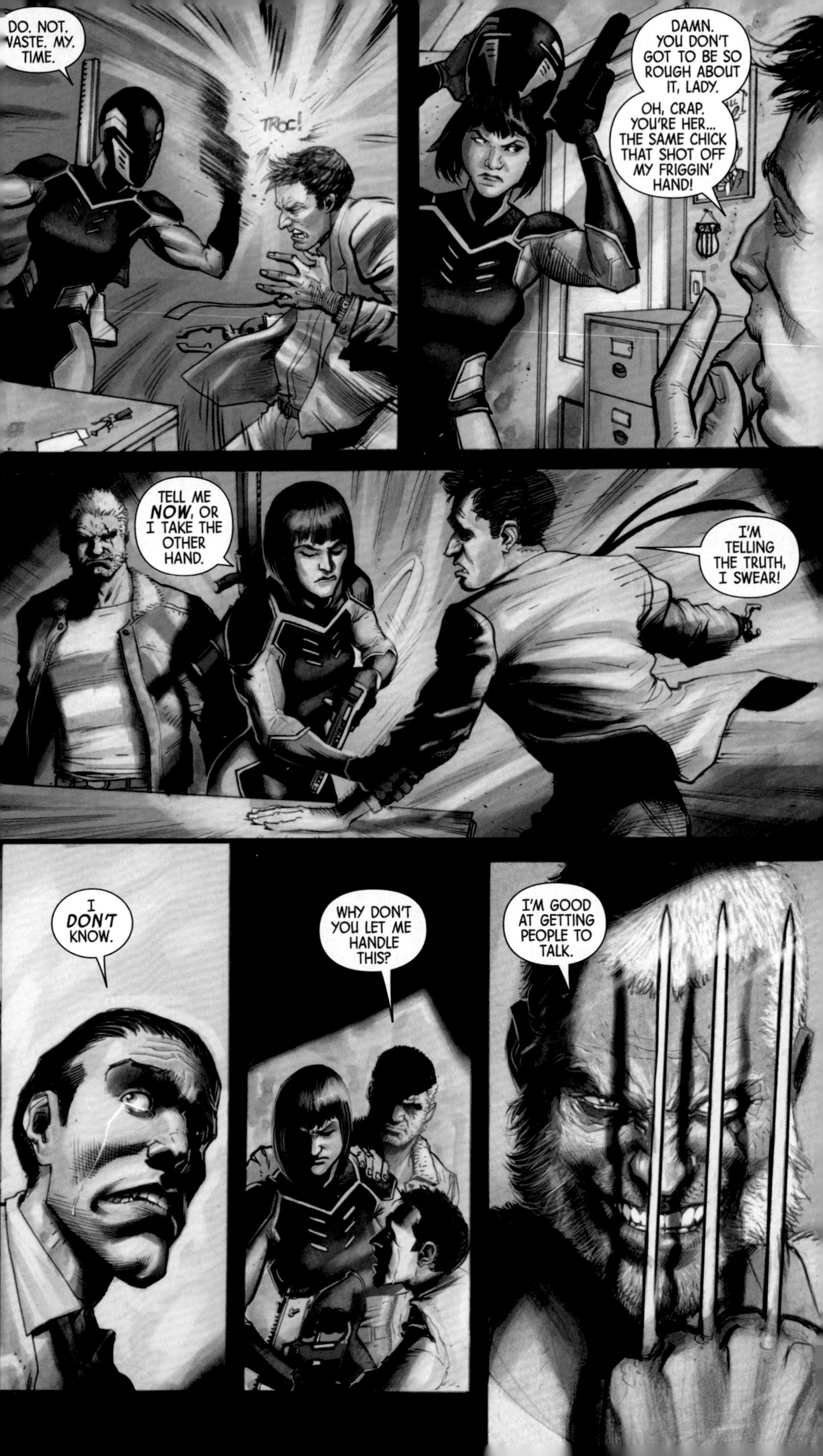
DO. NOT. WASTE. MY. TIME.
TROC!
DAMN. YOU DON'T GOT TO BE SO ROUGH ABOUT IT, LADY.
OH, CRAP. YOU'RE HER... THE SAME CHICK THAT SHOT OFF MY FRIGGIN' HAND!
TELL ME NOW, OR I TAKE THE OTHER HAND.
I'M TELLING THE TRUTH, I SWEAR!
I DON'T KNOW.
WHY DON'T YOU LET ME HANDLE THIS?
I'M GOOD AT GETTING PEOPLE TO TALK.

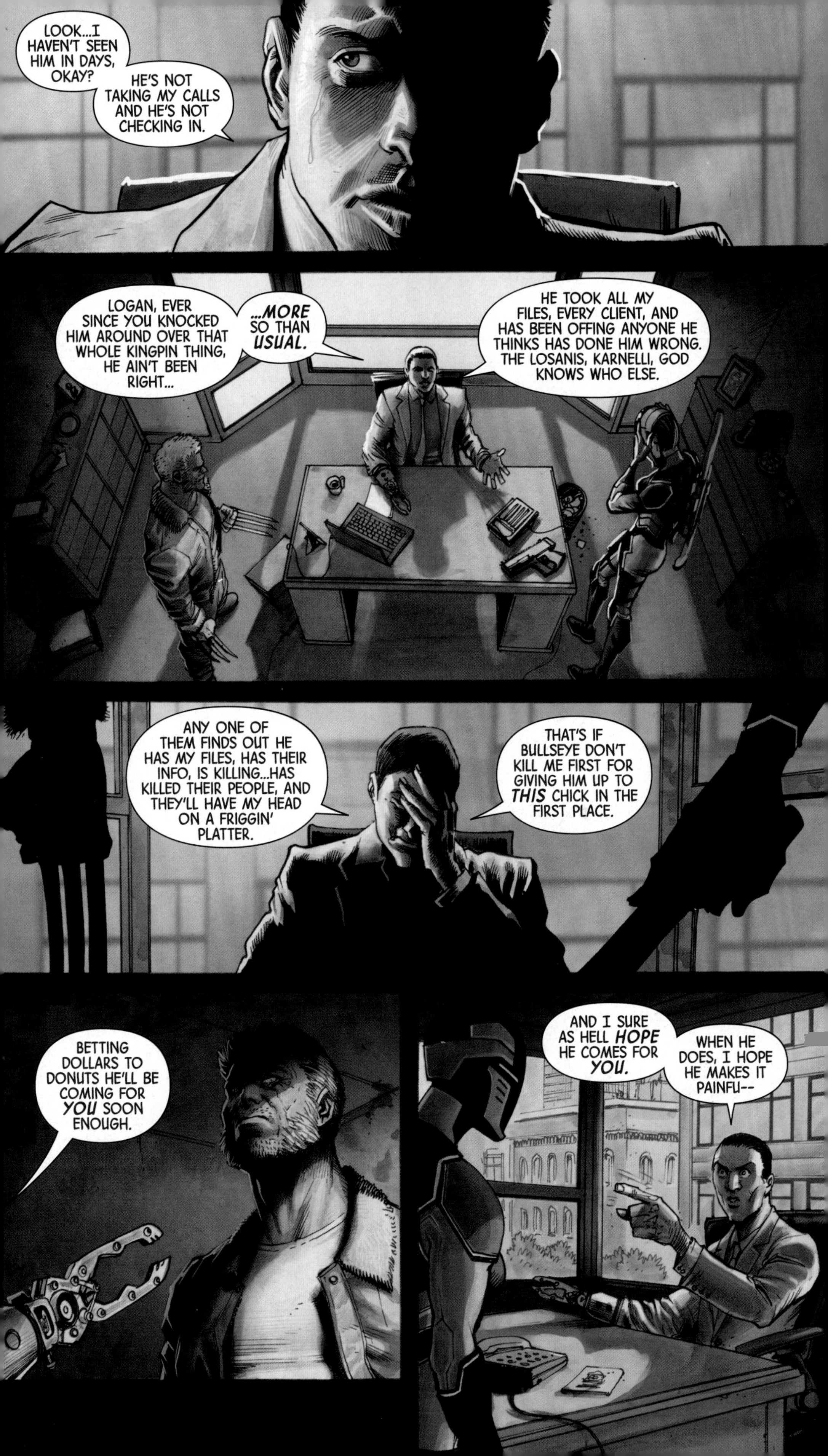
LOOK...I HAVEN'T SEEN HIM IN DAYS, OKAY?
HE'S NOT TAKING MY CALLS AND HE'S NOT CHECKING IN.
LOGAN, EVER SINCE YOU KNOCKED HIM AROUND OVER THAT WHOLE KINGPIN THING, HE AIN'T BEEN RIGHT...
...MORE SO THAN USUAL.
HE TOOK ALL MY FILES, EVERY CLIENT, AND HAS BEEN OFFING ANYONE HE THINKS HAS DONE HIM WRONG. THE LOSANIS, KARNELLI, GOD KNOWS WHO ELSE.
ANY ONE OF THEM FINDS OUT HE HAS MY FILES, HAS THEIR INFO, IS KILLING...HAS KILLED THEIR PEOPLE, AND THEY'LL HAVE MY HEAD ON A FRIGGIN' PLATTER.
THAT'S IF BULLSEYE DON'T KILL ME FIRST FOR GIVING HIM UP TO THIS CHICK IN THE FIRST PLACE.
BETTING DOLLARS TO DONUTS HE'LL BE COMING FOR YOU SOON ENOUGH.
AND I SURE AS HELL HOPE HE COMES FOR YOU.
WHEN HE DOES, I HOPE HE MAKES IT PAINFU--

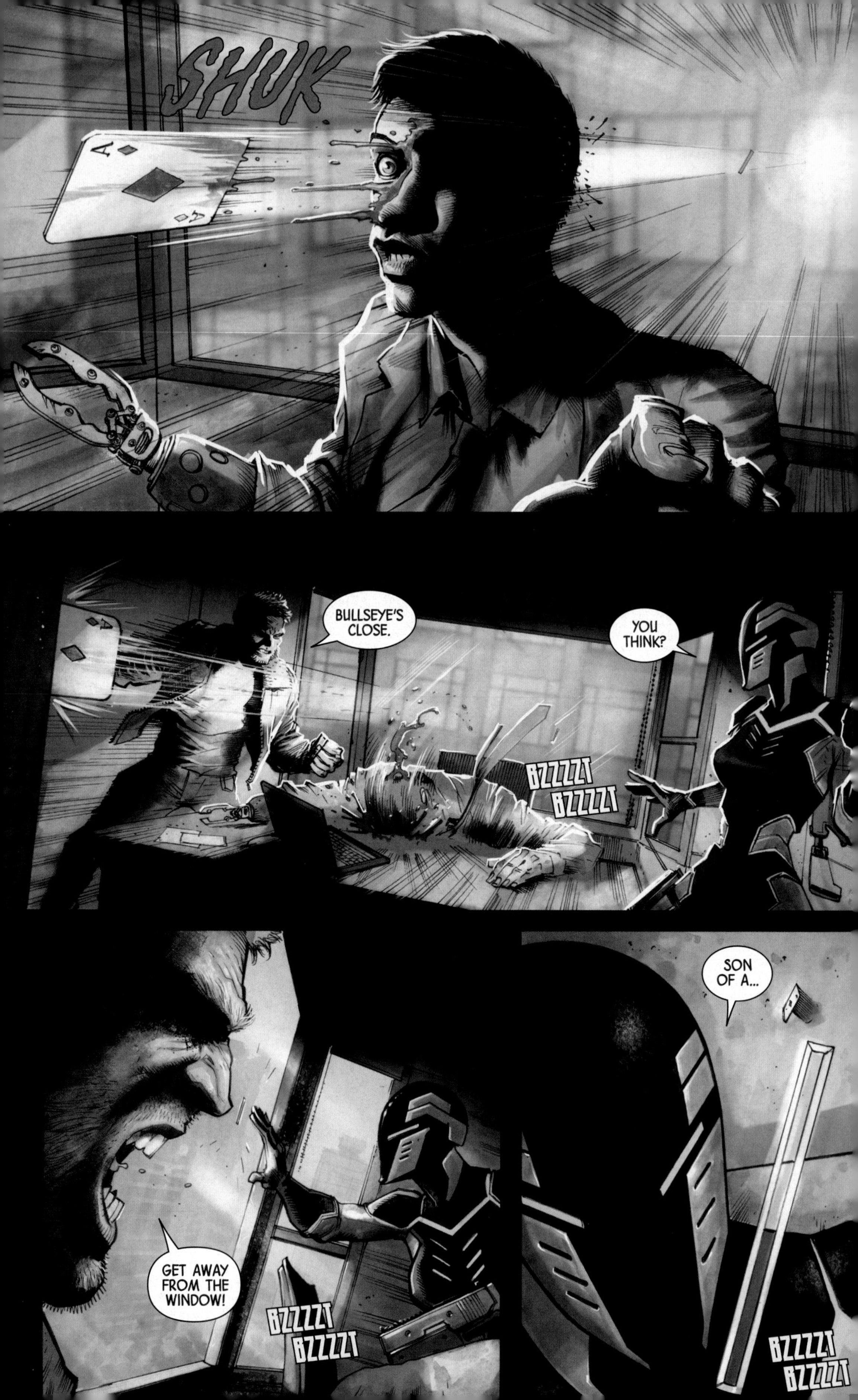
SHUK
BULLSEYE'S CLOSE.
YOU THINK?
BZZZZT
BZZZZT
GET AWAY FROM THE WINDOW!
BZZZZT
BZZZZT
SON OF A...
BZZZZT
BZZZZT

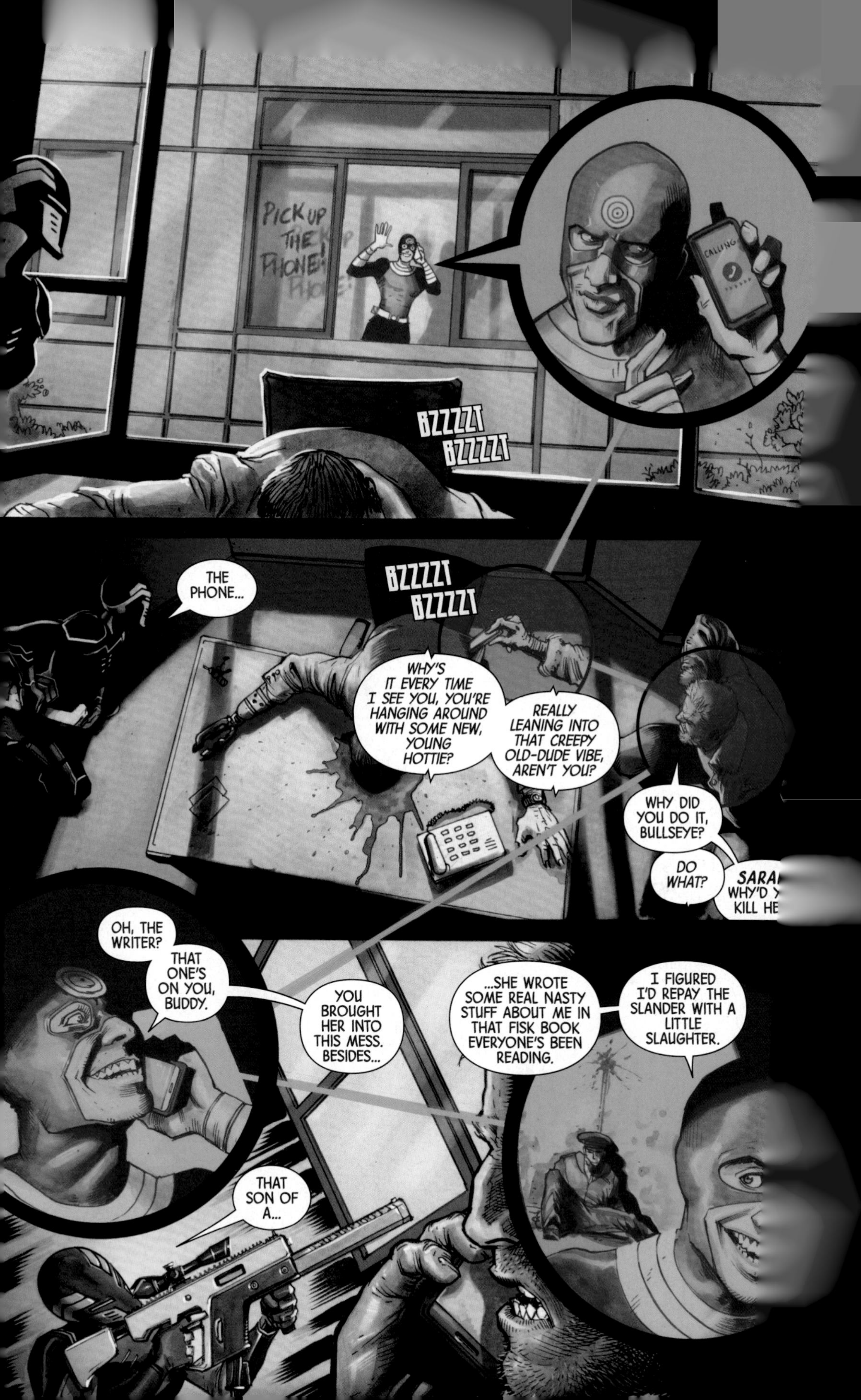
PICK UP THE PHONE!
BZZZZT BZZZZT
THE PHONE...
BZZZZT BZZZZT
WHY'S IT EVERY TIME I SEE YOU, YOU'RE HANGING AROUND WITH SOME NEW, YOUNG HOTTIE?
REALLY LEANING INTO THAT CREEPY OLD-DUDE VIBE, AREN'T YOU?
WHY DID YOU DO IT, BULLSEYE?
DO WHAT?
SARA
WHY'D Y
KILL HE
OH, THE WRITER?
THAT ONE'S ON YOU, BUDDY.
YOU BROUGHT HER INTO THIS MESS. BESIDES...
...SHE WROTE SOME REAL NASTY STUFF ABOUT ME IN THAT FISK BOOK EVERYONE'S BEEN READING.
I FIGURED I'D REPAY THE SLANDER WITH A LITTLE SLAUGHTER.
THAT SON OF A...

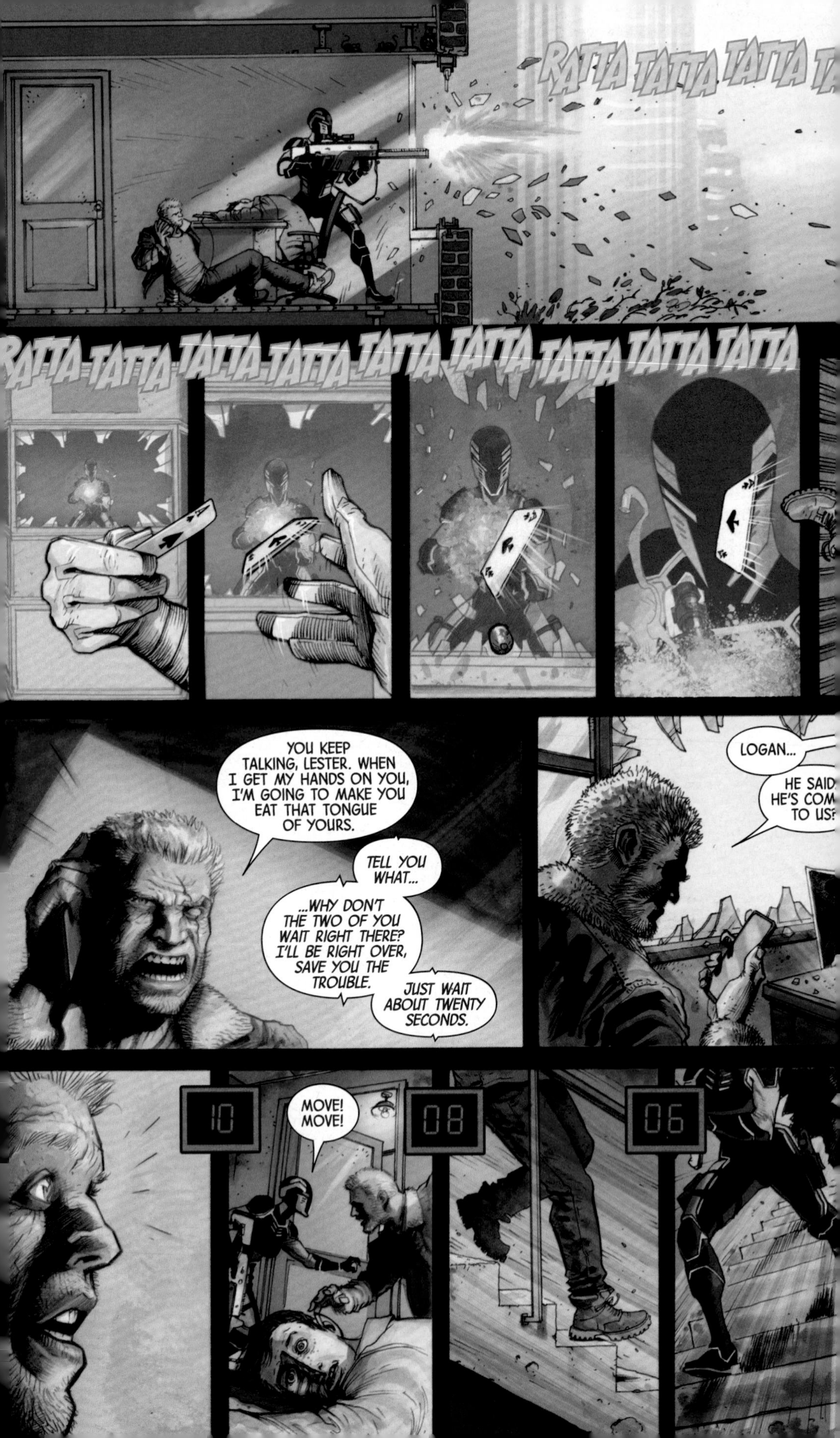
RATTA TATTA TATTA TA
RATTA TATTA TATTA TATTA TATTA TATTA TATTA TATTA TATTA
YOU KEEP TALKING, LESTER. WHEN I GET MY HANDS ON YOU, I'M GOING TO MAKE YOU EAT THAT TONGUE OF YOURS.
TELL YOU WHAT...
...WHY DON'T THE TWO OF YOU WAIT RIGHT THERE? I'LL BE RIGHT OVER, SAVE YOU THE TROUBLE.
JUST WAIT ABOUT TWENTY SECONDS.
LOGAN...
HE SAID
HE'S COM
TO US!
10
MOVE! MOVE!
08
06

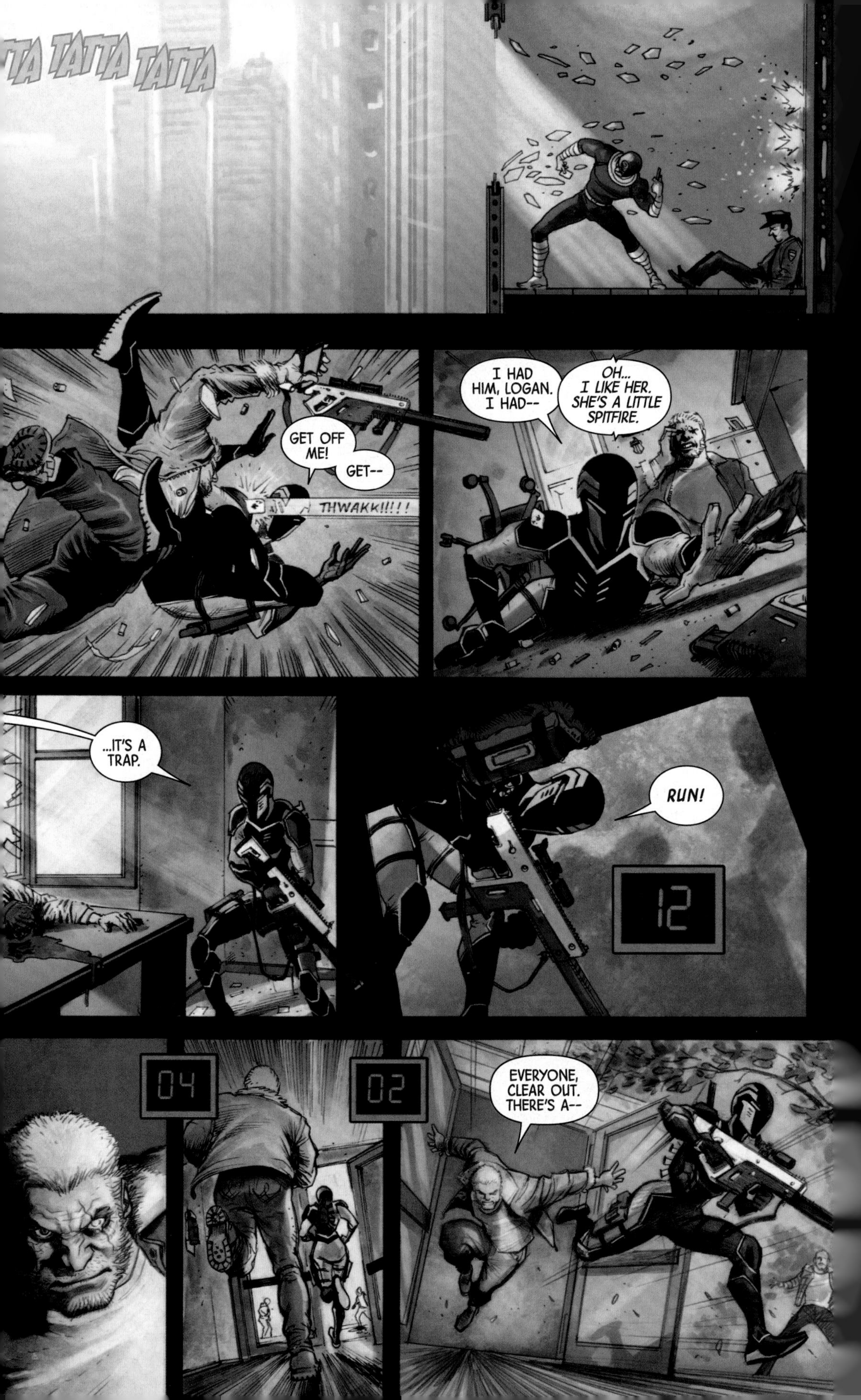
TA TATTA TATTA
GET OFF ME!
GET--
THWAKK!!!!!
I HAD HIM, LOGAN. I HAD--
OH... I LIKE HER. SHE'S A LITTLE SPITFIRE.
...IT'S A TRAP.
RUN!
12
04
02
EVERYONE, CLEAR OUT. THERE'S A--

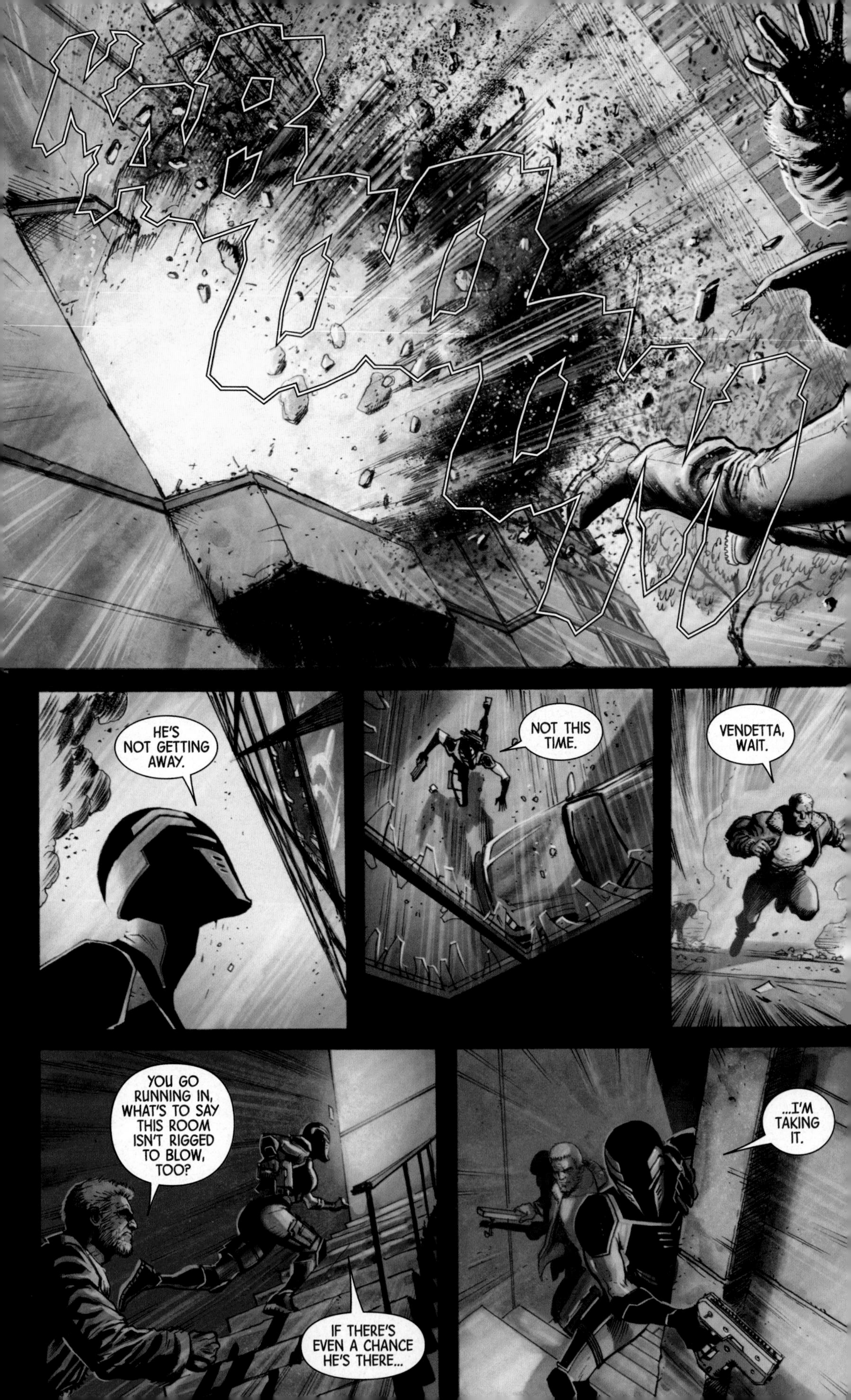
HE'S NOT GETTING AWAY.
NOT THIS TIME.
VENDETTA, WAIT.
YOU GO RUNNING IN, WHAT'S TO SAY THIS ROOM ISN'T RIGGED TO BLOW, TOO?
IF THERE'S EVEN A CHANCE HE'S THERE...
...I'M TAKING IT.

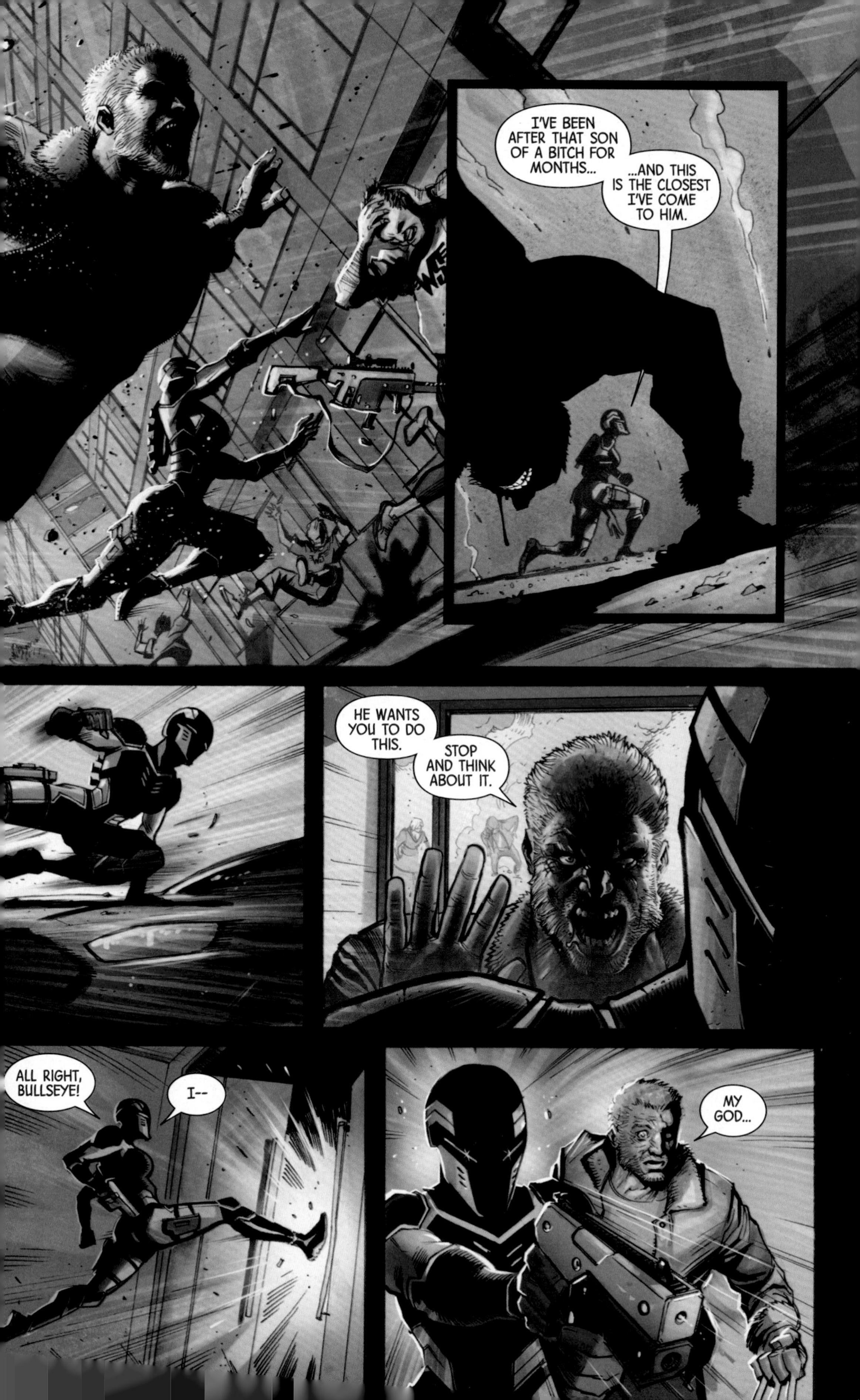
I'VE BEEN AFTER THAT SON OF A BITCH FOR MONTHS...
...AND THIS IS THE CLOSEST I'VE COME TO HIM.
HE WANTS YOU TO DO THIS.
STOP AND THINK ABOUT IT.
ALL RIGHT, BULLSEYE!
I--
MY GOD...

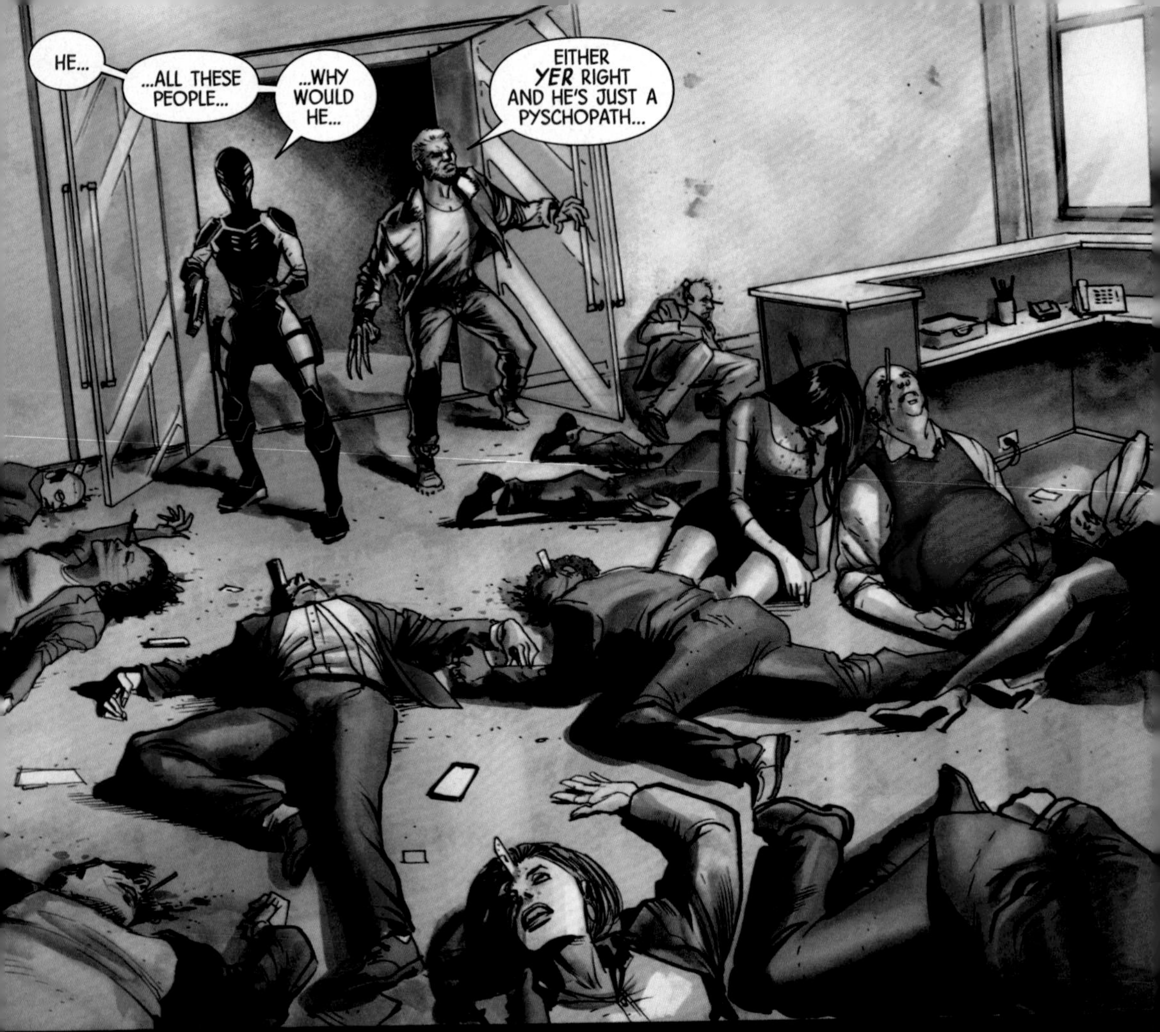
HE...
...ALL THESE PEOPLE...
...WHY WOULD HE...
EITHER YER RIGHT AND HE'S JUST A PYSCHOPATH...

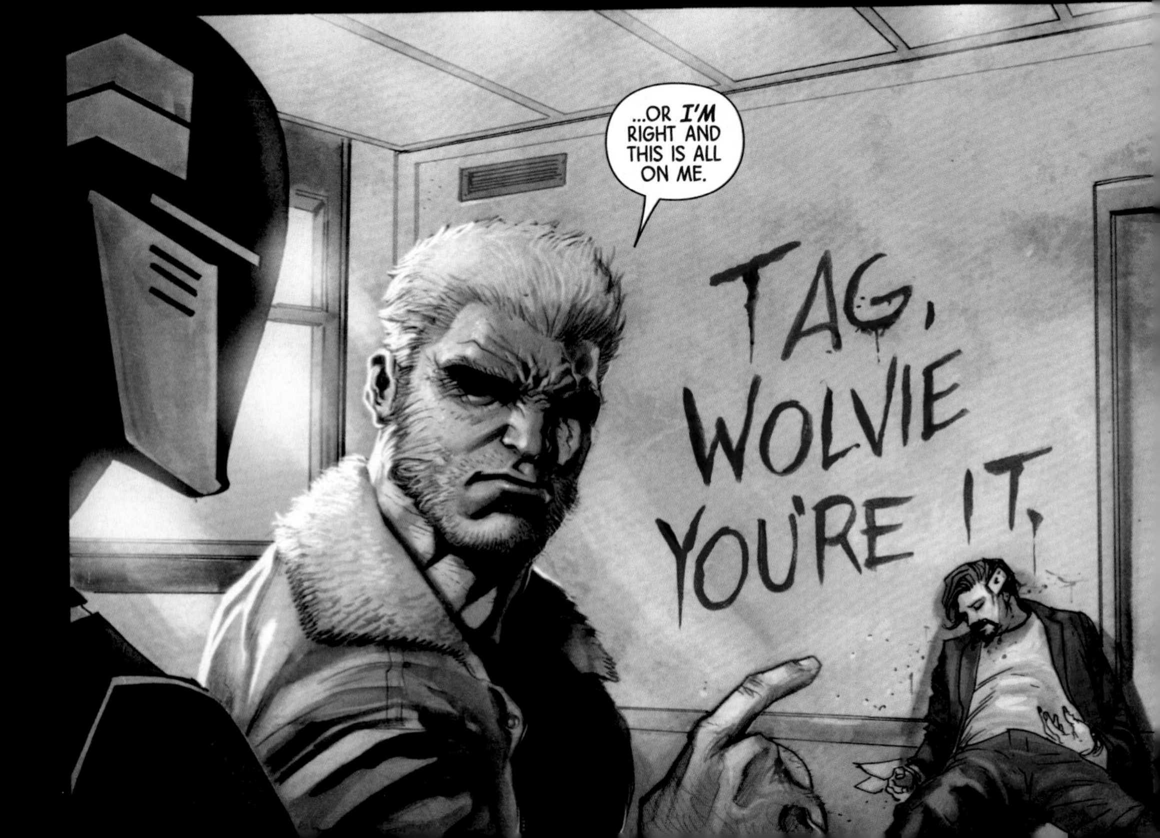
...OR I'M RIGHT AND THIS IS ALL ON ME.
TAG, WOLVIE YOU'RE IT.

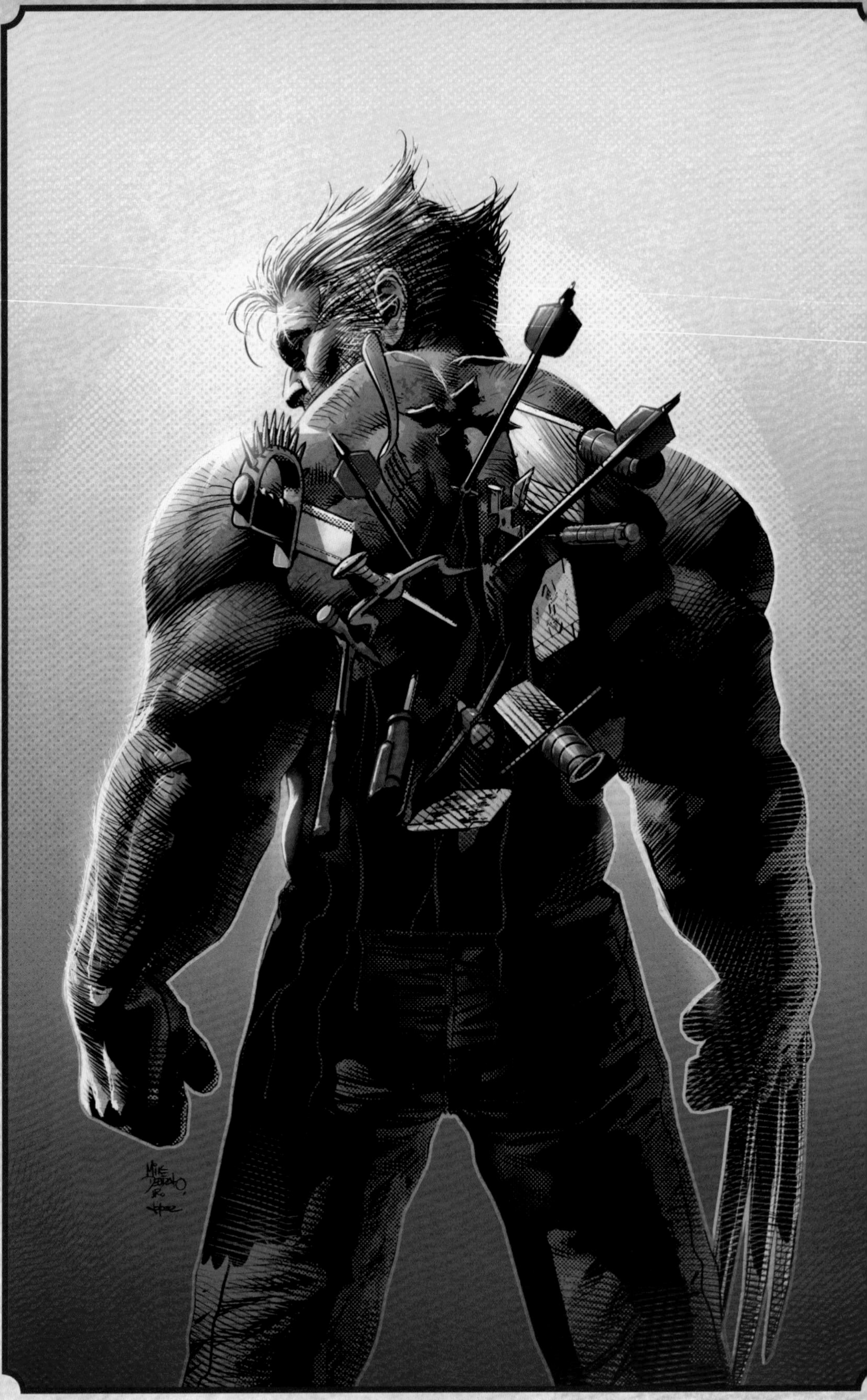

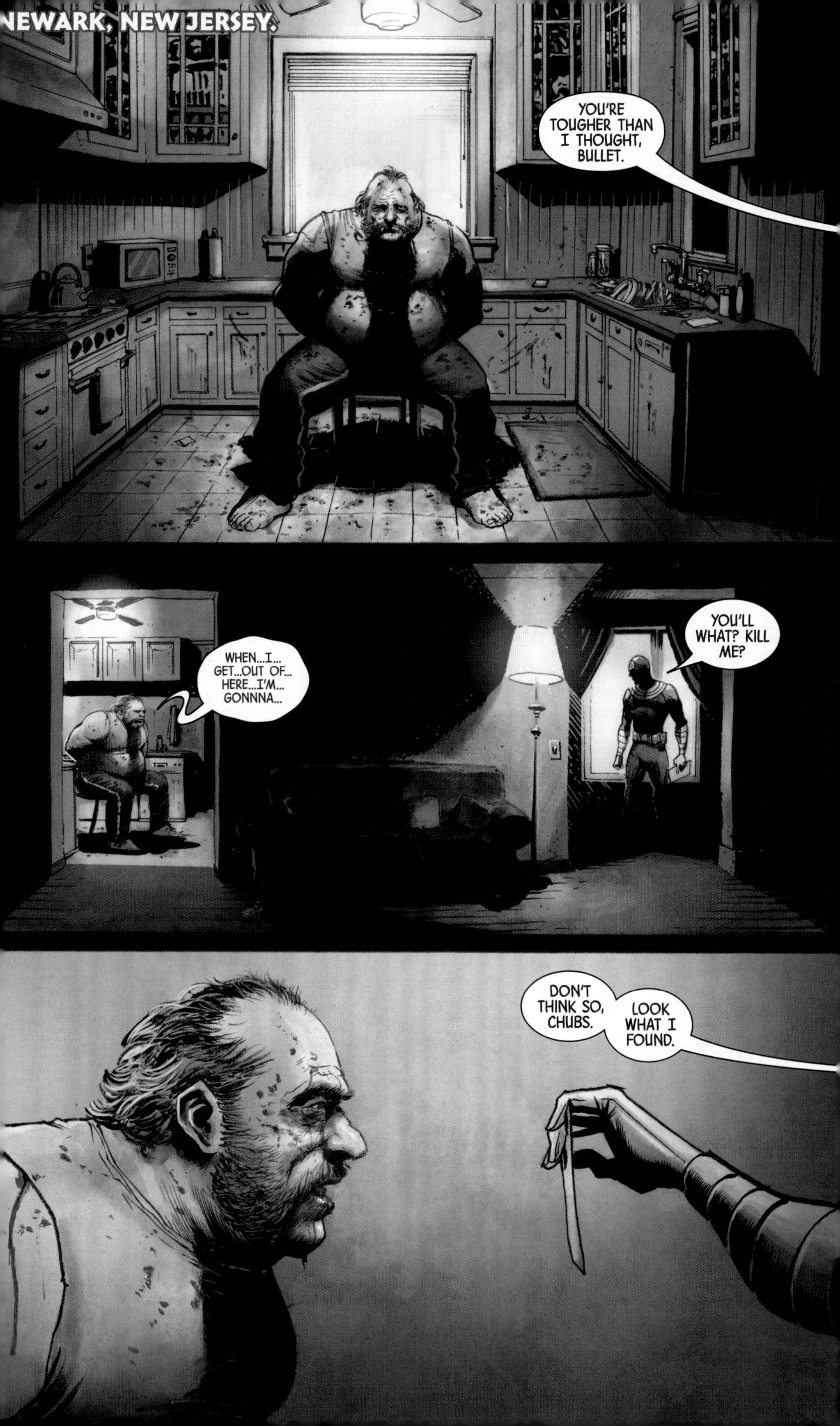
NEWARK, NEW JERSEY.
YOU'RE TOUGHER THAN I THOUGHT, BULLET.
WHEN...I... GET...OUT OF... HERE...I'M... GONNNA...
YOU'LL WHAT? KILL ME?
DON'T THINK SO, CHUBS.
LOOK WHAT I FOUND.

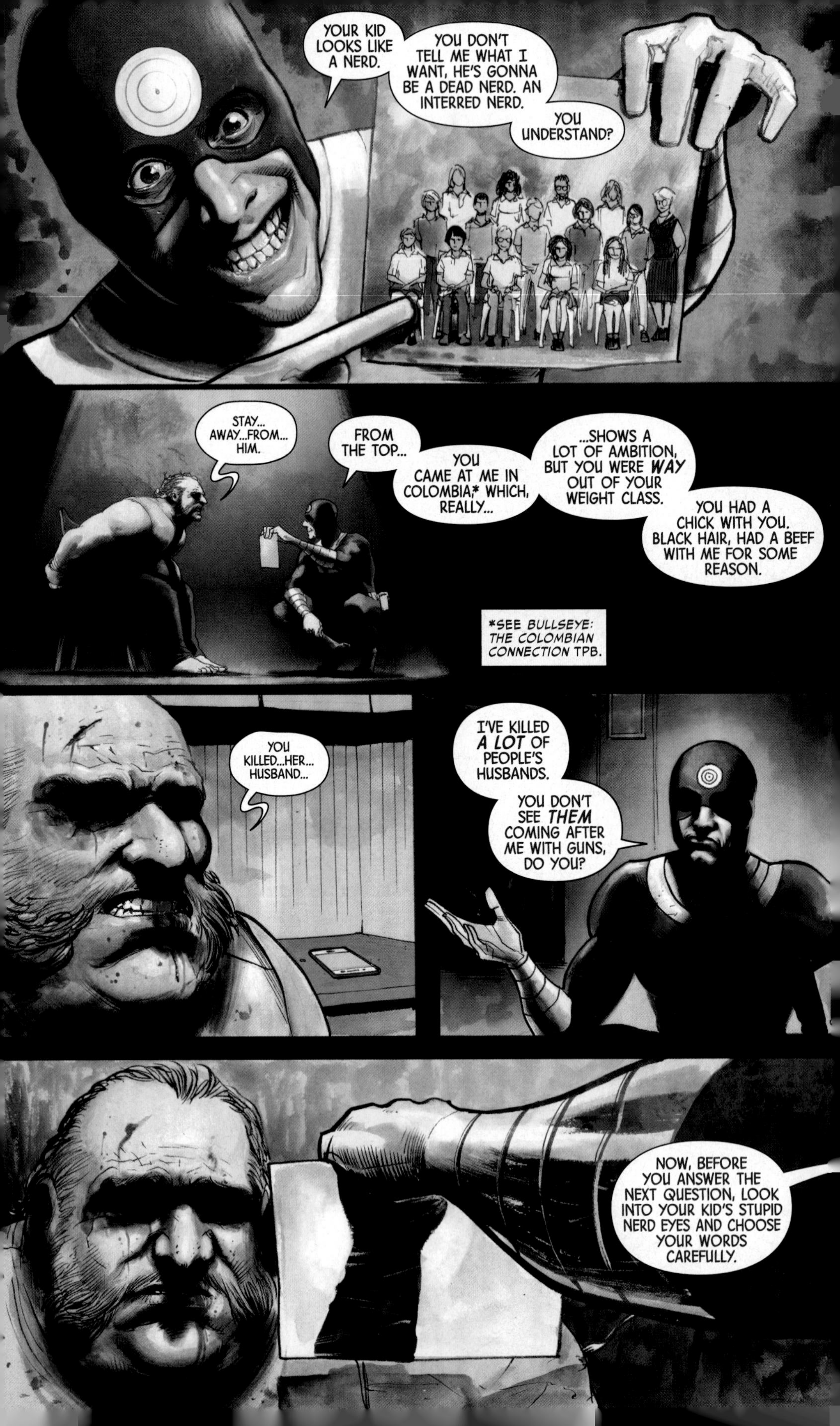
YOUR KID LOOKS LIKE A NERD.
YOU DON'T TELL ME WHAT I WANT, HE'S GONNA BE A DEAD NERD. AN INTERRED NERD.
YOU UNDERSTAND?
STAY... AWAY...FROM... HIM.
FROM THE TOP...
YOU CAME AT ME IN COLOMBIA,* WHICH, REALLY...
...SHOWS A LOT OF AMBITION, BUT YOU WERE *WAY* OUT OF YOUR WEIGHT CLASS.
YOU HAD A CHICK WITH YOU. BLACK HAIR, HAD A BEEF WITH ME FOR SOME REASON.
*SEE *BULLSEYE: THE COLOMBIAN CONNECTION* TPB.
YOU KILLED...HER... HUSBAND...
I'VE KILLED *A LOT* OF PEOPLE'S HUSBANDS.
YOU DON'T SEE *THEM* COMING AFTER ME WITH GUNS, DO YOU?
NOW, BEFORE YOU ANSWER THE NEXT QUESTION, LOOK INTO YOUR KID'S STUPID NERD EYES AND CHOOSE YOUR WORDS CAREFULLY.

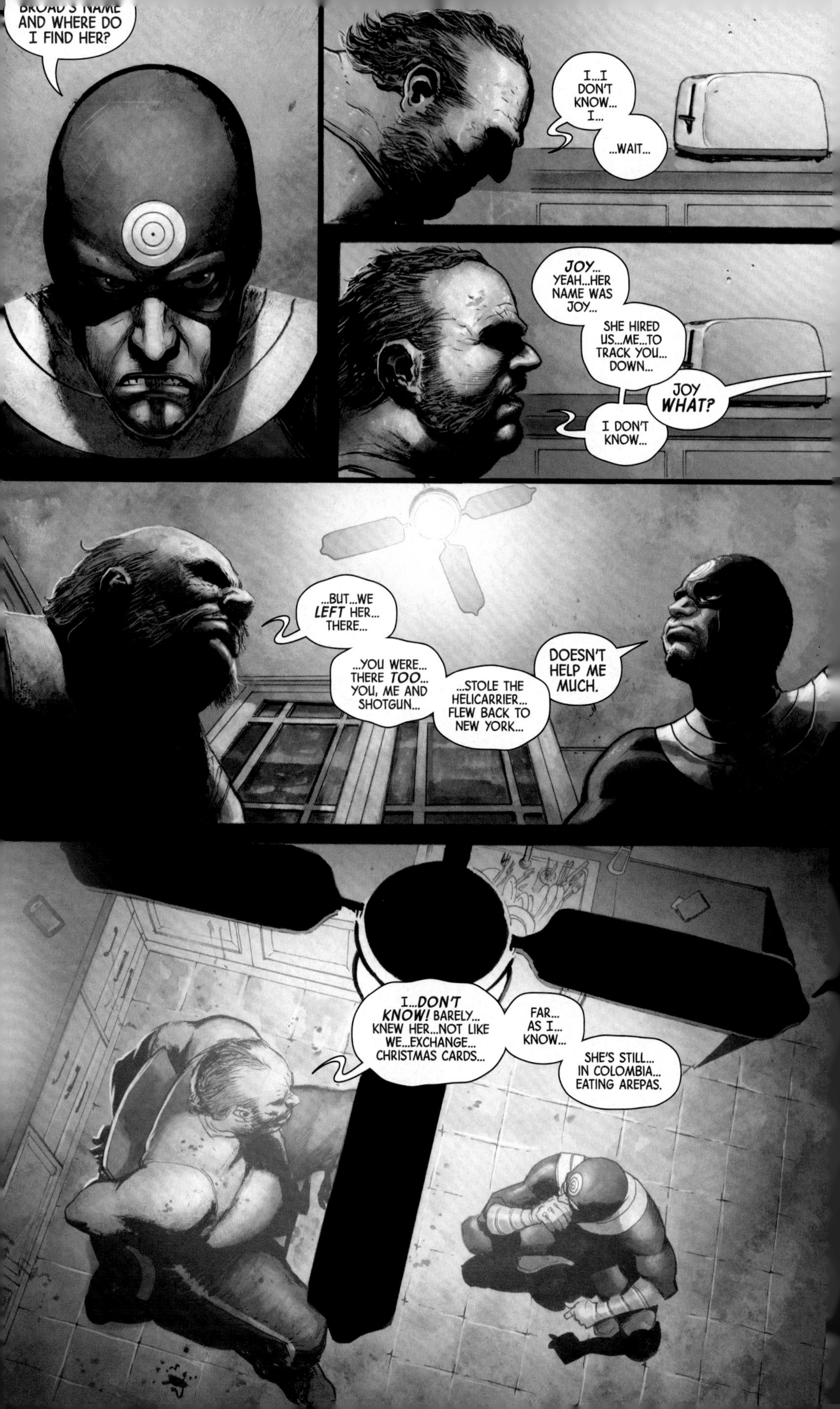

AND WHERE DO I FIND HER?
I...I DON'T KNOW... I...
...WAIT...
JOY... YEAH...HER NAME WAS JOY...
SHE HIRED US...ME...TO TRACK YOU... DOWN...
JOY WHAT?
I DON'T KNOW...
...BUT...WE LEFT HER... THERE...
...YOU WERE... THERE TOO... YOU, ME AND SHOTGUN...
...STOLE THE HELICARRIER... FLEW BACK TO NEW YORK...
DOESN'T HELP ME MUCH.
I...DON'T KNOW! BARELY... KNEW HER...NOT LIKE WE...EXCHANGE... CHRISTMAS CARDS...
FAR... AS I... KNOW...
SHE'S STILL... IN COLOMBIA... EATING AREPAS.

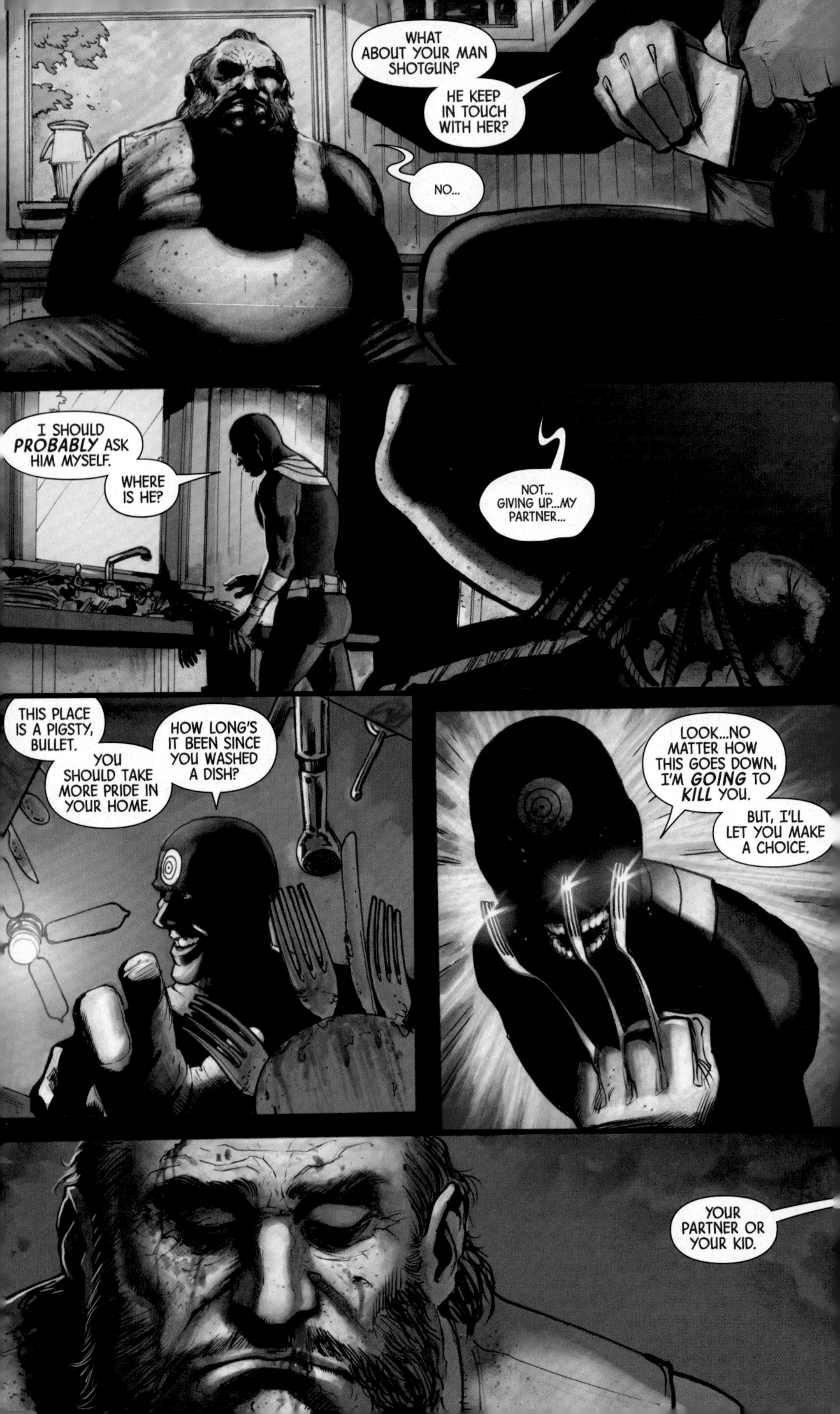
WHAT ABOUT YOUR MAN SHOTGUN?
HE KEEP IN TOUCH WITH HER?
NO...
I SHOULD PROBABLY ASK HIM MYSELF.
WHERE IS HE?
NOT... GIVING UP...MY PARTNER...
THIS PLACE IS A PIGSTY, BULLET.
YOU SHOULD TAKE MORE PRIDE IN YOUR HOME.
HOW LONG'S IT BEEN SINCE YOU WASHED A DISH?
LOOK...NO MATTER HOW THIS GOES DOWN, I'M GOING TO KILL YOU.
BUT, I'LL LET YOU MAKE A CHOICE.
YOUR PARTNER OR YOUR KID.

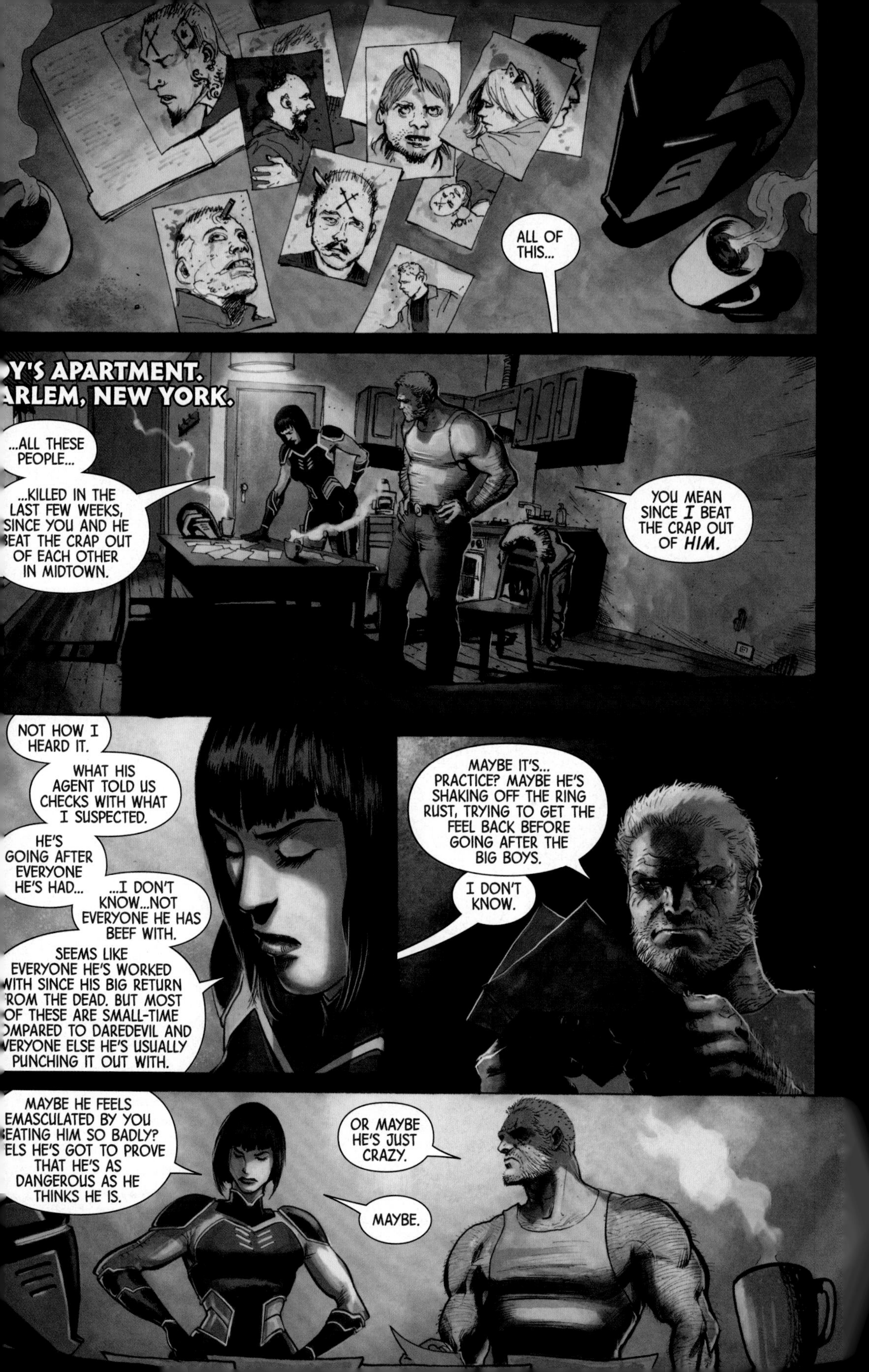
ALL OF THIS...
Y'S APARTMENT. ARLEM, NEW YORK.
...ALL THESE PEOPLE...
...KILLED IN THE LAST FEW WEEKS, SINCE YOU AND HE BEAT THE CRAP OUT OF EACH OTHER IN MIDTOWN.
YOU MEAN SINCE I BEAT THE CRAP OUT OF HIM.
NOT HOW I HEARD IT.
WHAT HIS AGENT TOLD US CHECKS WITH WHAT I SUSPECTED.
HE'S GOING AFTER EVERYONE HE'S HAD...
...I DON'T KNOW...NOT EVERYONE HE HAS BEEF WITH.
SEEMS LIKE EVERYONE HE'S WORKED WITH SINCE HIS BIG RETURN FROM THE DEAD. BUT MOST OF THESE ARE SMALL-TIME COMPARED TO DAREDEVIL AND EVERYONE ELSE HE'S USUALLY PUNCHING IT OUT WITH.
MAYBE IT'S... PRACTICE? MAYBE HE'S SHAKING OFF THE RING RUST, TRYING TO GET THE FEEL BACK BEFORE GOING AFTER THE BIG BOYS.
I DON'T KNOW.
MAYBE HE FEELS EMASCULATED BY YOU BEATING HIM SO BADLY? FEELS HE'S GOT TO PROVE THAT HE'S AS DANGEROUS AS HE THINKS HE IS.
OR MAYBE HE'S JUST CRAZY.
MAYBE.

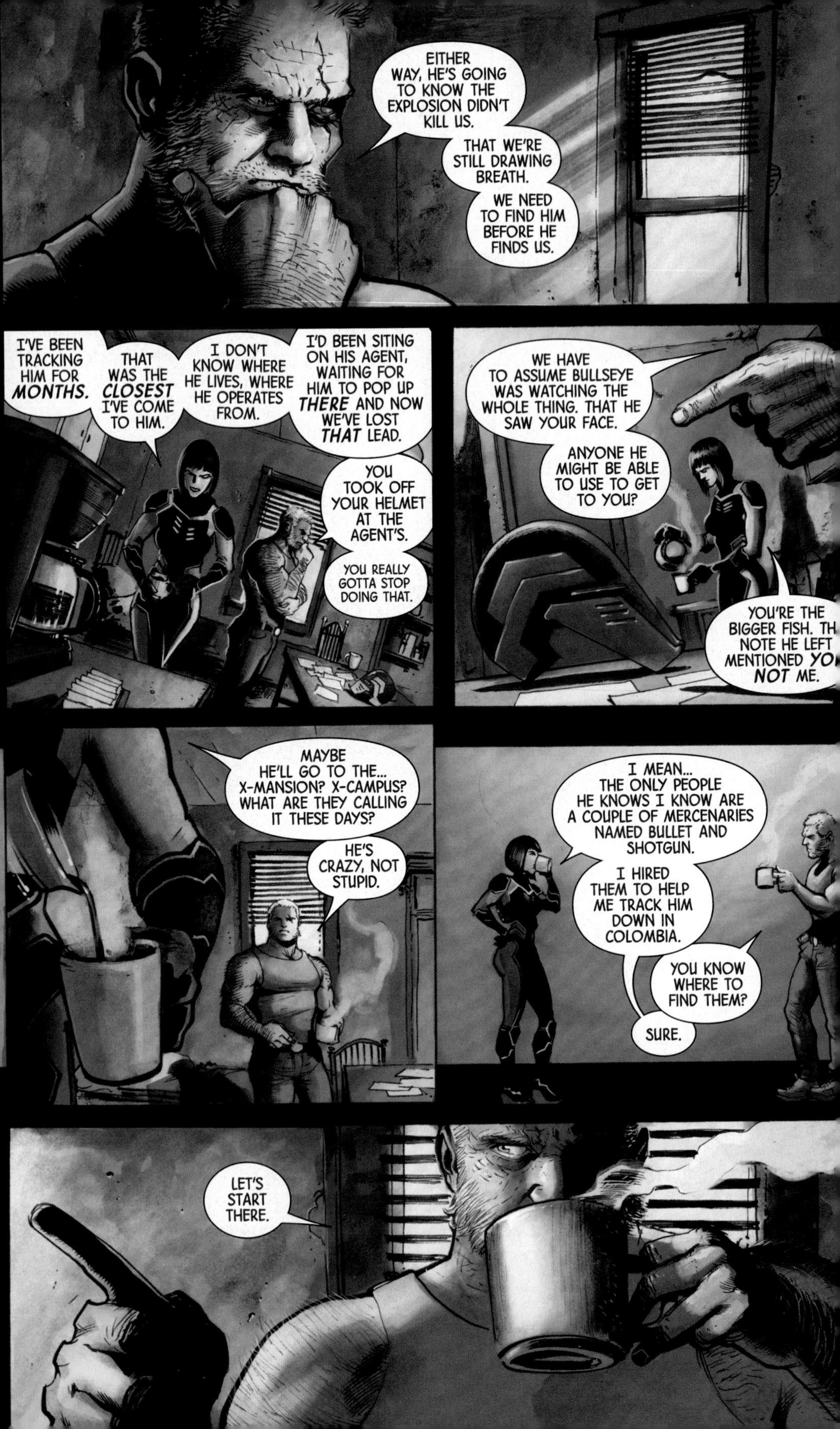

EITHER WAY, HE'S GOING TO KNOW THE EXPLOSION DIDN'T KILL US.
THAT WE'RE STILL DRAWING BREATH.
WE NEED TO FIND HIM BEFORE HE FINDS US.
I'VE BEEN TRACKING HIM FOR MONTHS.
THAT WAS THE CLOSEST I'VE COME TO HIM.
I DON'T KNOW WHERE HE LIVES, WHERE HE OPERATES FROM.
I'D BEEN SITING ON HIS AGENT, WAITING FOR HIM TO POP UP THERE AND NOW WE'VE LOST THAT LEAD.
YOU TOOK OFF YOUR HELMET AT THE AGENT'S.
YOU REALLY GOTTA STOP DOING THAT.
WE HAVE TO ASSUME BULLSEYE WAS WATCHING THE WHOLE THING. THAT HE SAW YOUR FACE.
ANYONE HE MIGHT BE ABLE TO USE TO GET TO YOU?
YOU'RE THE BIGGER FISH. TH NOTE HE LEFT MENTIONED YO NOT ME.
MAYBE HE'LL GO TO THE... X-MANSION? X-CAMPUS? WHAT ARE THEY CALLING IT THESE DAYS?
HE'S CRAZY, NOT STUPID.
I MEAN... THE ONLY PEOPLE HE KNOWS I KNOW ARE A COUPLE OF MERCENARIES NAMED BULLET AND SHOTGUN.
I HIRED THEM TO HELP ME TRACK HIM DOWN IN COLOMBIA.
YOU KNOW WHERE TO FIND THEM?
SURE.
LET'S START THERE.

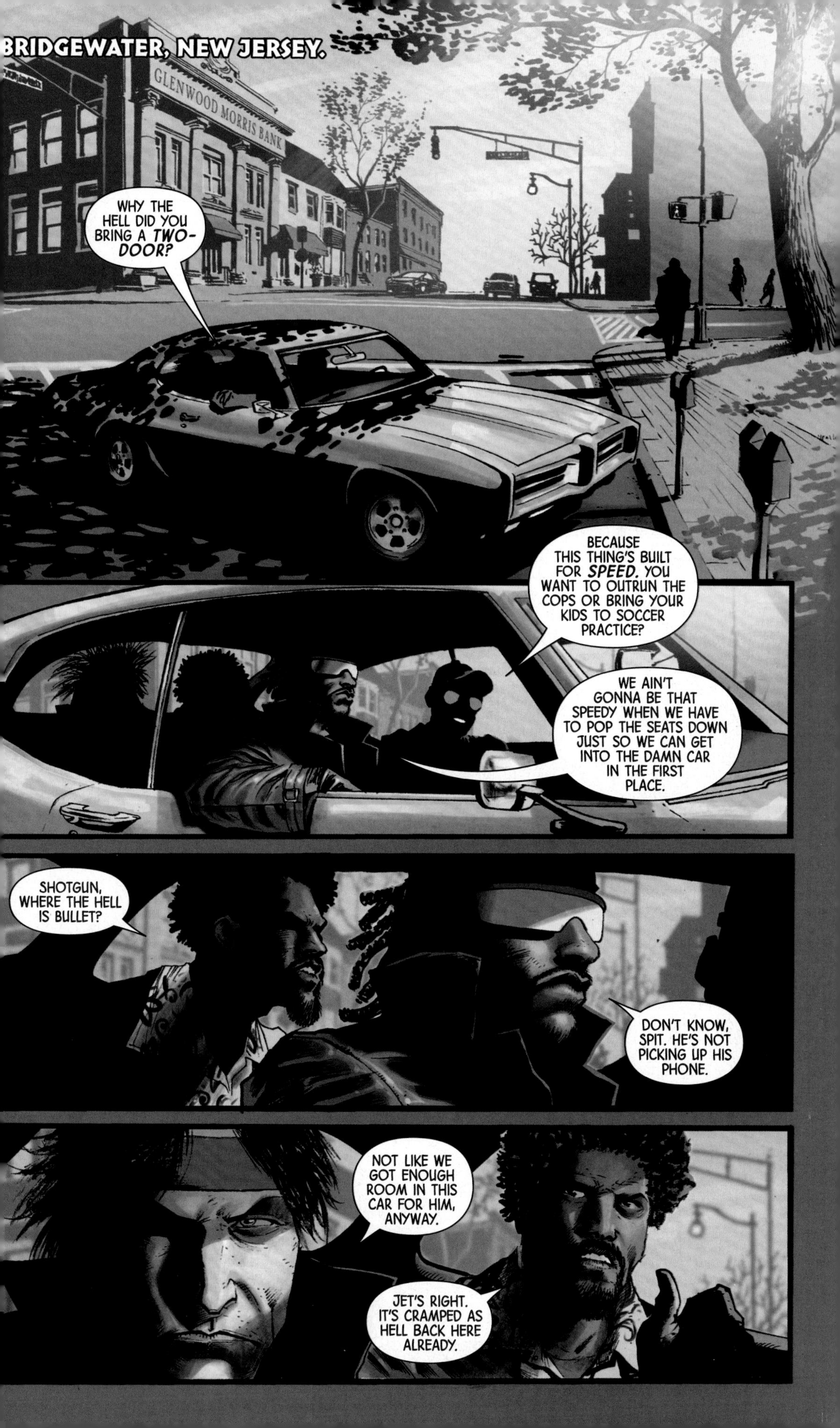
BRIDGEWATER, NEW JERSEY.
GLENWOOD MORRIS BANK
WHY THE HELL DID YOU BRING A *TWO-DOOR?*
BECAUSE THIS THING'S BUILT FOR ***SPEED.*** YOU WANT TO OUTRUN THE COPS OR BRING YOUR KIDS TO SOCCER PRACTICE?
WE AIN'T GONNA BE THAT SPEEDY WHEN WE HAVE TO POP THE SEATS DOWN JUST SO WE CAN GET INTO THE DAMN CAR IN THE FIRST PLACE.
SHOTGUN, WHERE THE HELL IS BULLET?
DON'T KNOW, SPIT. HE'S NOT PICKING UP HIS PHONE.
NOT LIKE WE GOT ENOUGH ROOM IN THIS CAR FOR HIM, ANYWAY.
JET'S RIGHT. IT'S CRAMPED AS HELL BACK HERE ALREADY.

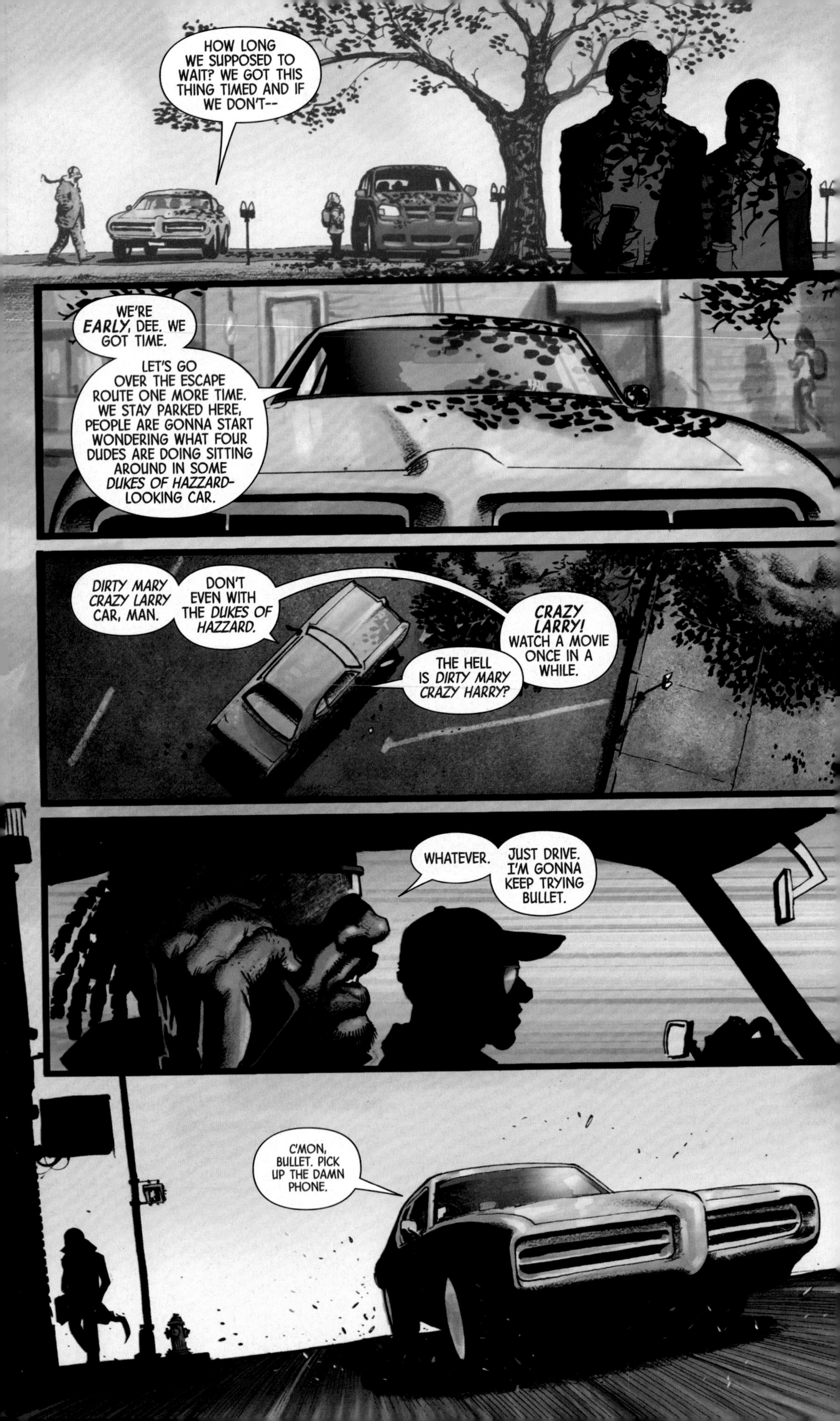
HOW LONG WE SUPPOSED TO WAIT? WE GOT THIS THING TIMED AND IF WE DON'T--
WE'RE *EARLY*, DEE. WE GOT TIME.
LET'S GO OVER THE ESCAPE ROUTE ONE MORE TIME. WE STAY PARKED HERE, PEOPLE ARE GONNA START WONDERING WHAT FOUR DUDES ARE DOING SITTING AROUND IN SOME *DUKES OF HAZZARD*-LOOKING CAR.
DIRTY MARY CRAZY LARRY CAR, MAN.
DON'T EVEN WITH THE *DUKES OF HAZZARD.*
THE HELL IS *DIRTY MARY CRAZY HARRY?*
CRAZY LARRY! WATCH A MOVIE ONCE IN A WHILE.
WHATEVER.
JUST DRIVE. I'M GONNA KEEP TRYING BULLET.
C'MON, BULLET. PICK UP THE DAMN PHONE.

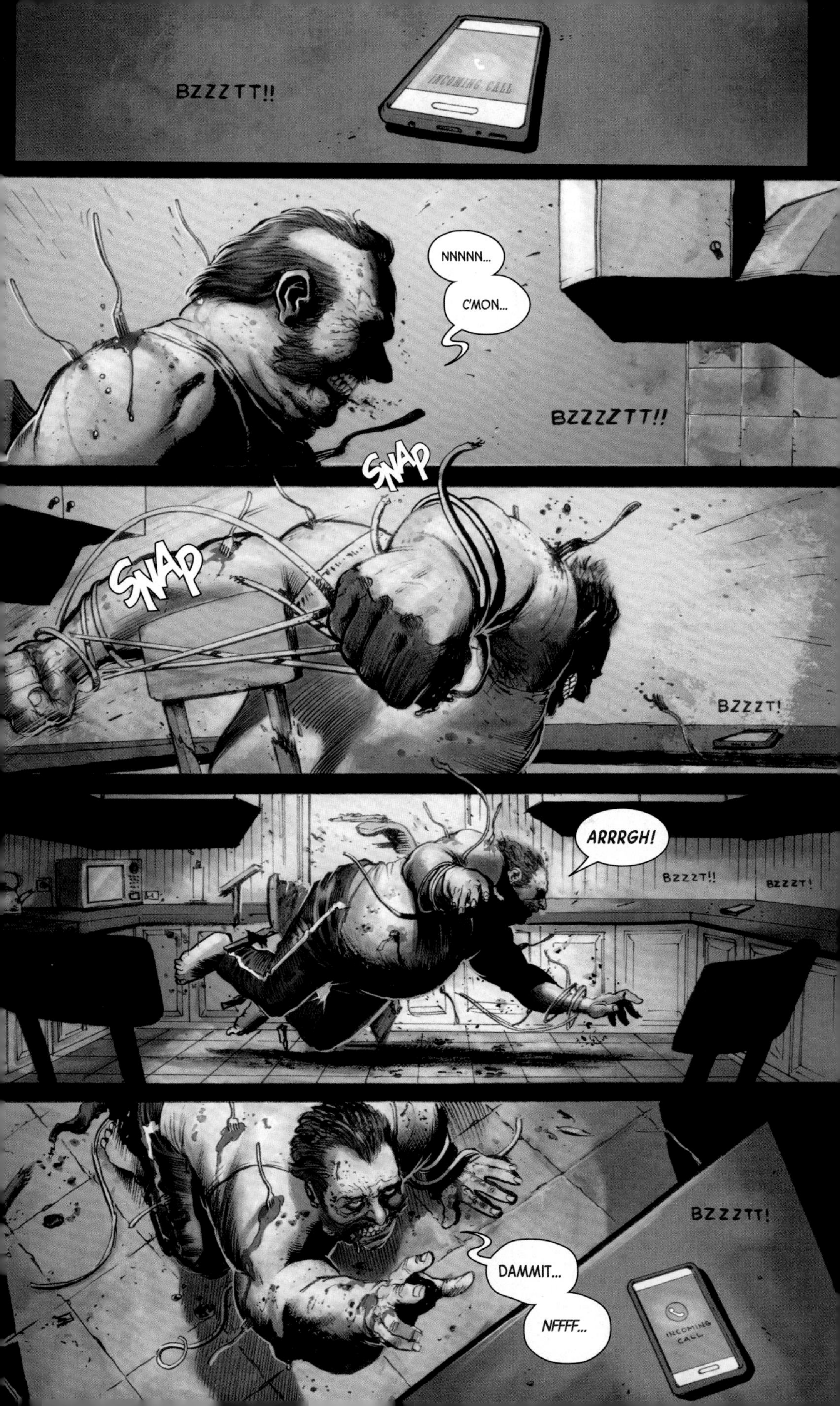
INCOMING CALL
BZZZTT!!
NNNNN...
C'MON...
BZZZZTT!!
SNAP
SNAP
BZZZT!
ARRRGH!
BZZZT!!
BZZZT!
BZZZTT!
DAMMIT...
NFFFF...
INCOMING CALL

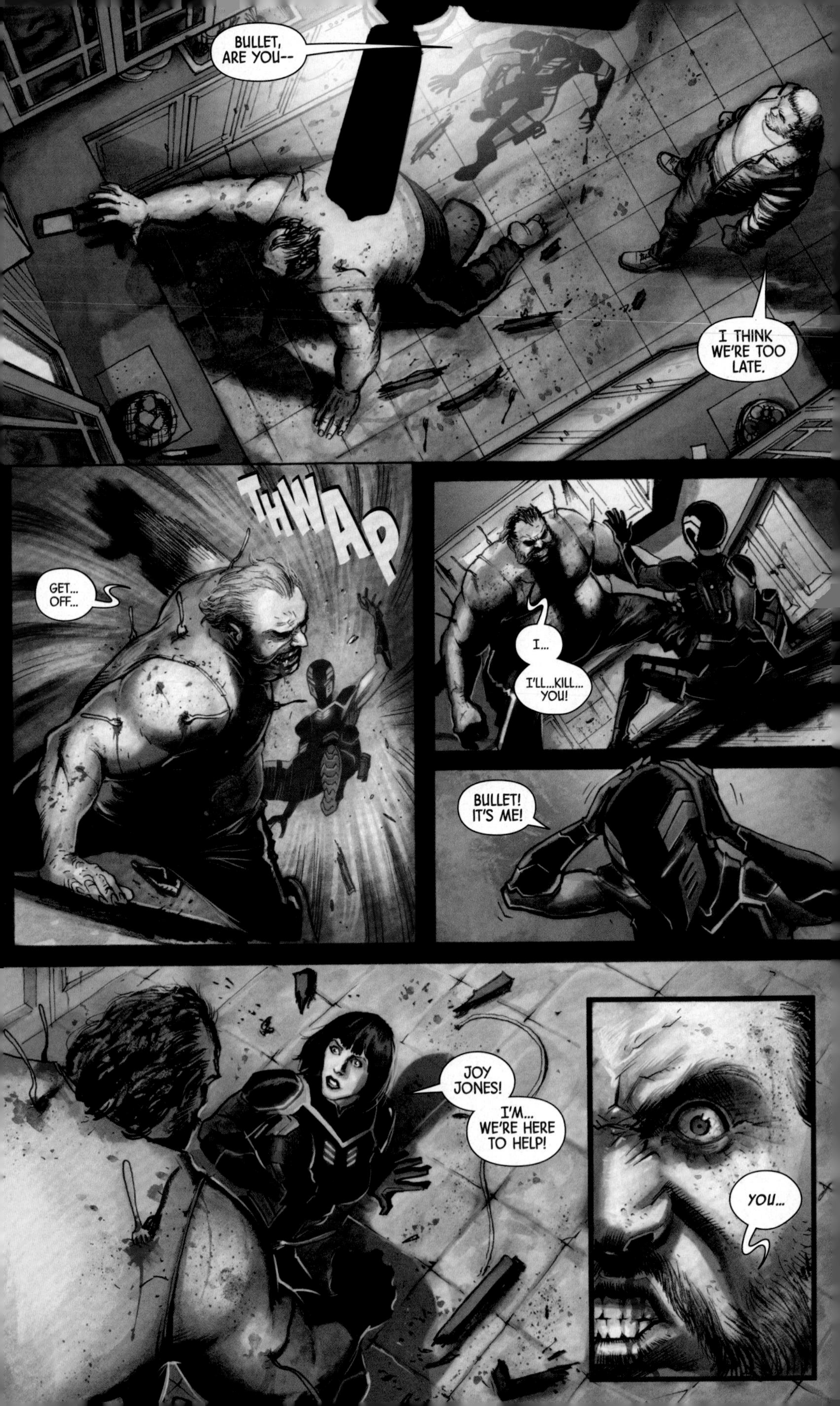
BULLET, ARE YOU--
I THINK WE'RE TOO LATE.
THWAP
GET... OFF...
I...
I'LL...KILL... YOU!
BULLET! IT'S ME!
JOY JONES!
I'M... WE'RE HERE TO HELP!
YOU...

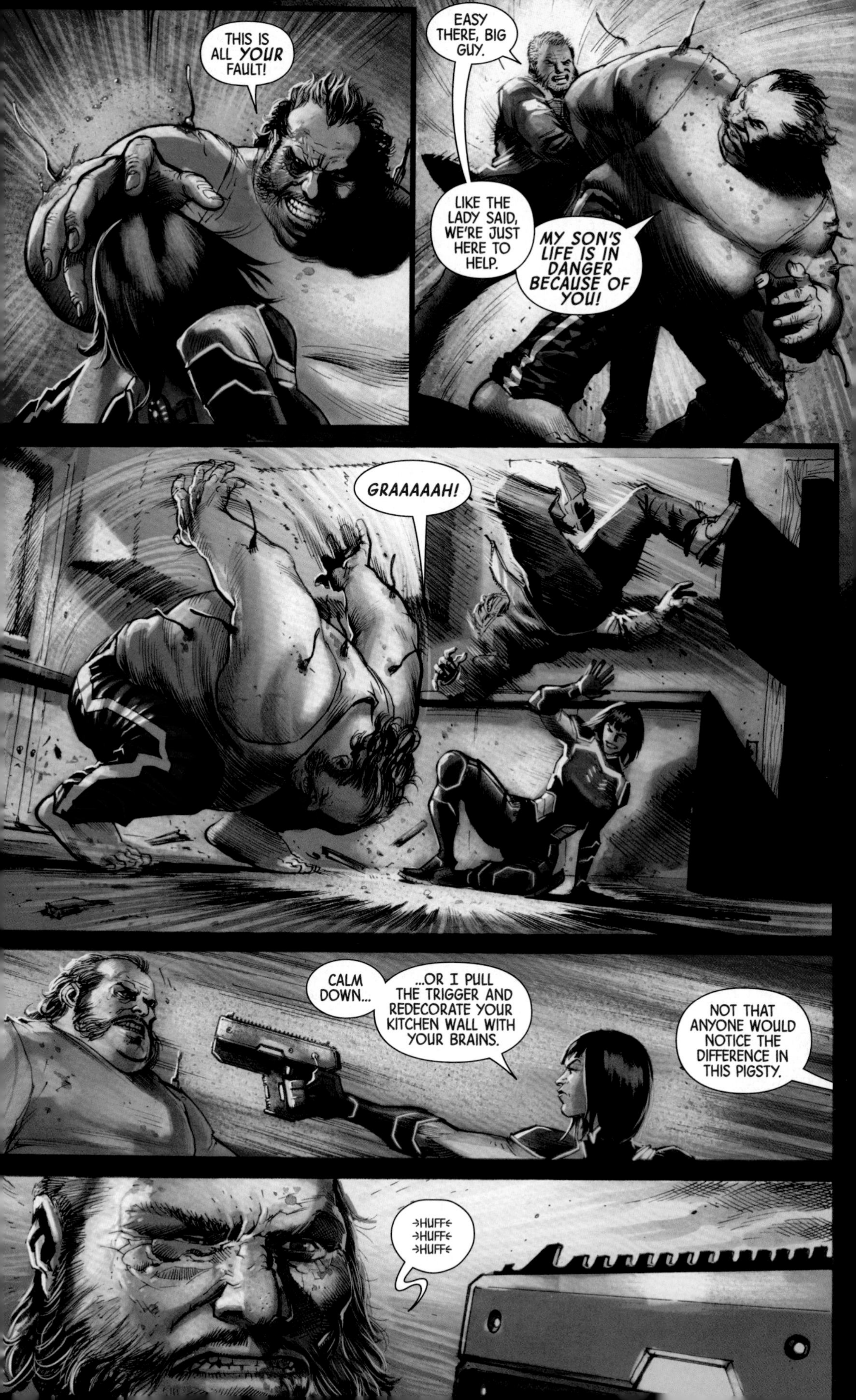
THIS IS ALL *YOUR* FAULT!
EASY THERE, BIG GUY.
LIKE THE LADY SAID, WE'RE JUST HERE TO HELP.
MY SON'S LIFE IS IN DANGER BECAUSE OF YOU!
GRAAAAAH!
CALM DOWN...
...OR I PULL THE TRIGGER AND REDECORATE YOUR KITCHEN WALL WITH YOUR BRAINS.
NOT THAT ANYONE WOULD NOTICE THE DIFFERENCE IN THIS PIGSTY.
›HUFF‹
›HUFF‹
›HUFF‹

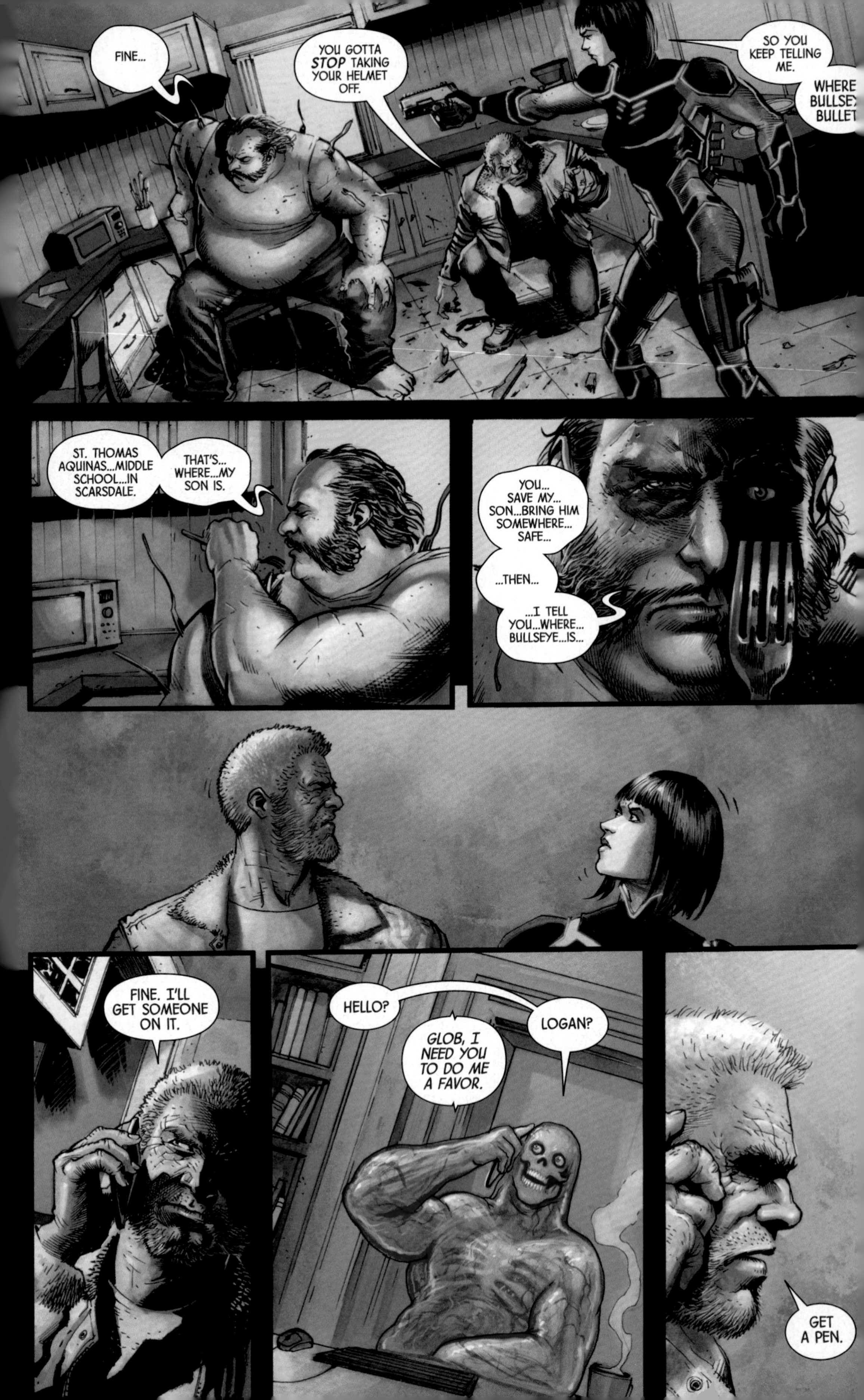
FINE...
YOU GOTTA STOP TAKING YOUR HELMET OFF.
SO YOU KEEP TELLING ME.
WHERE BULLSEY BULLET
ST. THOMAS AQUINAS...MIDDLE SCHOOL...IN SCARSDALE.
THAT'S... WHERE...MY SON IS.
YOU... SAVE MY... SON...BRING HIM SOMEWHERE... SAFE...
...THEN...
...I TELL YOU...WHERE... BULLSEYE...IS...
FINE. I'LL GET SOMEONE ON IT.
HELLO?
LOGAN?
GLOB, I NEED YOU TO DO ME A FAVOR.
GET A PEN.

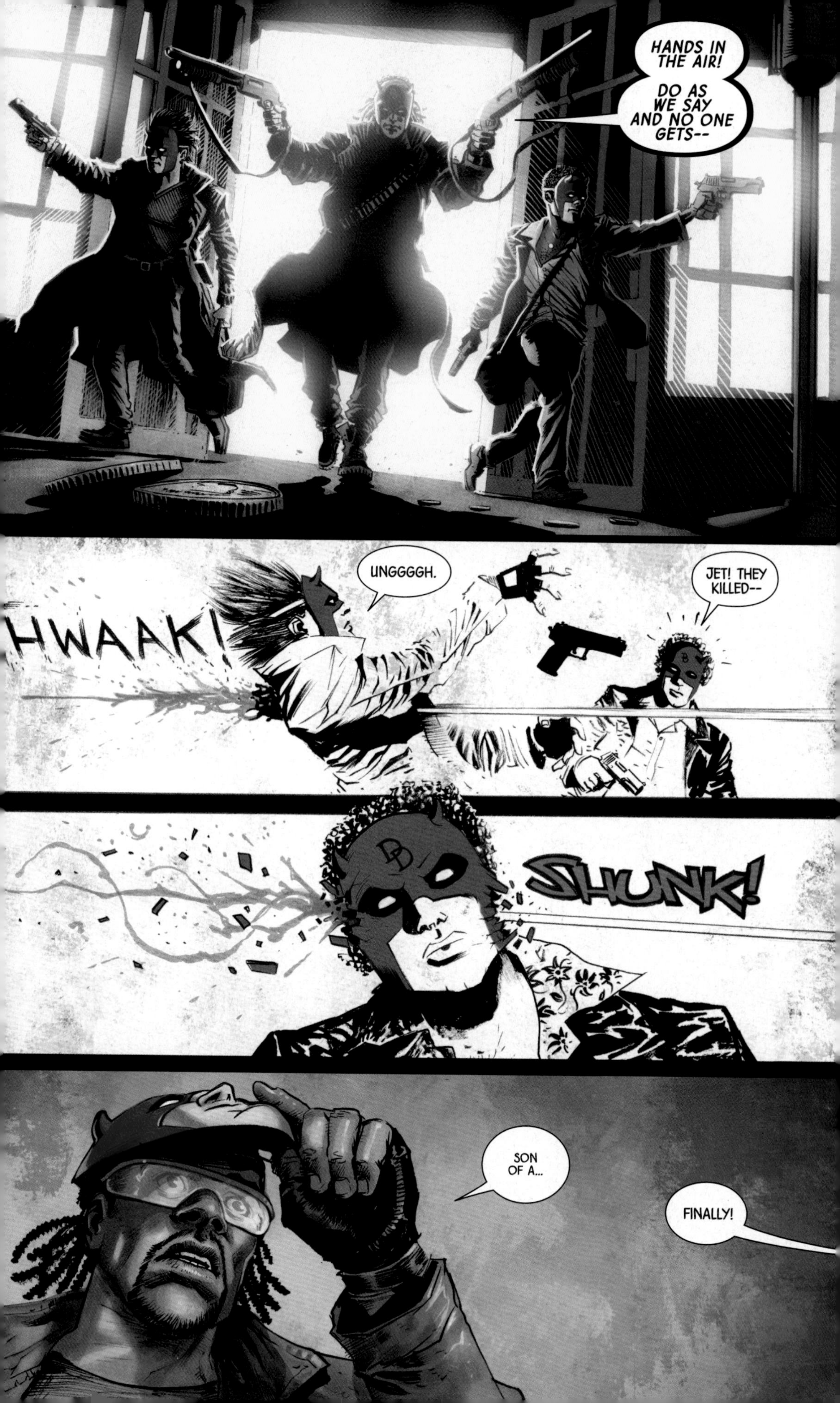
HANDS IN THE AIR!
DO AS WE SAY AND NO ONE GETS--
HWAAK!
UNGGGGH.
JET! THEY KILLED--
SHUNK!
SON OF A...
FINALLY!

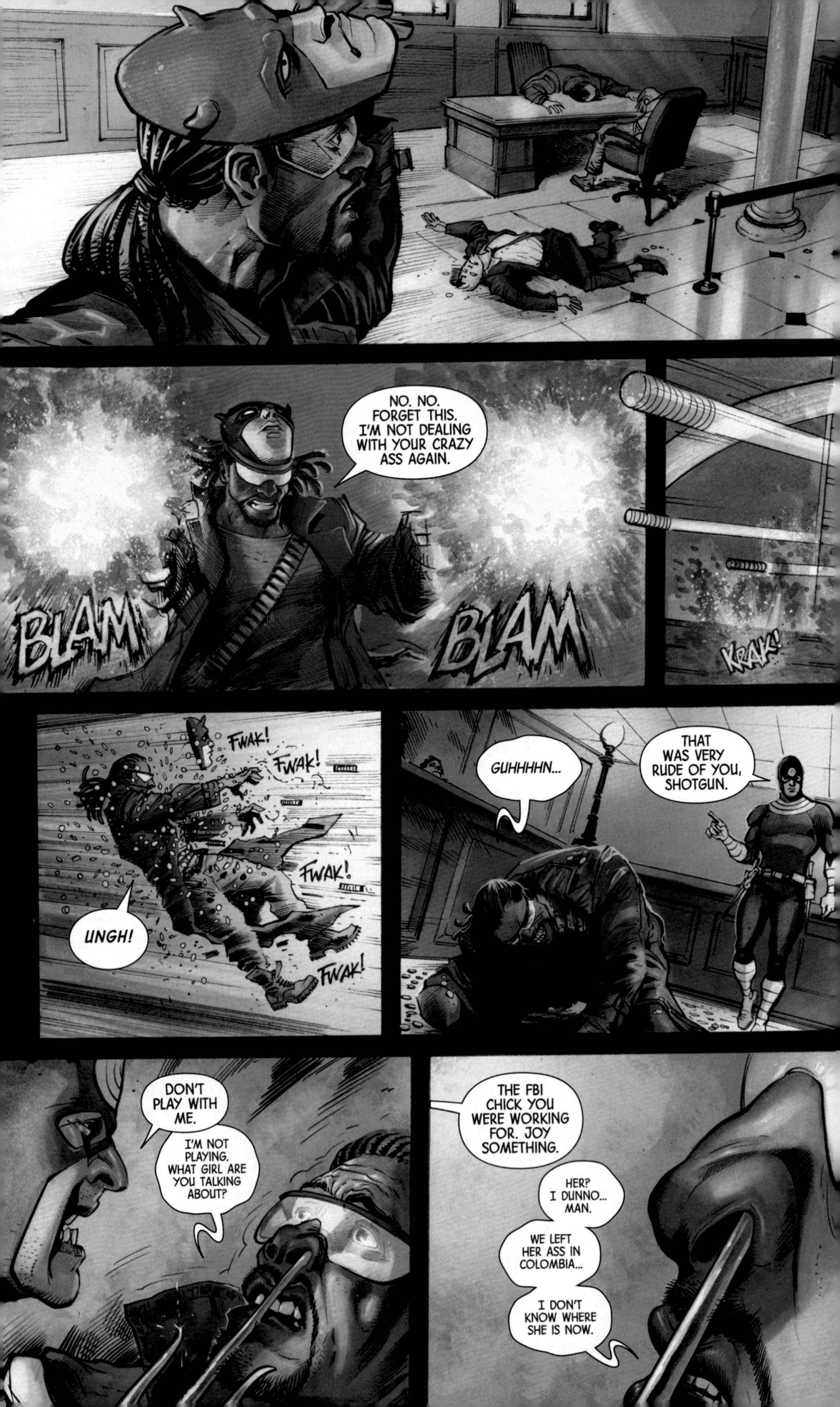

NO. NO. FORGET THIS. I'M NOT DEALING WITH YOUR CRAZY ASS AGAIN.
BLAM
BLAM
KRAK!
FWAK!
FWAK!
FWAK!
FWAK!
UNGH!
GUHHHHN...
THAT WAS VERY RUDE OF YOU, SHOTGUN.
DON'T PLAY WITH ME.
I'M NOT PLAYING. WHAT GIRL ARE YOU TALKING ABOUT?
THE FBI CHICK YOU WERE WORKING FOR. JOY SOMETHING.
HER? I DUNNO... MAN.
WE LEFT HER ASS IN COLOMBIA...
I DON'T KNOW WHERE SHE IS NOW.

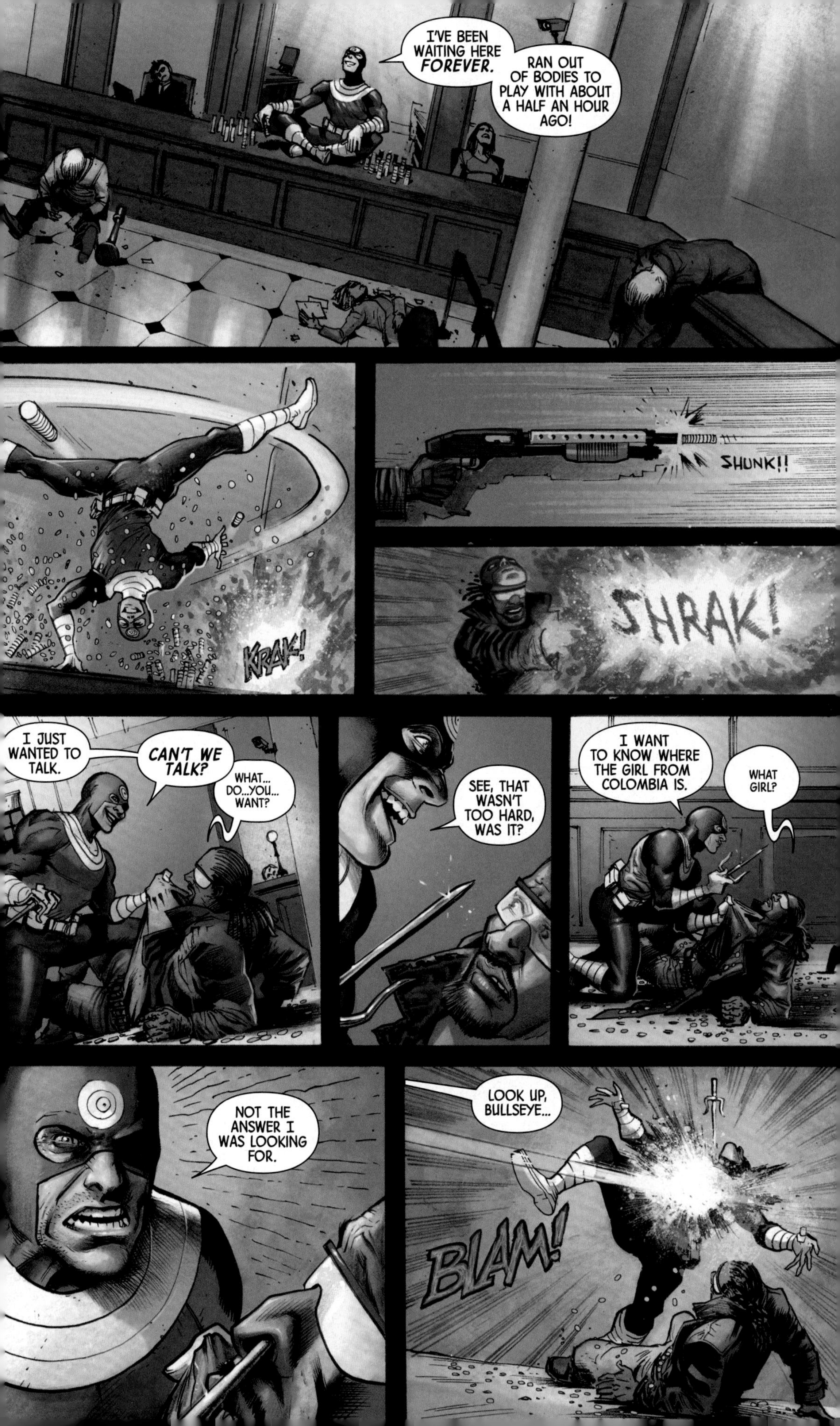
I'VE BEEN WAITING HERE *FOREVER.*
RAN OUT OF BODIES TO PLAY WITH ABOUT A HALF AN HOUR AGO!
KRAK!
SHUNK!!
SHRAK!
I JUST WANTED TO TALK.
CAN'T WE TALK?
WHAT... DO...YOU... WANT?
SEE, THAT WASN'T TOO HARD, WAS IT?
I WANT TO KNOW WHERE THE GIRL FROM COLOMBIA IS.
WHAT GIRL?
NOT THE ANSWER I WAS LOOKING FOR.
LOOK UP, BULLSEYE...
BLAM!

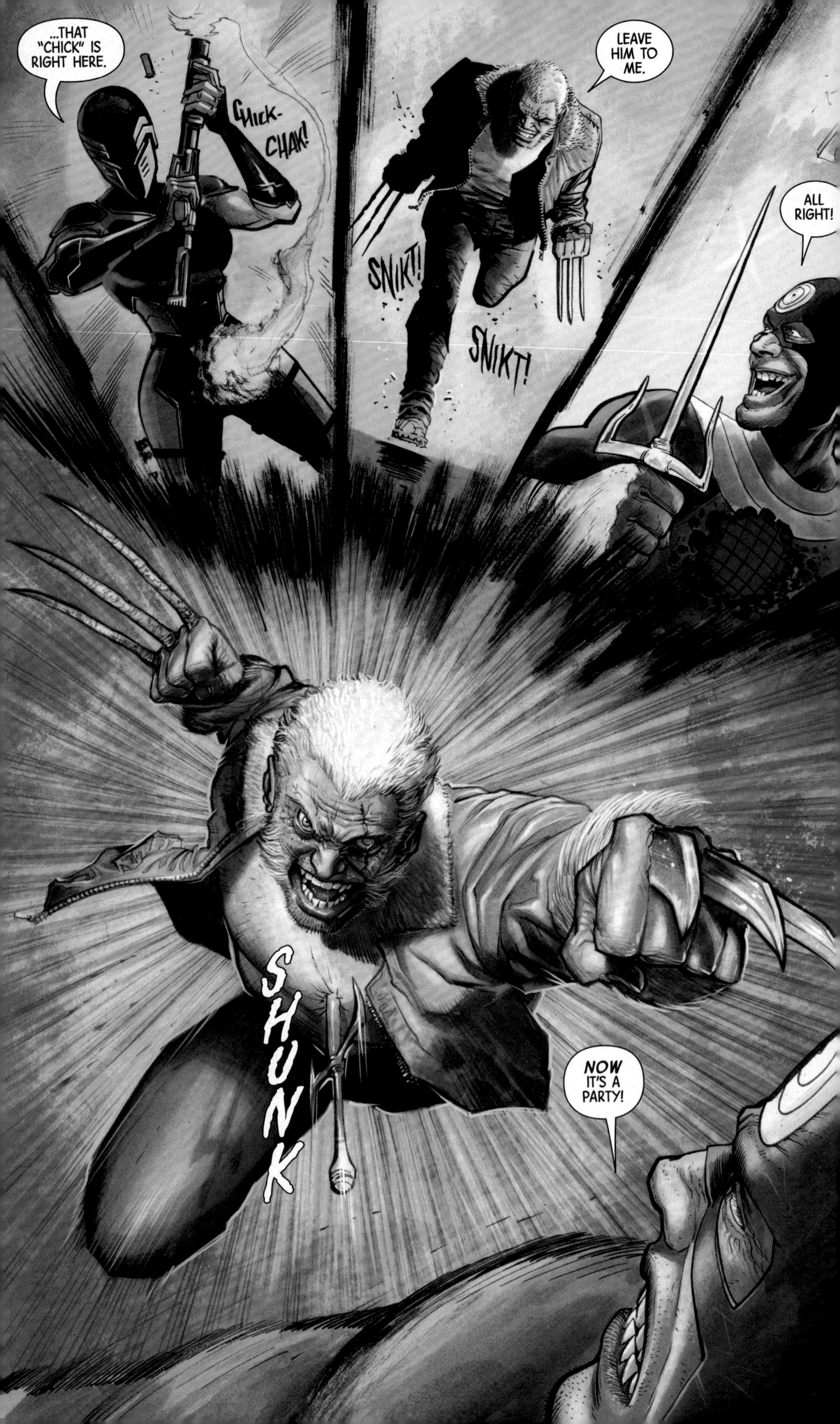

...THAT "CHICK" IS RIGHT HERE.
CHICK-CHAK!
LEAVE HIM TO ME.
SNIKT!
SNIKT!
ALL RIGHT!
SHUNK
NOW IT'S A PARTY!

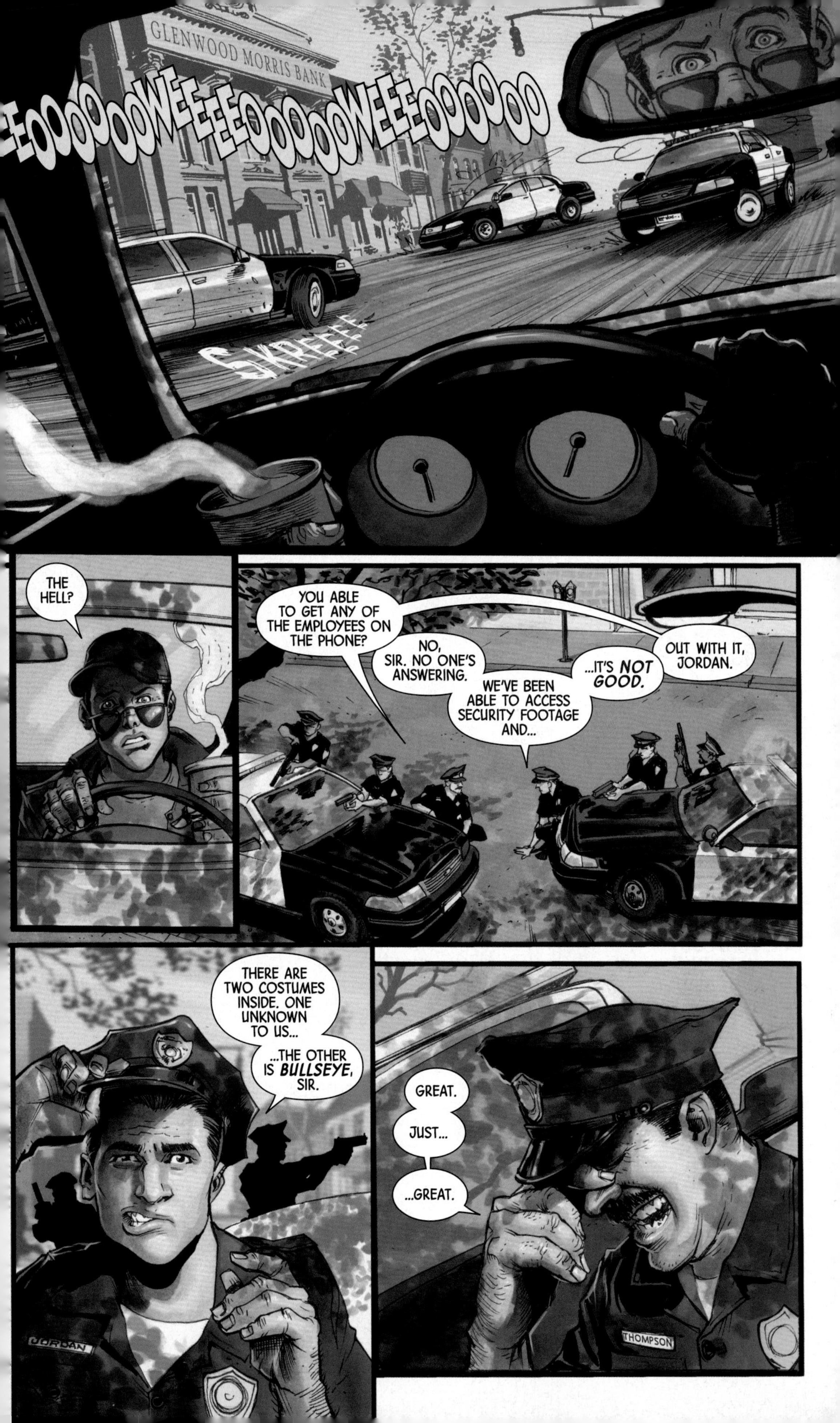
GLENWOOD MORRIS BANK
EEOOOOOOWEEEEOOOOOWEEEOOOOO
SKREEEE
THE HELL?
YOU ABLE TO GET ANY OF THE EMPLOYEES ON THE PHONE?
NO, SIR. NO ONE'S ANSWERING.
WE'VE BEEN ABLE TO ACCESS SECURITY FOOTAGE AND...
...IT'S NOT GOOD.
OUT WITH IT, JORDAN.
THERE ARE TWO COSTUMES INSIDE. ONE UNKNOWN TO US...
...THE OTHER IS BULLSEYE, SIR.
JORDAN
GREAT.
JUST...
...GREAT.
THOMPSON

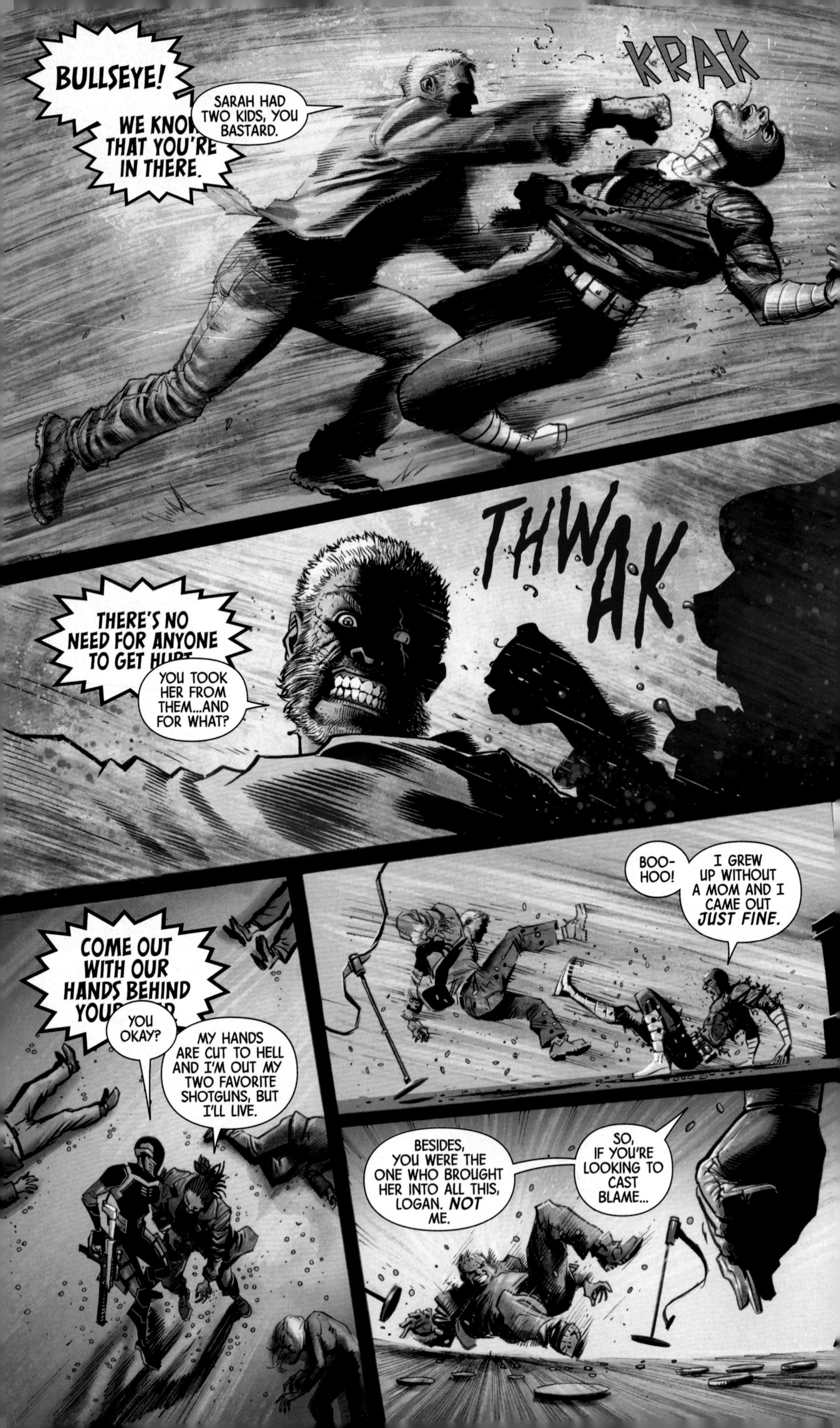
BULLSEYE!
WE KNOW THAT YOU'RE IN THERE.
SARAH HAD TWO KIDS, YOU BASTARD.
KRAK
THWAK
THERE'S NO NEED FOR ANYONE TO GET HURT
YOU TOOK HER FROM THEM...AND FOR WHAT?
BOO-HOO!
I GREW UP WITHOUT A MOM AND I CAME OUT JUST FINE.
COME OUT WITH OUR HANDS BEHIND YOUR
YOU OKAY?
MY HANDS ARE CUT TO HELL AND I'M OUT MY TWO FAVORITE SHOTGUNS, BUT I'LL LIVE.
SO, IF YOU'RE LOOKING TO CAST BLAME...
BESIDES, YOU WERE THE ONE WHO BROUGHT HER INTO ALL THIS, LOGAN. NOT ME.

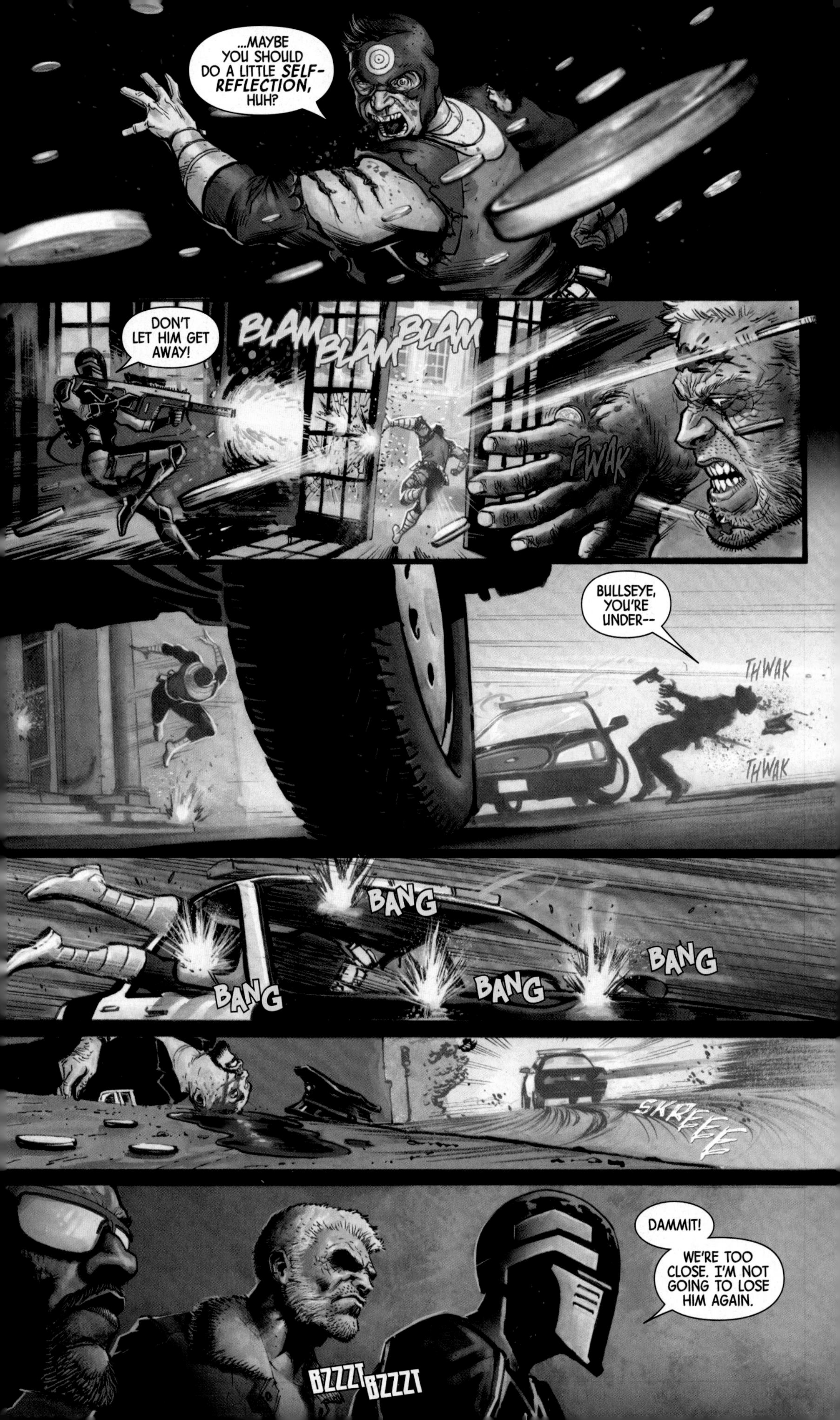
...MAYBE YOU SHOULD DO A LITTLE SELF-REFLECTION, HUH?
DON'T LET HIM GET AWAY!
BLAM BLAM BLAM BLAM
FWAK
BULLSEYE, YOU'RE UNDER--
THWAK
THWAK
BANG
BANG
BANG
BANG
SKREEEE
DAMMIT!
WE'RE TOO CLOSE. I'M NOT GOING TO LOSE HIM AGAIN.
BZZZT BZZZT

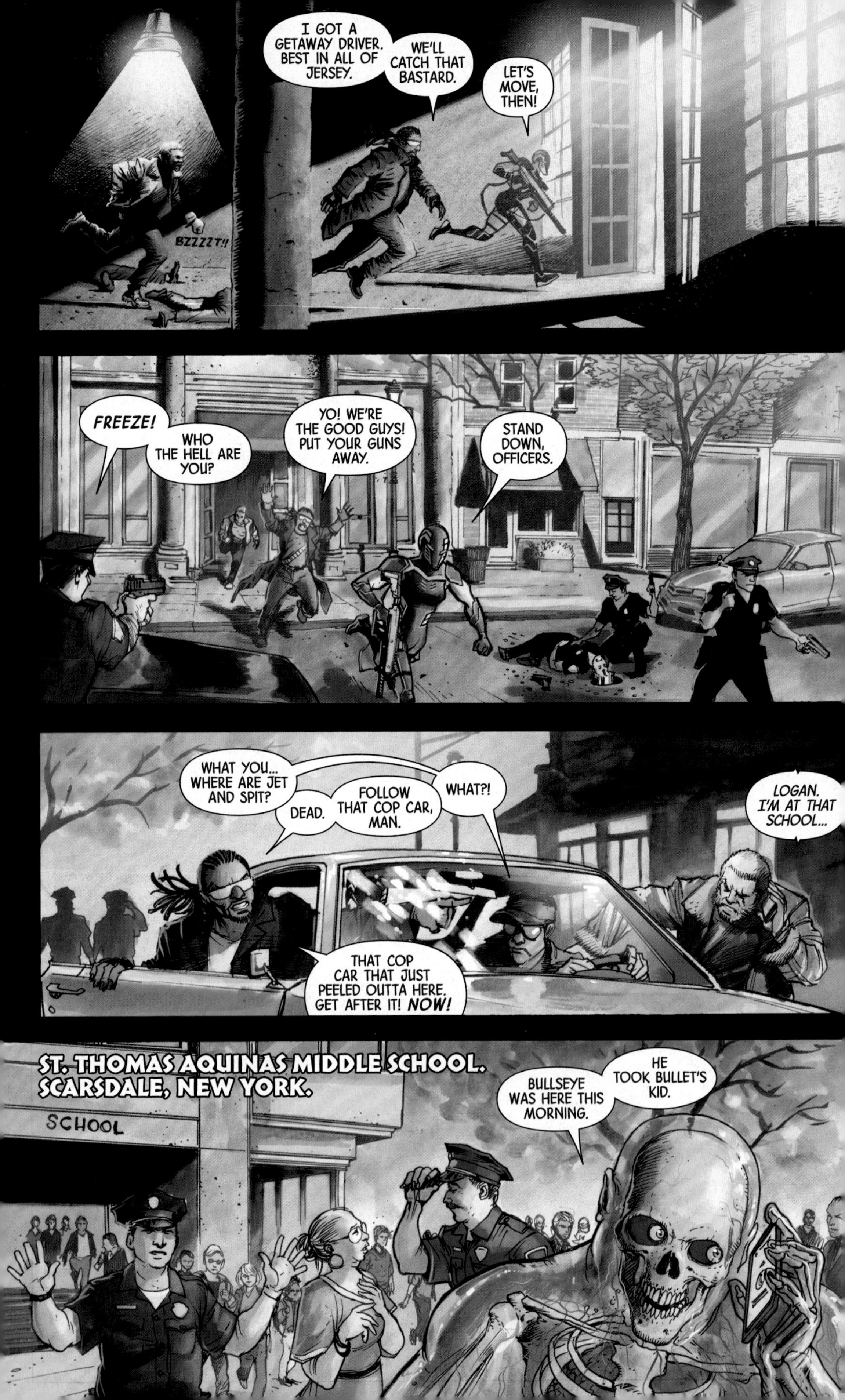
BZZZZT!!
I GOT A GETAWAY DRIVER. BEST IN ALL OF JERSEY.
WE'LL CATCH THAT BASTARD.
LET'S MOVE, THEN!
FREEZE!
WHO THE HELL ARE YOU?
YO! WE'RE THE GOOD GUYS! PUT YOUR GUNS AWAY.
STAND DOWN, OFFICERS.
WHAT YOU... WHERE ARE JET AND SPIT?
DEAD.
WHAT?!
FOLLOW THAT COP CAR, MAN.
THAT COP CAR THAT JUST PEELED OUTTA HERE. GET AFTER IT! NOW!
LOGAN. I'M AT THAT SCHOOL...
ST. THOMAS AQUINAS MIDDLE SCHOOL. SCARSDALE, NEW YORK.
SCHOOL
BULLSEYE WAS HERE THIS MORNING.
HE TOOK BULLET'S KID.

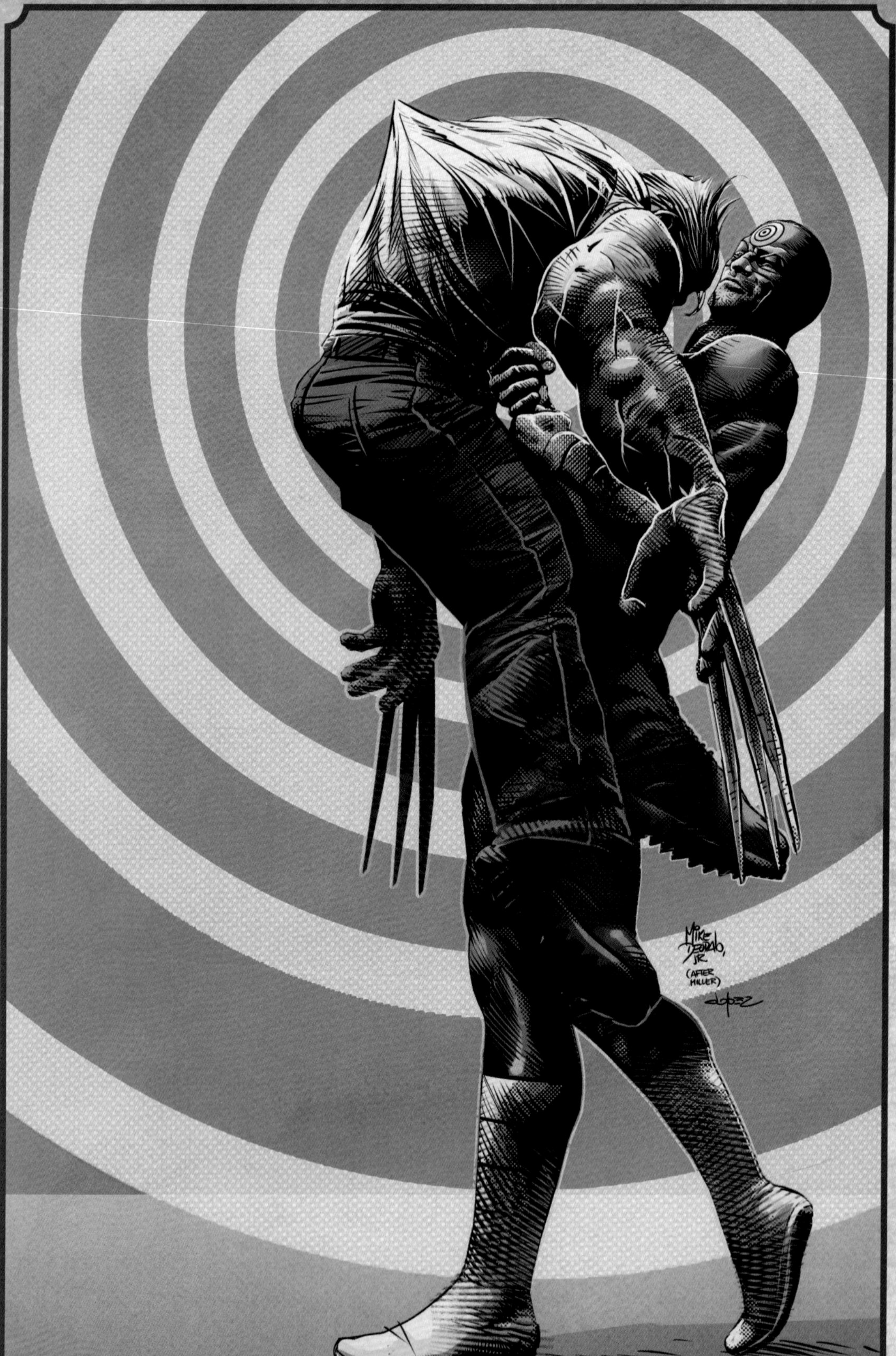
(AFTER MILLER)

45

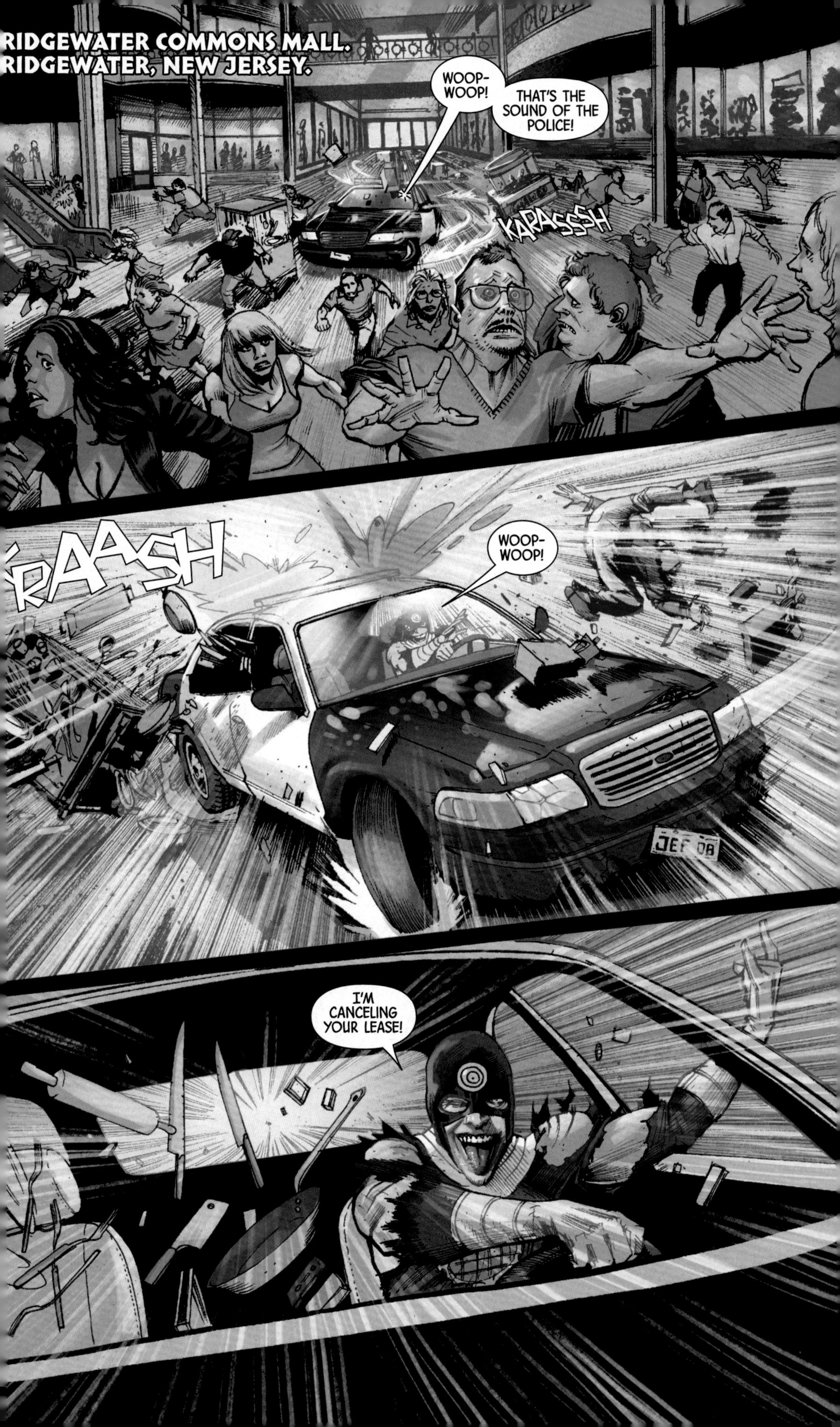
RIDGEWATER COMMONS MALL.
RIDGEWATER, NEW JERSEY.
WOOP-WOOP!
THAT'S THE SOUND OF THE POLICE!
KARASSSH
'RAASH
WOOP-WOOP!
JEF 08
I'M CANCELING YOUR LEASE!

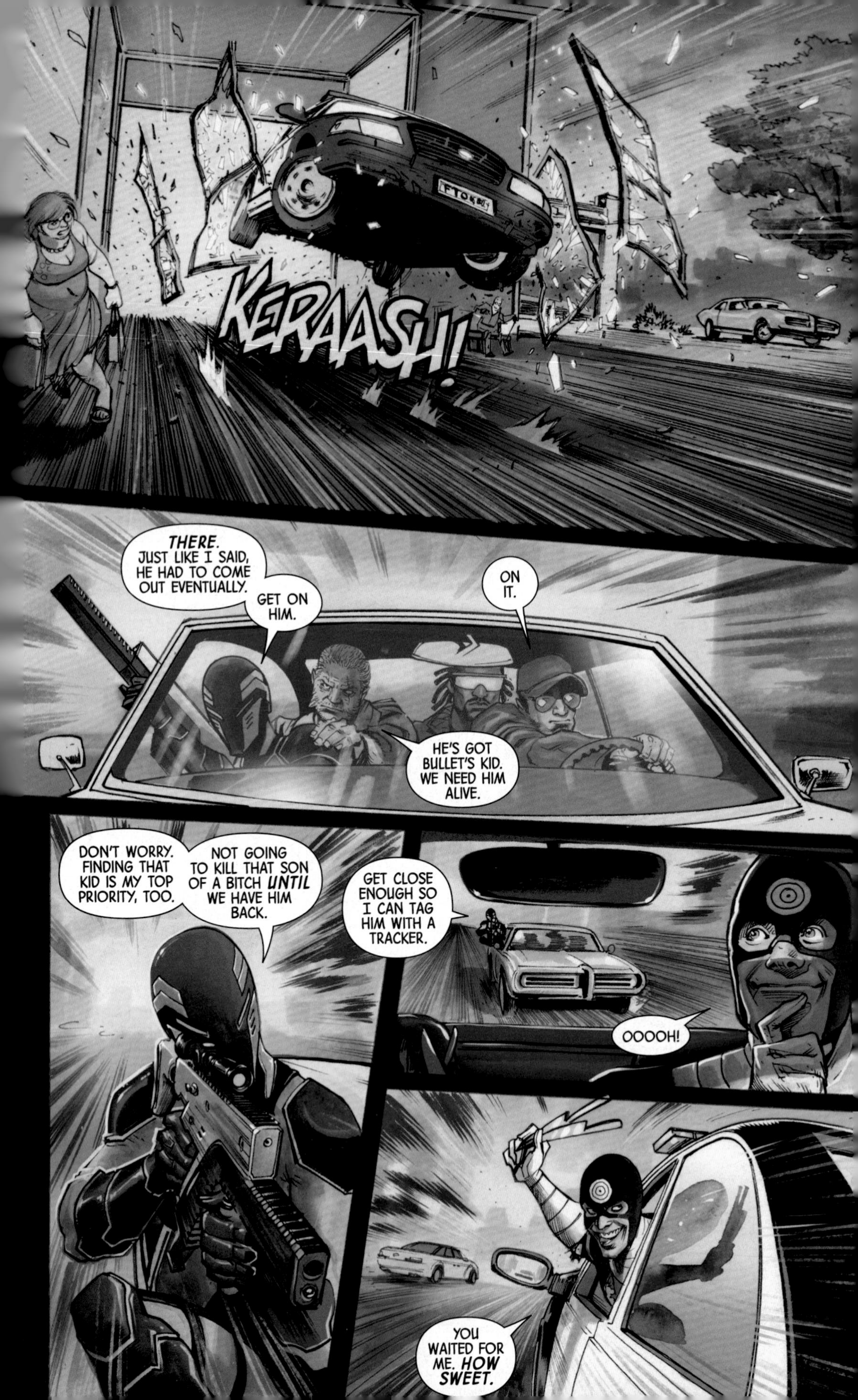
KERAASH!
THERE. JUST LIKE I SAID, HE HAD TO COME OUT EVENTUALLY.
GET ON HIM.
ON IT.
HE'S GOT BULLET'S KID. WE NEED HIM ALIVE.
DON'T WORRY. FINDING THAT KID IS MY TOP PRIORITY, TOO.
NOT GOING TO KILL THAT SON OF A BITCH UNTIL WE HAVE HIM BACK.
GET CLOSE ENOUGH SO I CAN TAG HIM WITH A TRACKER.
OOOOH!
YOU WAITED FOR ME. HOW SWEET.

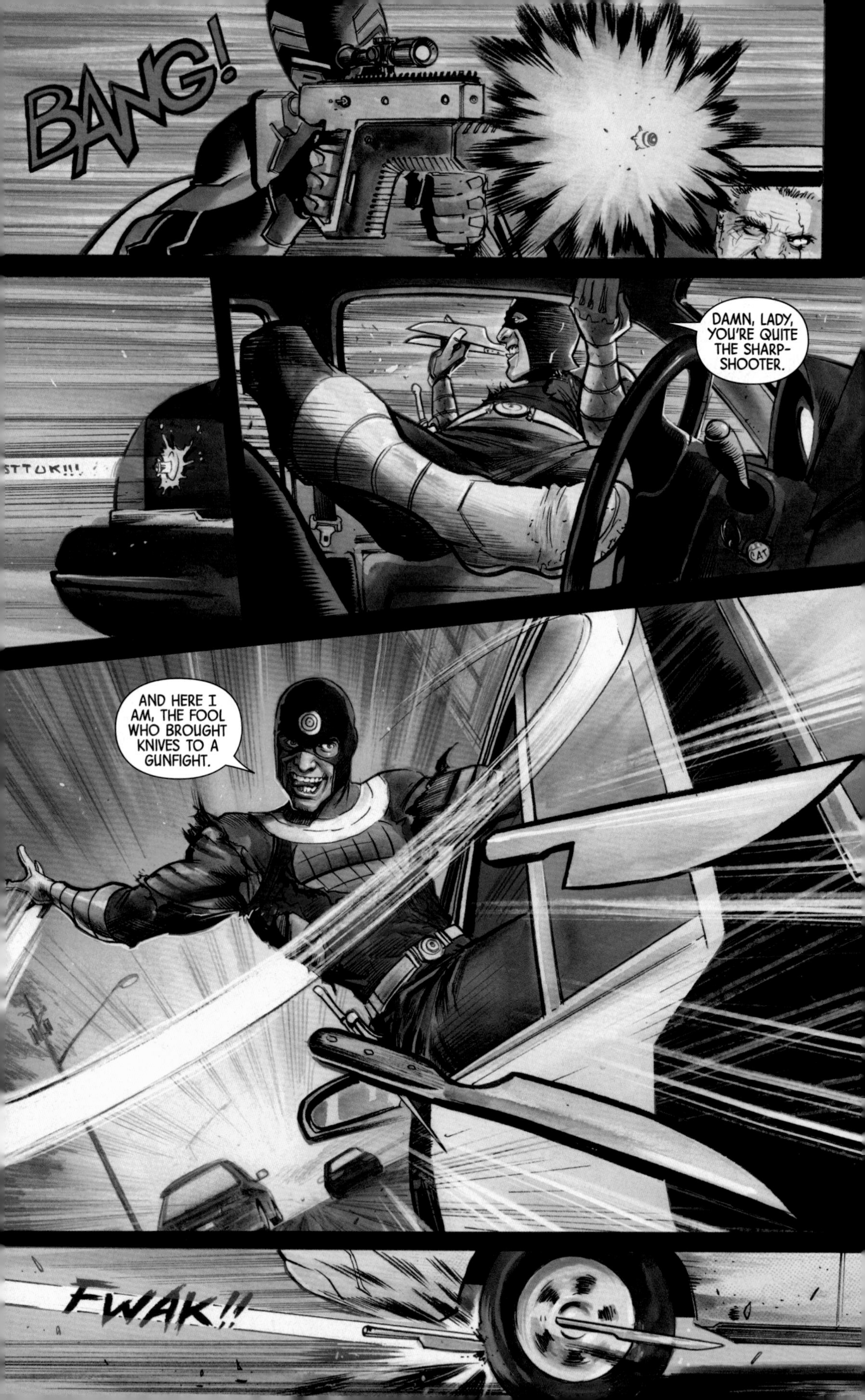
BANG!
DAMN, LADY, YOU'RE QUITE THE SHARP-SHOOTER.
STTUK!!!
AND HERE I AM, THE FOOL WHO BROUGHT KNIVES TO A GUNFIGHT.
FWAK!!

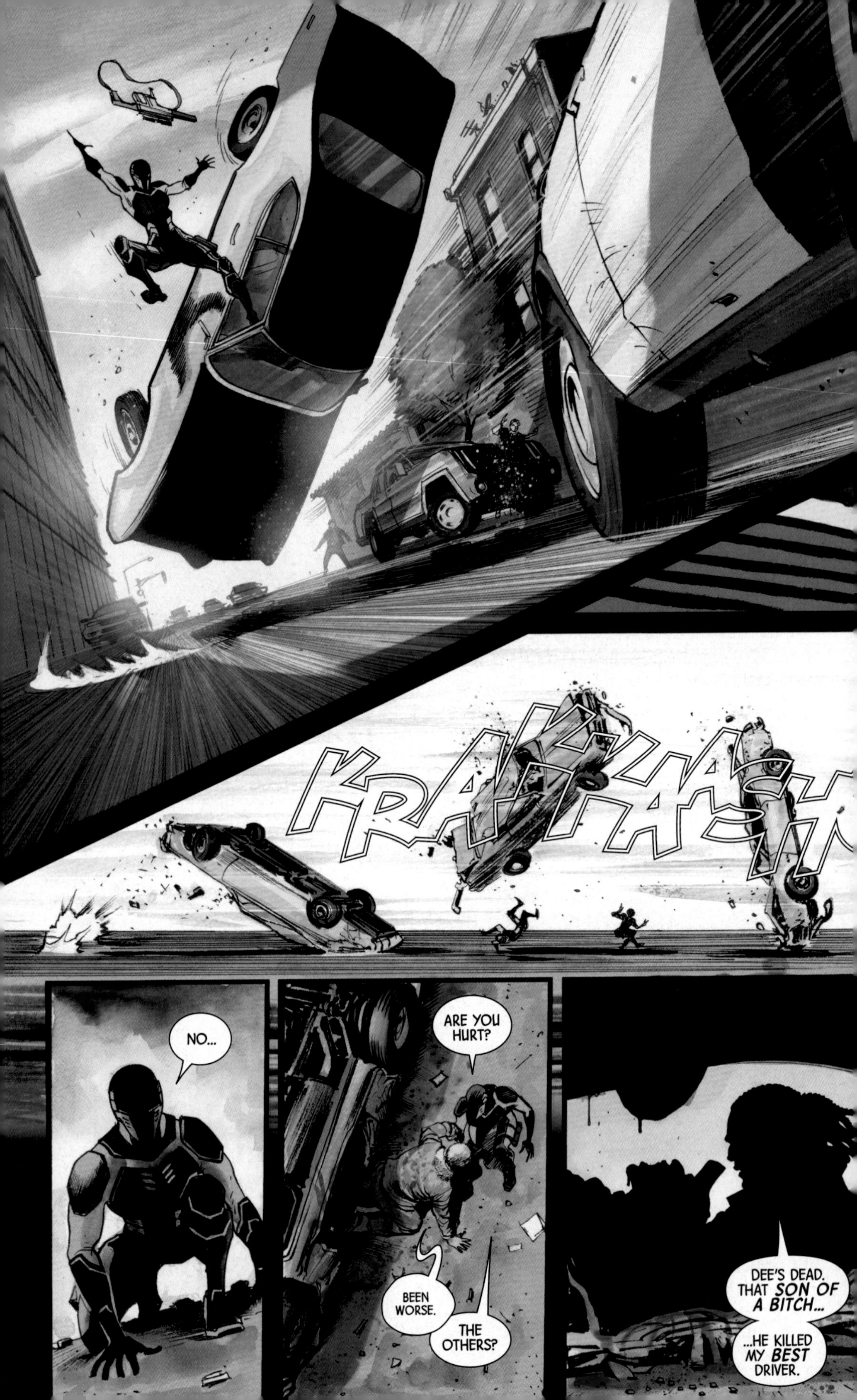
KRAAASH
NO...
ARE YOU HURT?
BEEN WORSE.
THE OTHERS?
DEE'S DEAD. THAT SON OF A BITCH...
...HE KILLED MY BEST DRIVER.

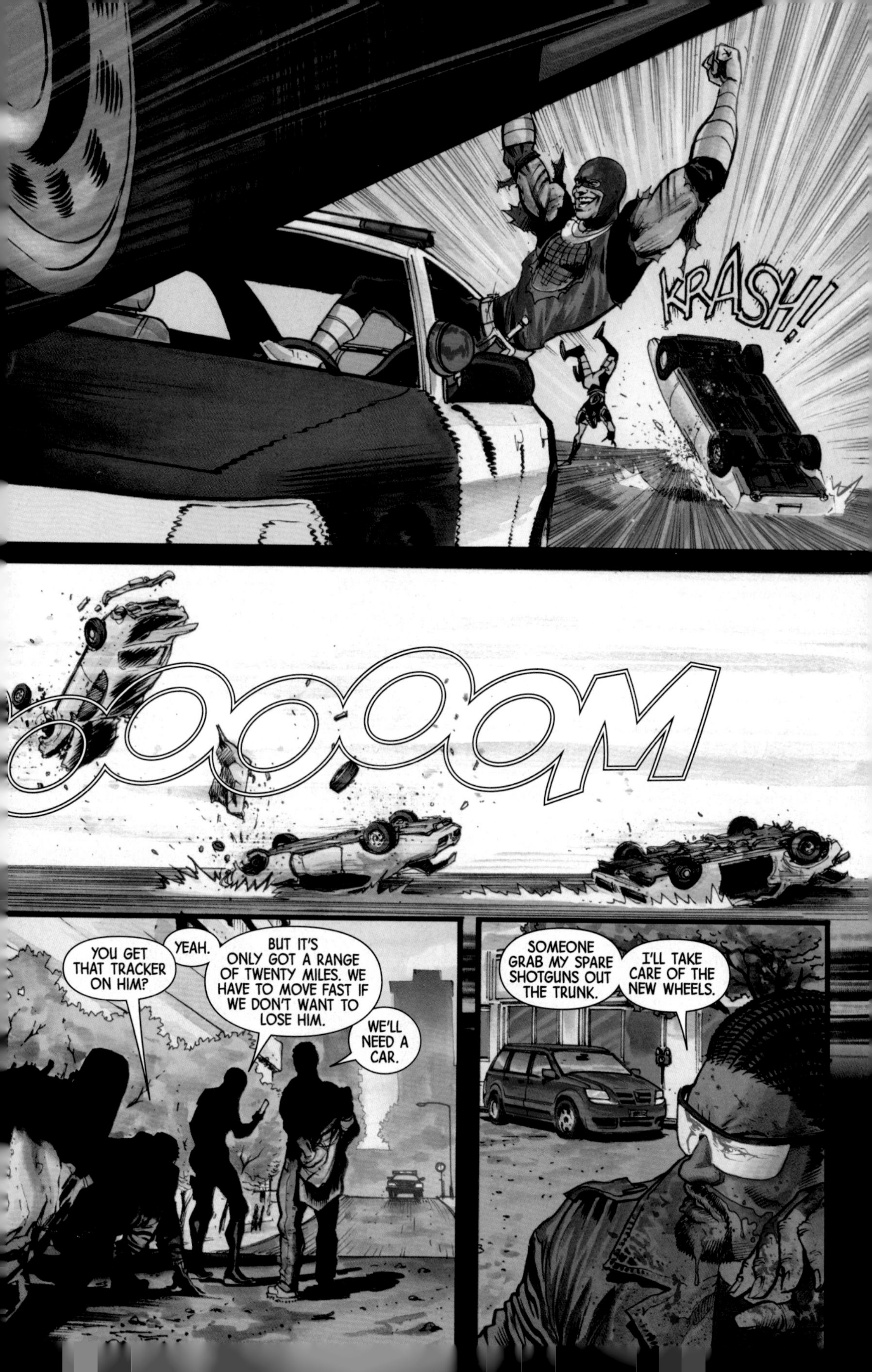
KRASH!
BOOOOOM
YOU GET THAT TRACKER ON HIM?
YEAH.
BUT IT'S ONLY GOT A RANGE OF TWENTY MILES. WE HAVE TO MOVE FAST IF WE DON'T WANT TO LOSE HIM.
WE'LL NEED A CAR.
SOMEONE GRAB MY SPARE SHOTGUNS OUT THE TRUNK.
I'LL TAKE CARE OF THE NEW WHEELS.

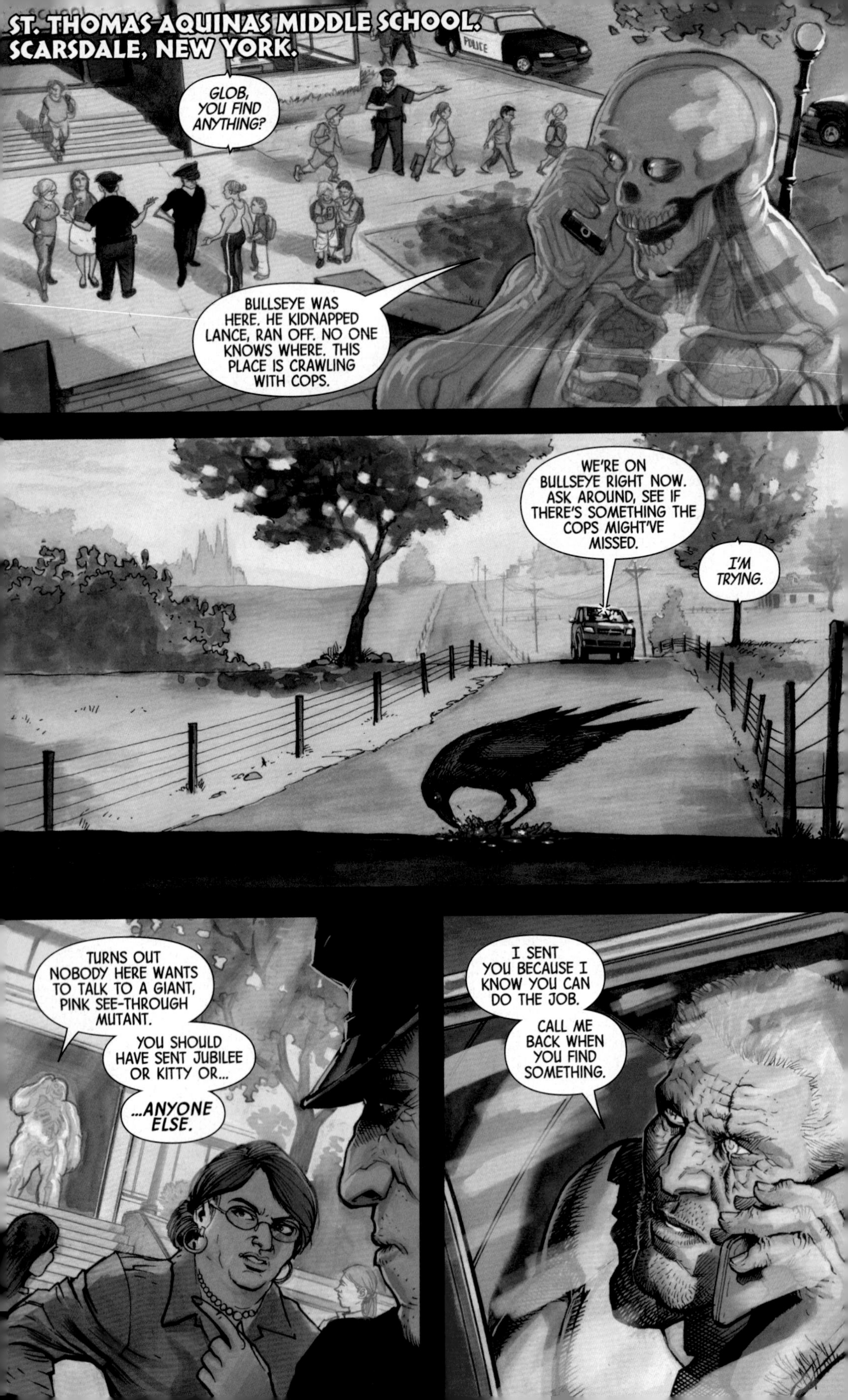

ST. THOMAS AQUINAS MIDDLE SCHOOL. SCARSDALE, NEW YORK.
GLOB, YOU FIND ANYTHING?
BULLSEYE WAS HERE. HE KIDNAPPED LANCE, RAN OFF. NO ONE KNOWS WHERE. THIS PLACE IS CRAWLING WITH COPS.
WE'RE ON BULLSEYE RIGHT NOW. ASK AROUND, SEE IF THERE'S SOMETHING THE COPS MIGHT'VE MISSED.
I'M TRYING.
TURNS OUT NOBODY HERE WANTS TO TALK TO A GIANT, PINK SEE-THROUGH MUTANT.
YOU SHOULD HAVE SENT JUBILEE OR KITTY OR...
...ANYONE ELSE.
I SENT YOU BECAUSE I KNOW YOU CAN DO THE JOB.
CALL ME BACK WHEN YOU FIND SOMETHING.

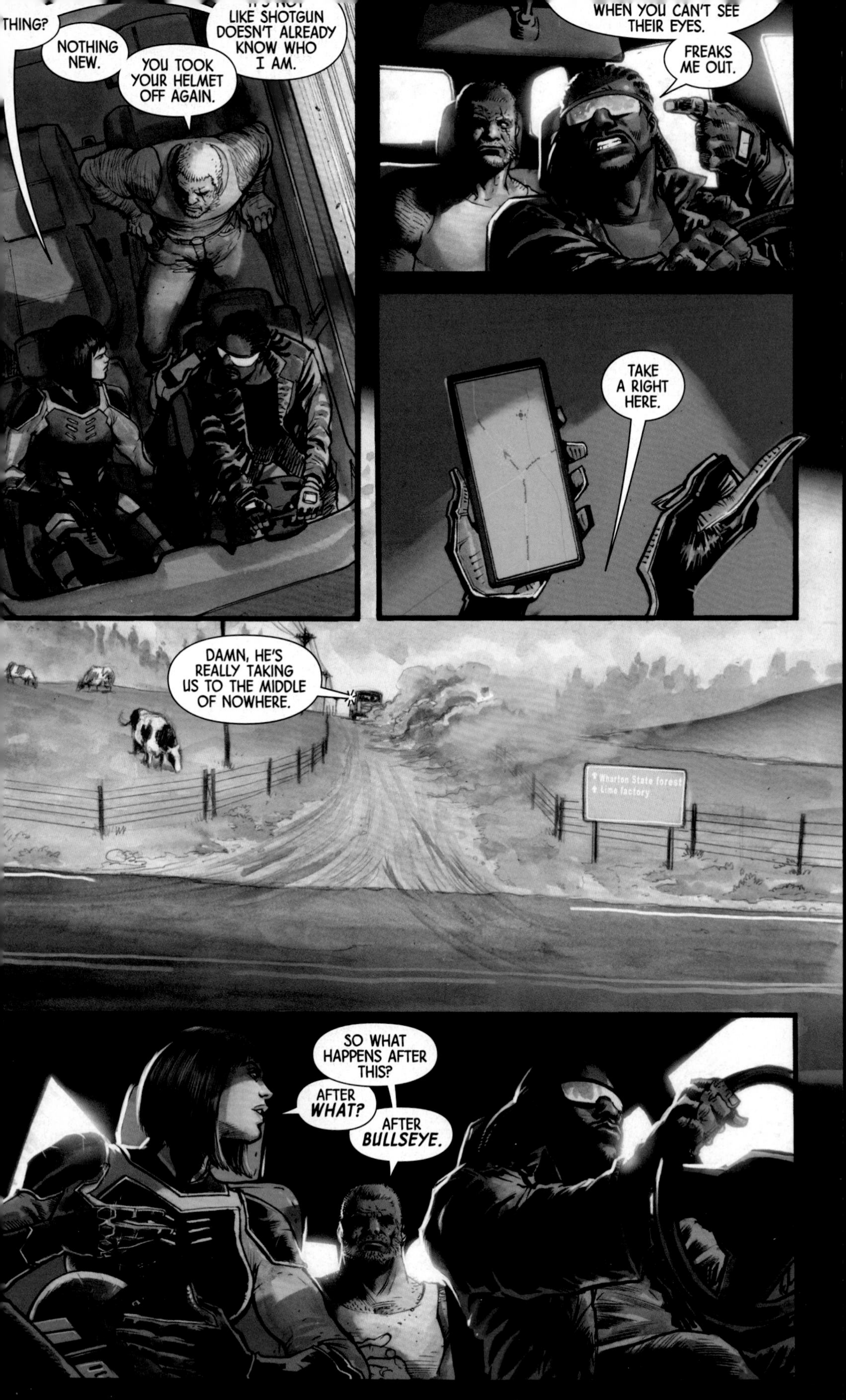
THING?
NOTHING NEW.
YOU TOOK YOUR HELMET OFF AGAIN.
LIKE SHOTGUN DOESN'T ALREADY KNOW WHO I AM.
WHEN YOU CAN'T SEE THEIR EYES.
FREAKS ME OUT.
TAKE A RIGHT HERE.
DAMN, HE'S REALLY TAKING US TO THE MIDDLE OF NOWHERE.
Wharton State forest
Lime factory
SO WHAT HAPPENS AFTER THIS?
AFTER *WHAT?*
AFTER *BULLSEYE.*

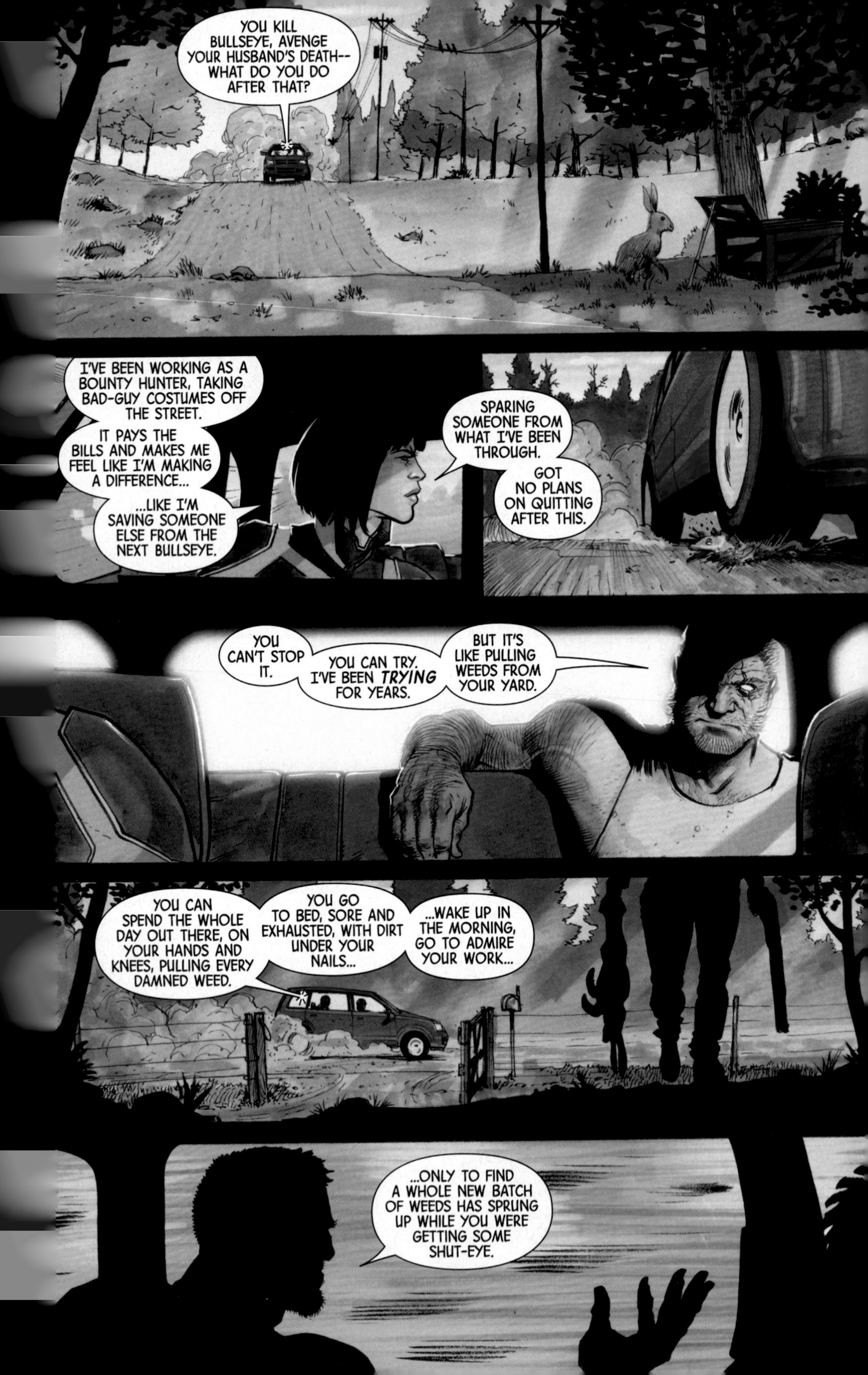
YOU KILL BULLSEYE, AVENGE YOUR HUSBAND'S DEATH-- WHAT DO YOU DO AFTER THAT?
I'VE BEEN WORKING AS A BOUNTY HUNTER, TAKING BAD-GUY COSTUMES OFF THE STREET.
IT PAYS THE BILLS AND MAKES ME FEEL LIKE I'M MAKING A DIFFERENCE...
...LIKE I'M SAVING SOMEONE ELSE FROM THE NEXT BULLSEYE.
SPARING SOMEONE FROM WHAT I'VE BEEN THROUGH.
GOT NO PLANS ON QUITTING AFTER THIS.
YOU CAN'T STOP IT.
YOU CAN TRY. I'VE BEEN *TRYING* FOR YEARS.
BUT IT'S LIKE PULLING WEEDS FROM YOUR YARD.
YOU CAN SPEND THE WHOLE DAY OUT THERE, ON YOUR HANDS AND KNEES, PULLING EVERY DAMNED WEED.
YOU GO TO BED, SORE AND EXHAUSTED, WITH DIRT UNDER YOUR NAILS...
...WAKE UP IN THE MORNING, GO TO ADMIRE YOUR WORK...
...ONLY TO FIND A WHOLE NEW BATCH OF WEEDS HAS SPRUNG UP WHILE YOU WERE GETTING SOME SHUT-EYE.

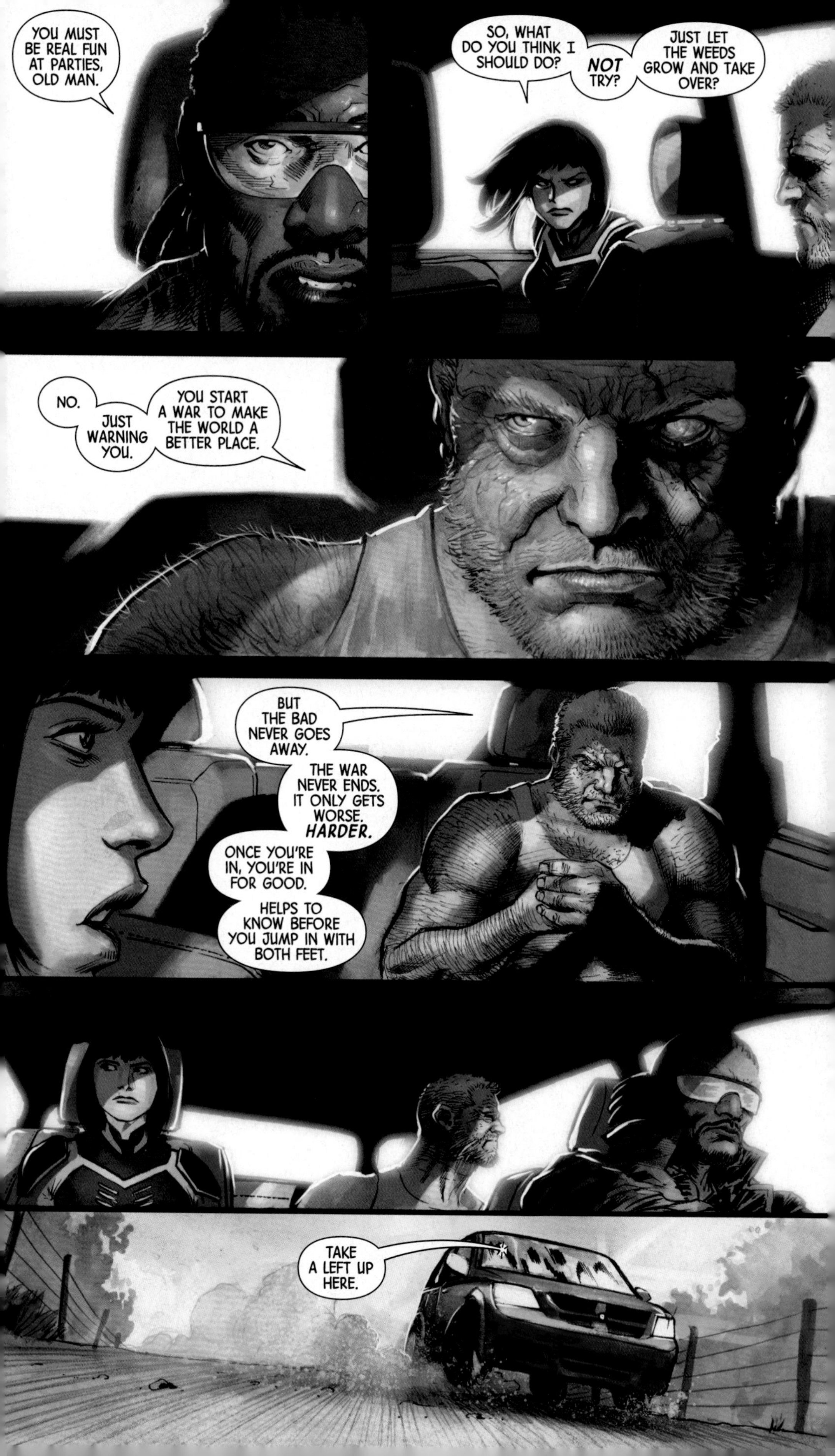
YOU MUST BE REAL FUN AT PARTIES, OLD MAN.
SO, WHAT DO YOU THINK I SHOULD DO?
NOT TRY?
JUST LET THE WEEDS GROW AND TAKE OVER?
NO.
JUST WARNING YOU.
YOU START A WAR TO MAKE THE WORLD A BETTER PLACE.
BUT THE BAD NEVER GOES AWAY.
THE WAR NEVER ENDS. IT ONLY GETS WORSE. HARDER.
ONCE YOU'RE IN, YOU'RE IN FOR GOOD.
HELPS TO KNOW BEFORE YOU JUMP IN WITH BOTH FEET.
TAKE A LEFT UP HERE.

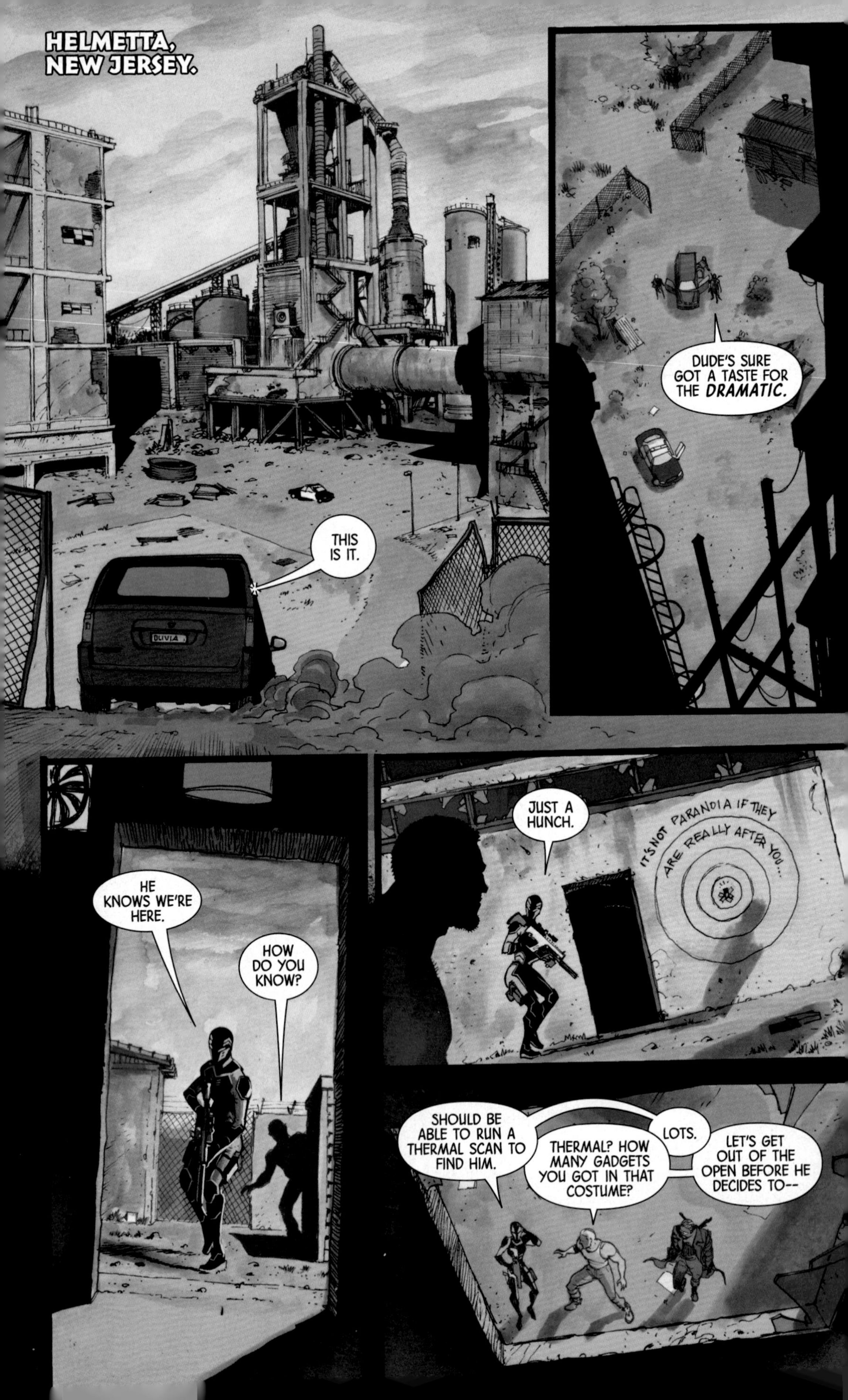

HELMETTA, NEW JERSEY.
THIS IS IT.
DUDE'S SURE GOT A TASTE FOR THE DRAMATIC.
HE KNOWS WE'RE HERE.
HOW DO YOU KNOW?
JUST A HUNCH.
IT'S NOT PARANOIA IF THEY ARE REALLY AFTER YOU...
SHOULD BE ABLE TO RUN A THERMAL SCAN TO FIND HIM.
THERMAL? HOW MANY GADGETS YOU GOT IN THAT COSTUME?
LOTS.
LET'S GET OUT OF THE OPEN BEFORE HE DECIDES TO--

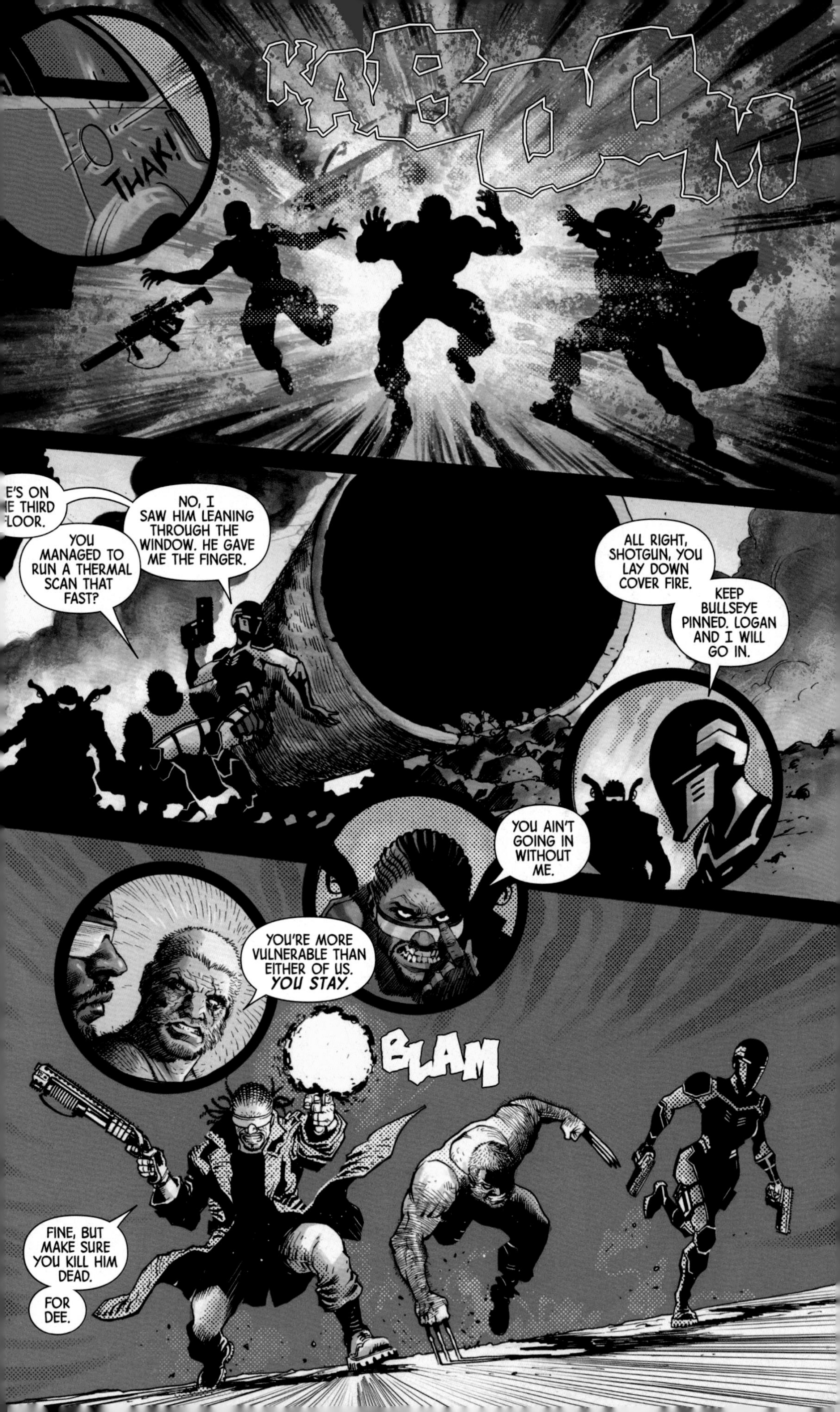
THAK!
KABOOOM
E'S ON
E THIRD
FLOOR.
YOU MANAGED TO RUN A THERMAL SCAN THAT FAST?
NO, I SAW HIM LEANING THROUGH THE WINDOW. HE GAVE ME THE FINGER.
ALL RIGHT, SHOTGUN, YOU LAY DOWN COVER FIRE.
KEEP BULLSEYE PINNED. LOGAN AND I WILL GO IN.
YOU AIN'T GOING IN WITHOUT ME.
YOU'RE MORE VULNERABLE THAN EITHER OF US. *YOU STAY.*
BLAM
FINE, BUT MAKE SURE YOU KILL HIM DEAD.
FOR DEE.

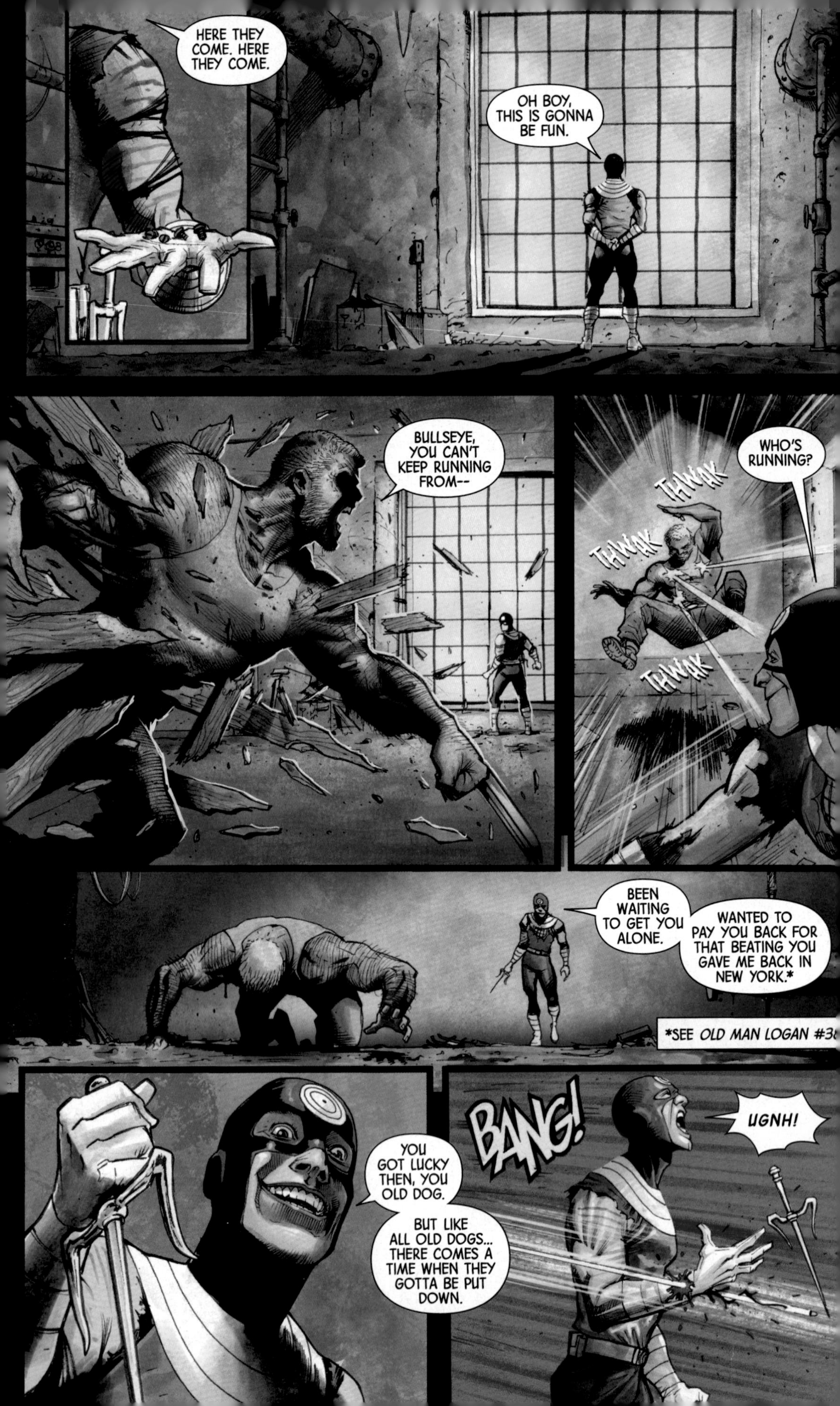
HERE THEY COME. HERE THEY COME.
OH BOY, THIS IS GONNA BE FUN.
BULLSEYE, YOU CAN'T KEEP RUNNING FROM--
WHO'S RUNNING?
THWAK
THWAK
THWAK
BEEN WAITING TO GET YOU ALONE.
WANTED TO PAY YOU BACK FOR THAT BEATING YOU GAVE ME BACK IN NEW YORK.*
*SEE OLD MAN LOGAN #3
YOU GOT LUCKY THEN, YOU OLD DOG.
BUT LIKE ALL OLD DOGS... THERE COMES A TIME WHEN THEY GOTTA BE PUT DOWN.
BANG!
UGNH!

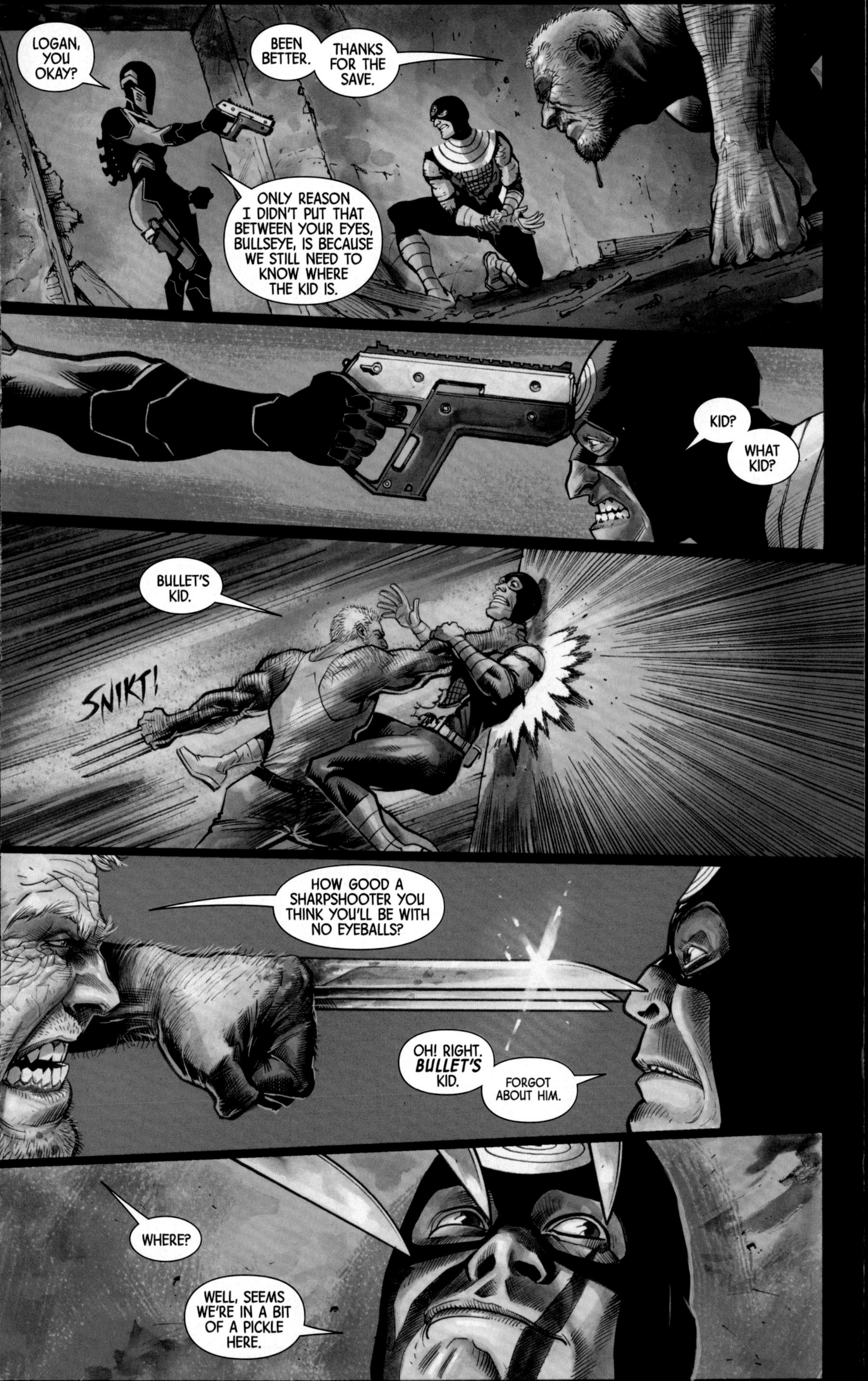
LOGAN, YOU OKAY?
BEEN BETTER.
THANKS FOR THE SAVE.
ONLY REASON I DIDN'T PUT THAT BETWEEN YOUR EYES, BULLSEYE, IS BECAUSE WE STILL NEED TO KNOW WHERE THE KID IS.
KID?
WHAT KID?
BULLET'S KID.
SNIKT!
HOW GOOD A SHARPSHOOTER YOU THINK YOU'LL BE WITH NO EYEBALLS?
OH! RIGHT. BULLET'S KID.
FORGOT ABOUT HIM.
WHERE?
WELL, SEEMS WE'RE IN A BIT OF A PICKLE HERE.

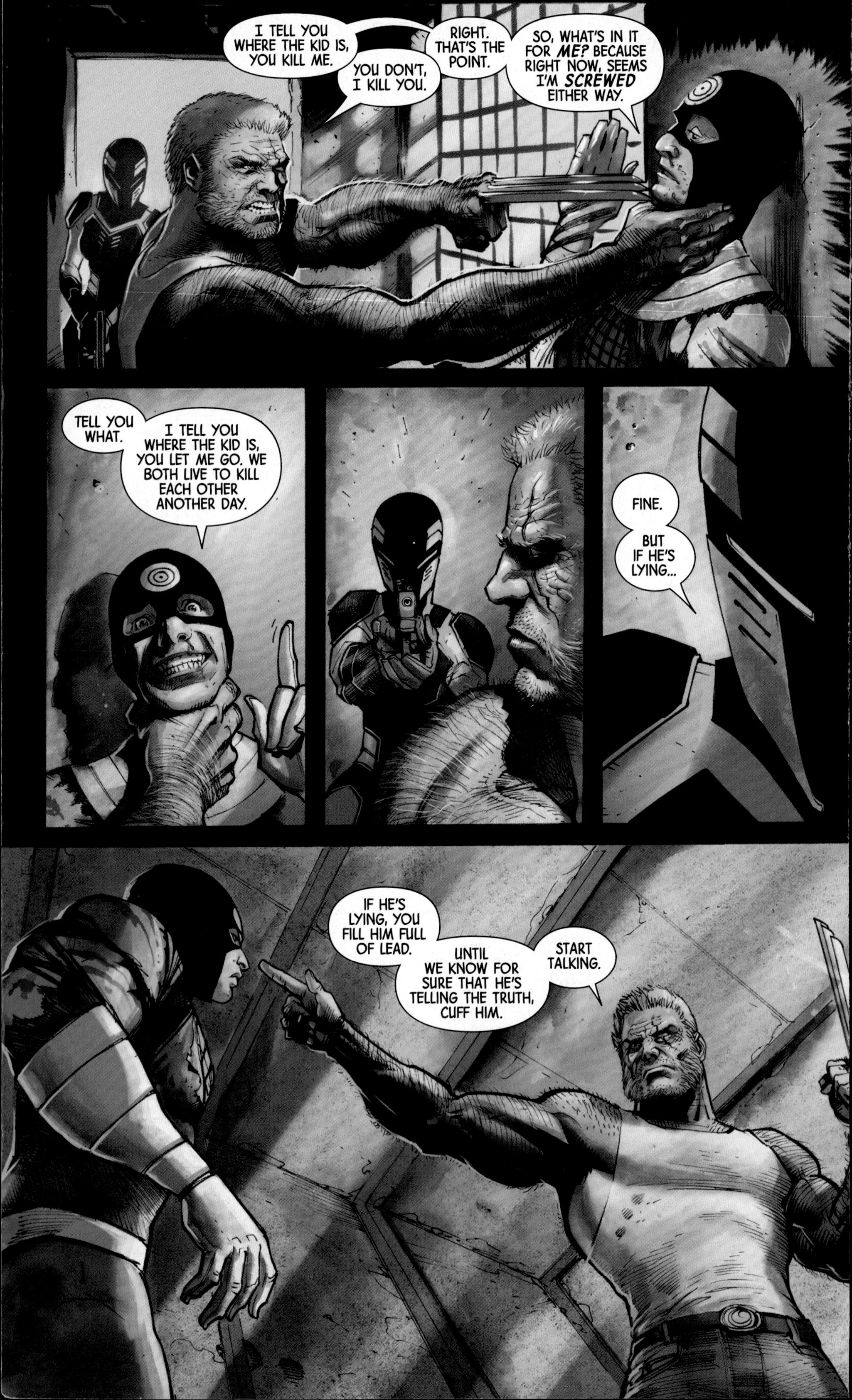
I TELL YOU WHERE THE KID IS, YOU KILL ME.
YOU DON'T, I KILL YOU.
RIGHT. THAT'S THE POINT.
SO, WHAT'S IN IT FOR ME? BECAUSE RIGHT NOW, SEEMS I'M SCREWED EITHER WAY.
TELL YOU WHAT.
I TELL YOU WHERE THE KID IS, YOU LET ME GO. WE BOTH LIVE TO KILL EACH OTHER ANOTHER DAY.
FINE.
BUT IF HE'S LYING...
IF HE'S LYING, YOU FILL HIM FULL OF LEAD.
UNTIL WE KNOW FOR SURE THAT HE'S TELLING THE TRUTH, CUFF HIM.
START TALKING.

WHITE PLAINS, NEW YORK. HALF AN HOUR LATER.

I'M AT THE ADDRESS. WHERE NOW?

WHERE IS HE? WHAT ROOM?

UPSTAIRS. SECOND BEDROOM ON THE RIGHT.

YOU GET THAT?

YEAH. ON MY WAY.

MUST BE HARD, LOGAN.

SHUT UP, BULLSEYE.

TRYING TO SAVE PEOPLE. PEOPLE LIKE SARAH.

"YOU PUT YOUR LIFE ON THE LINE."

TIME AND TIME AGAIN.

LANCE? MY NAME IS GLOB. I'M COMING IN.

DON'T BE AFRAID. I'M HERE TO HELP YOU.

AND YET...

A MOMENT BEFORE HE SAYS IT, I KNOW.

LOGAN. OH... HE'S--

AND IT MAKES ME SICK TO MY STOMACH.

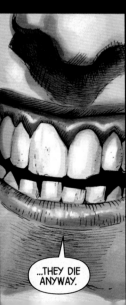

...THEY DIE ANYWAY.

LOGAN... HE'S DEAD.

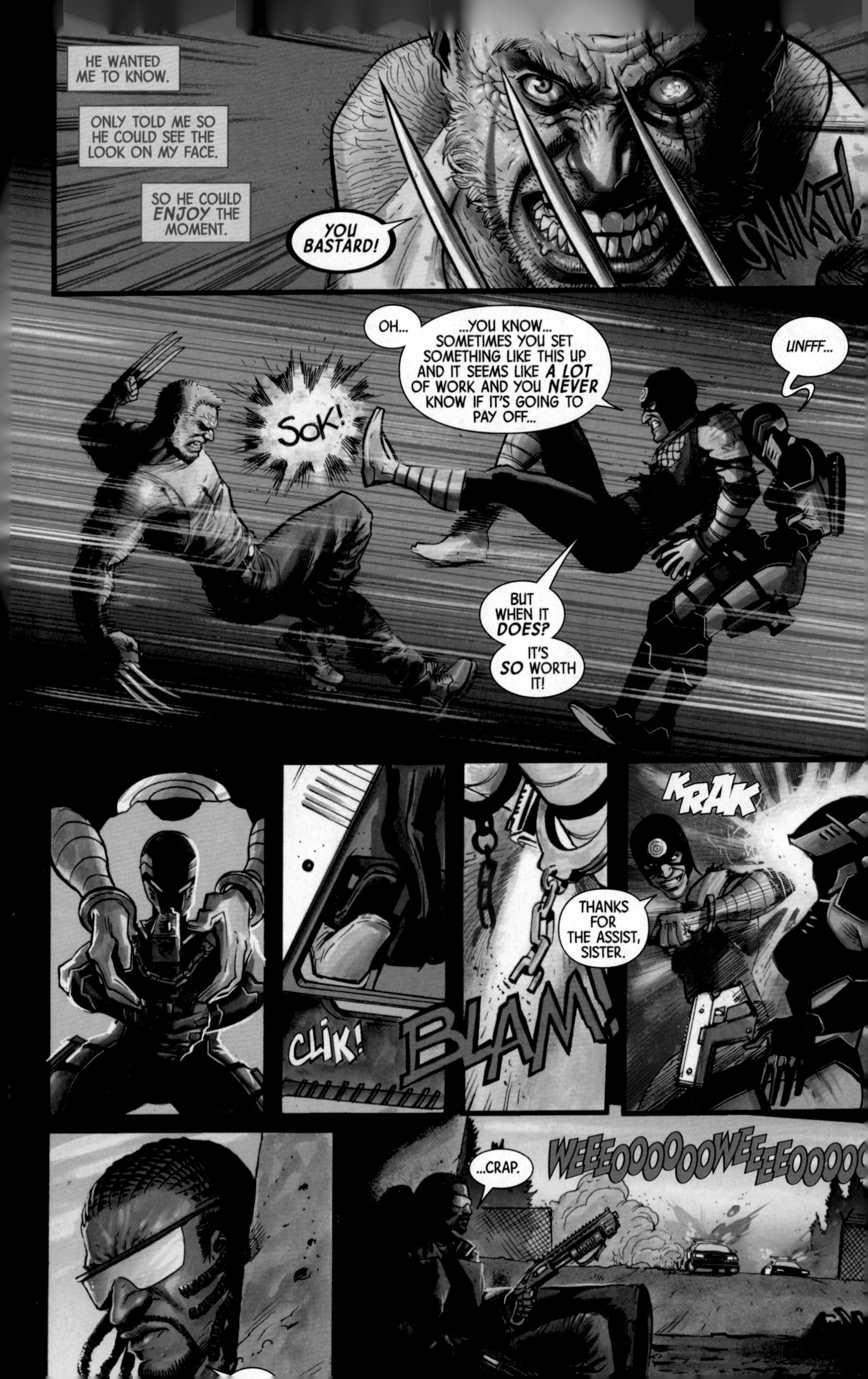

HE WANTED ME TO KNOW.
ONLY TOLD ME SO HE COULD SEE THE LOOK ON MY FACE.
SO HE COULD ENJOY THE MOMENT.
YOU BASTARD!
SNIKT!
OH...
...YOU KNOW... SOMETIMES YOU SET SOMETHING LIKE THIS UP AND IT SEEMS LIKE A LOT OF WORK AND YOU NEVER KNOW IF IT'S GOING TO PAY OFF...
UNFFF...
SOK!
BUT WHEN IT DOES?
IT'S SO WORTH IT!
CLIK!
BLAM!
KRAK
THANKS FOR THE ASSIST, SISTER.
...CRAP.
WEEEOOOOOOWEEEEOOOOO

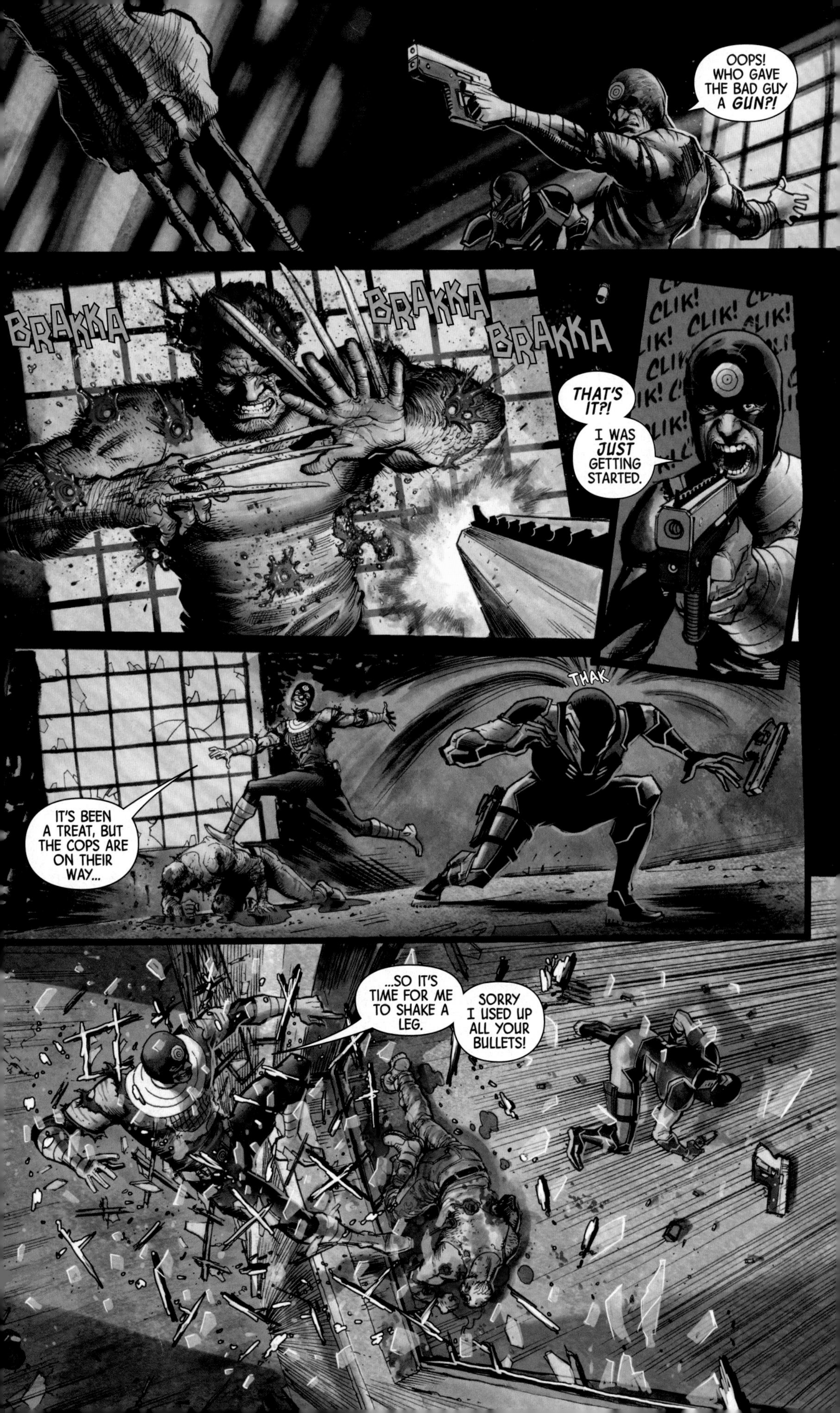
OOPS! WHO GAVE THE BAD GUY A GUN?!
BRAKKA
BRAKKA
BRAKKA
CLIK! CLIK! CLIK! CLIK! CLIK! CLIK! CLIK! CLIK!
THAT'S IT?!
I WAS JUST GETTING STARTED.
THAK
IT'S BEEN A TREAT, BUT THE COPS ARE ON THEIR WAY...
...SO IT'S TIME FOR ME TO SHAKE A LEG.
SORRY I USED UP ALL YOUR BULLETS!

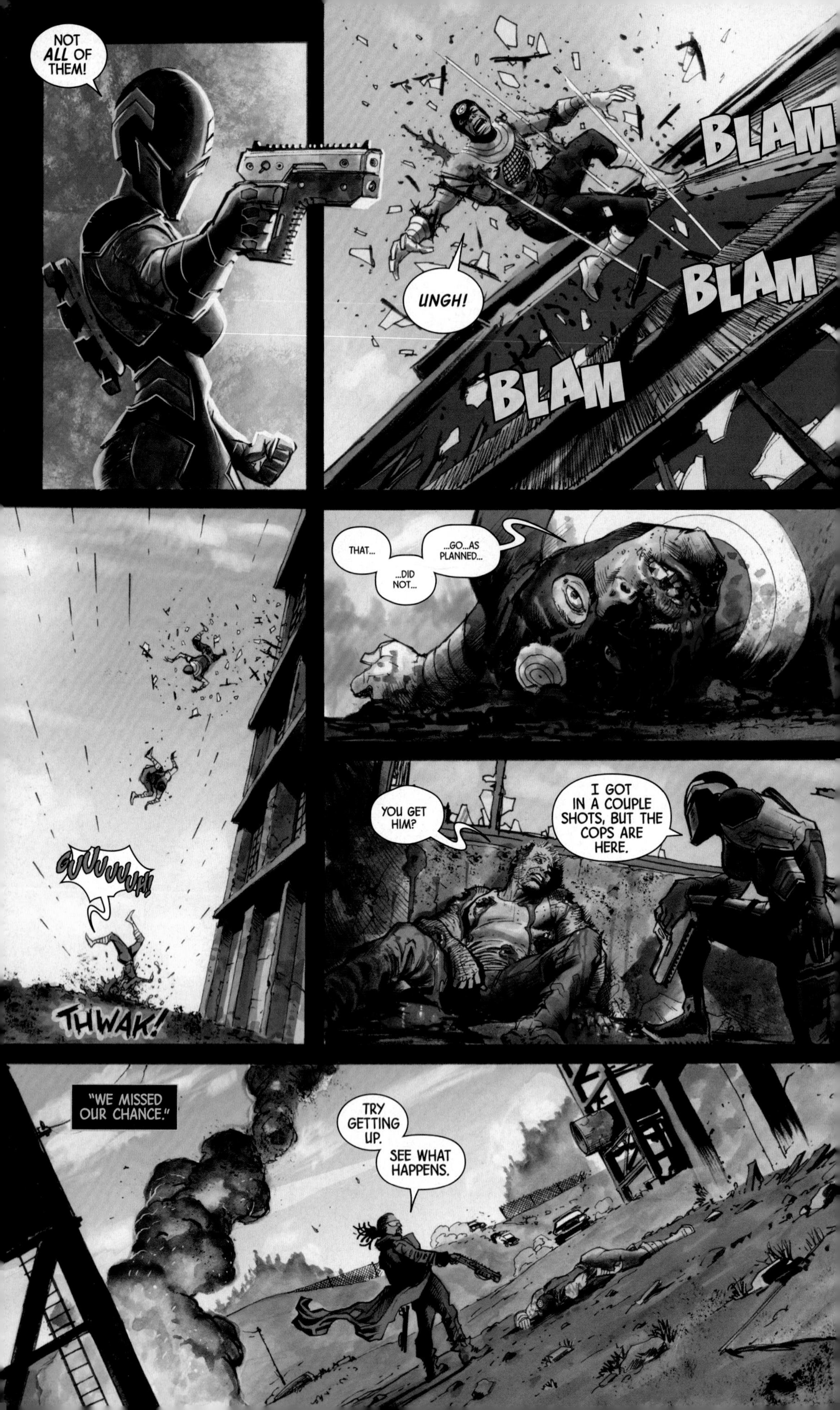
NOT ALL OF THEM!
BLAM
UNGH!
BLAM
BLAM
THAT...
...DID NOT...
...GO...AS PLANNED...
GUUUUUUH!
THWAK!
YOU GET HIM?
I GOT IN A COUPLE SHOTS, BUT THE COPS ARE HERE.
"WE MISSED OUR CHANCE."
TRY GETTING UP.
SEE WHAT HAPPENS.

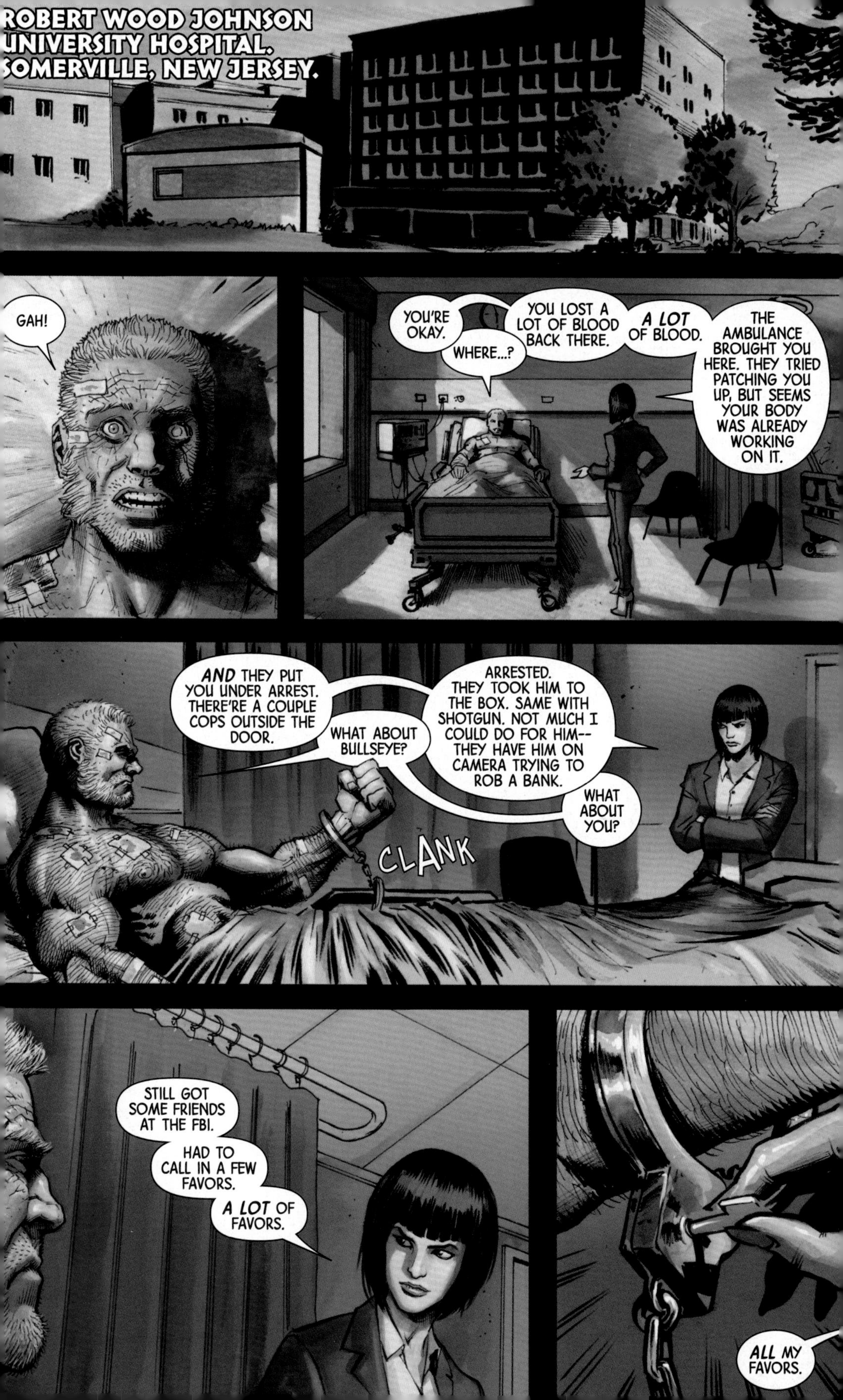
ROBERT WOOD JOHNSON UNIVERSITY HOSPITAL. SOMERVILLE, NEW JERSEY.
GAH!
YOU'RE OKAY.
WHERE...?
YOU LOST A LOT OF BLOOD BACK THERE.
A LOT OF BLOOD.
THE AMBULANCE BROUGHT YOU HERE. THEY TRIED PATCHING YOU UP, BUT SEEMS YOUR BODY WAS ALREADY WORKING ON IT.
AND THEY PUT YOU UNDER ARREST. THERE'RE A COUPLE COPS OUTSIDE THE DOOR.
WHAT ABOUT BULLSEYE?
ARRESTED. THEY TOOK HIM TO THE BOX. SAME WITH SHOTGUN. NOT MUCH I COULD DO FOR HIM-- THEY HAVE HIM ON CAMERA TRYING TO ROB A BANK.
WHAT ABOUT YOU?
CLANK
STILL GOT SOME FRIENDS AT THE FBI.
HAD TO CALL IN A FEW FAVORS.
A LOT OF FAVORS.
ALL MY FAVORS.

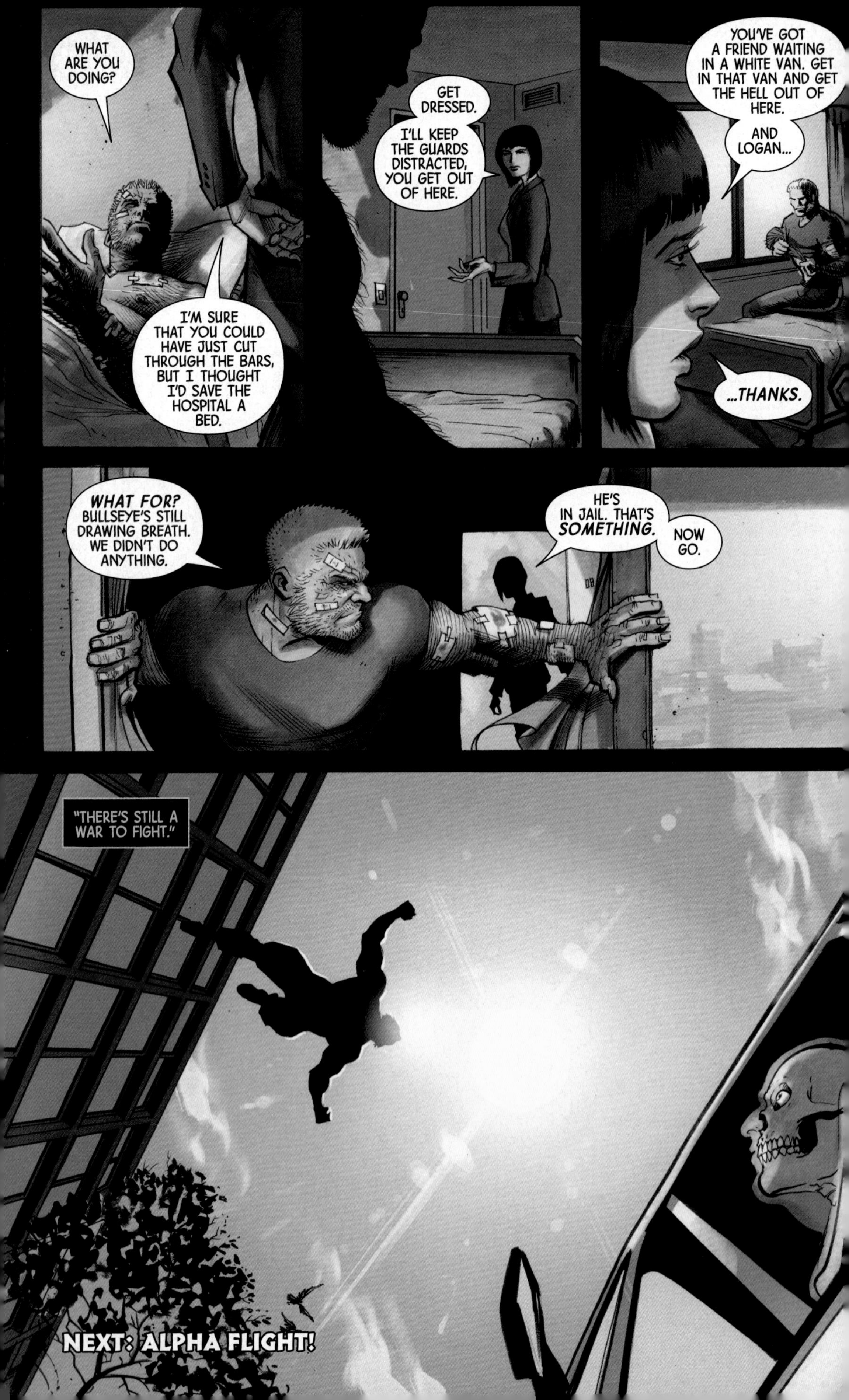
WHAT ARE YOU DOING?
I'M SURE THAT YOU COULD HAVE JUST CUT THROUGH THE BARS, BUT I THOUGHT I'D SAVE THE HOSPITAL A BED.
GET DRESSED.
I'LL KEEP THE GUARDS DISTRACTED, YOU GET OUT OF HERE.
YOU'VE GOT A FRIEND WAITING IN A WHITE VAN. GET IN THAT VAN AND GET THE HELL OUT OF HERE.
AND LOGAN...
...THANKS.
WHAT FOR? BULLSEYE'S STILL DRAWING BREATH. WE DIDN'T DO ANYTHING.
HE'S IN JAIL. THAT'S SOMETHING.
NOW GO.
"THERE'S STILL A WAR TO FIGHT."
NEXT: ALPHA FLIGHT!

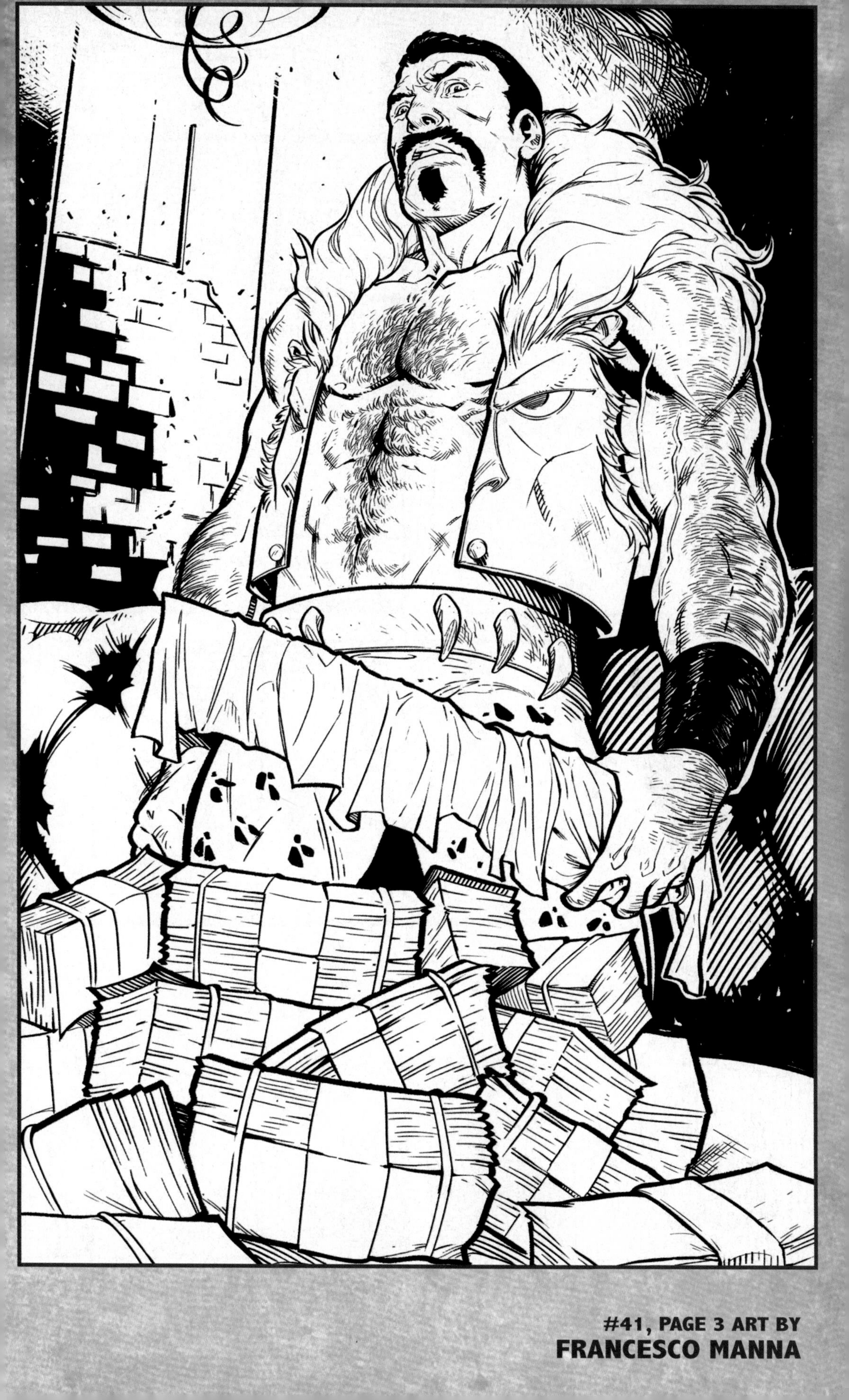

#41, PAGE 3 ART BY
FRANCESCO MANNA

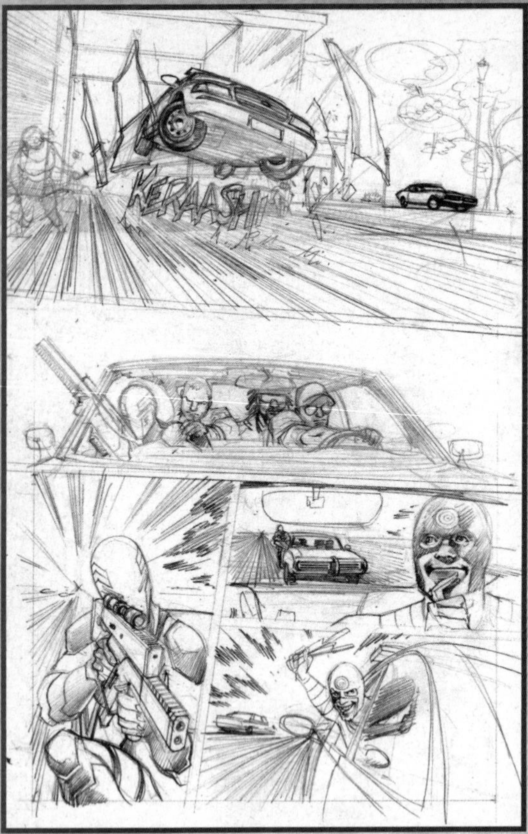
KERAASH!!

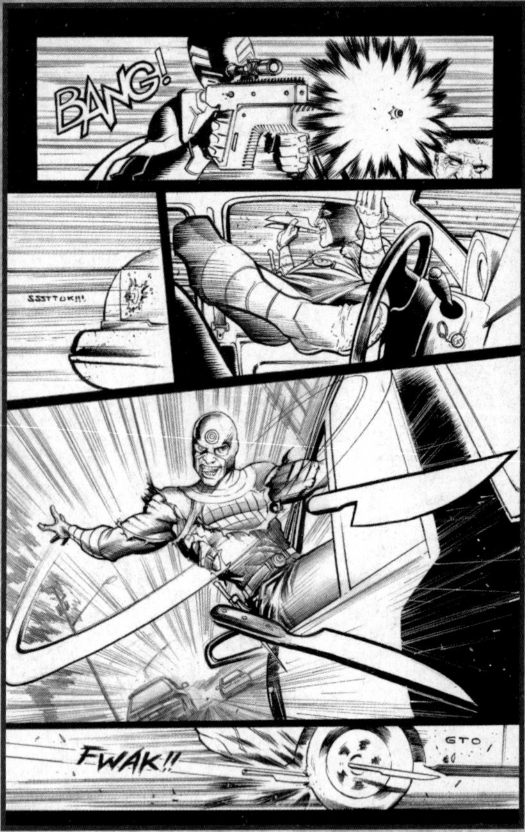
BANG!
SSSTTUK!!!
FWAK!!
GTO

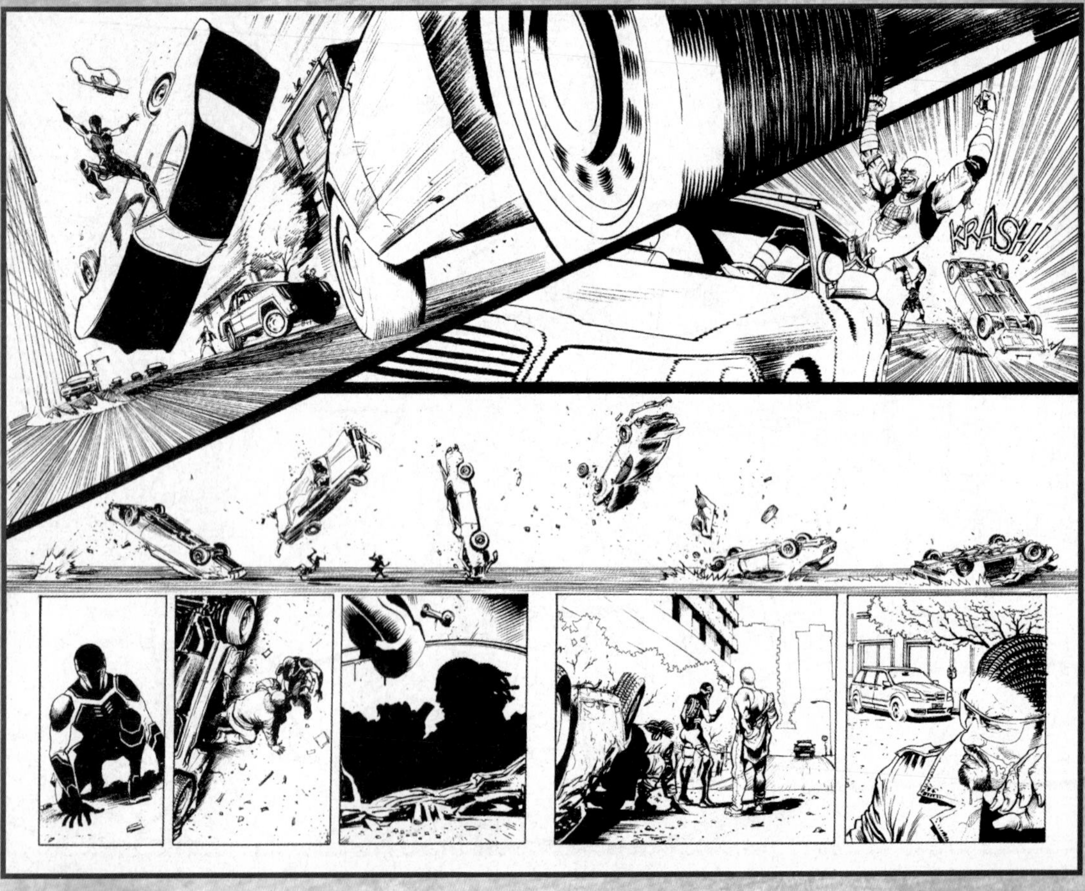
KRASH!!

#45, PAGES 2-5 ART BY
JUAN FERREYRA